THE GENDERED NEW WORLD ORDER

Routledge
New York and London

THE GENDERED NEW WORLD ORDER

Militarism, Development, and the Environment

edited by

Jennifer Turpin and Lois Ann Lorentzen

Published in 1996 by
Routledge
29 West 35th Street
New York, NY 10001

Published in
Great Britain by
Routledge
11 New Fetter Lane
London EC4P 4EE

Copyright © 1996 by
Routledge
Printed in the United
States of America on acid-
free paper.

Chapter 13 was originally
published in *Women and
Peace* by Betty Reardon,
SUNY Press, New York,
1994. Reprinted courtesy
of SUNY Press.

Library of Congress Cataloging-in-Publication Data

The gendered new world order : militarism, development, and the
    environment / edited by Jennifer Turpin and Lois Ann Lorentzen.
        p.   cm.
    Includes bibliographical references (p.   ) and index.
    ISBN 0-415-91517-1 (alk. paper). — ISBN 0-415-91518-X (pbk. :
alk. paper)
        1. Women—Government policy.   2. Women in development.
    3. Ecofeminism.   4. Women and war.   5. Women in politics.
    I. Turpin, Jennifer E.   II. Lorentzen, Lois Ann, 1952–   .
    HQ1236.G4625   1996
    305.4—dc20   96-21006
                                                        CIP

CONTENTS

ACKNOWLEDGMENTS

THIS BOOK emerged from a seminar we co-taught at the University of San Francisco in spring 1994, following our participation in a "Gender, Justice, and Development" workshop at the University of Massachusetts, Amherst. Funding for our seminar was provided by Louise M. Davies. We are grateful to the Davies Advisory Board, and especially Associate Dean Gerardo Marín, for their assistance. We received additional funding from Interfaith Hunger Appeal in the form of a matching curriculum grant. Our ongoing research has been funded in part by the Faculty Development Fund at USF. Dean Stanley Nel has always encouraged us and supported our work in very concrete ways.

We thank our partners, Robert Elias and Gerardo Marín, for their unfailing moral, intellectual, and emotional support. Finally, we thank each other—working together has been deeply rewarding.

To Madeleine
and
To Hannah and Tucker
our future

INTRODUCTION: THE GENDERED NEW WORLD ORDER

Lois Ann Lorentzen and Jennifer Turpin

REFUGEES, POLLUTED waters, bombed villages, starving children, a global HIV/AIDS epidemic: our news bombards us with these seemingly disparate crises. Each of these problems characterizes the new world order—the order the Cold War left in its wake. For almost fifty years, the Cold War between the United States and the former Soviet Union threatened to destroy the planet. While the Cold War is over, its legacy remains in the forms of militarism, unequal development, and environmental crises. We contend that these problems are linked and gendered.

Rather than reducing poverty in the so-called Third World and within First World countries, the Cold War actually exacerbated development problems. The competition for military superiority promoted massive expenditures on weapons instead of on social problems, such as poverty, education, sanitation, health care, and sustainable food cultivation. Inequalities between peoples and nations were heightened so that overall, countries in the North prospered while those in the South remained poor and dependent on the rich countries that had originally colonized them. Current environment, development, and military conflicts reflect this legacy of colonialism as the North continues exploiting the South's resources, enforcing its will through world financial institutions and militaries, and leaving massive environmental destruction in its wake.

Yet these repercussions can be seen not only in those places we traditionally view as underdeveloped, such as Africa and India, but also in places typically excluded from development studies, such as the United States, Russia, and Eastern Europe. Ironically, in some of the more affluent countries like the United States, many people live in poverty, especially women and people of color. These people have been impoverished, or at least deprived of any assistance for their poverty, because resources were spent instead on the expanding military, thus creating significant pockets of underdevelopment in the developed world. Russians and Eastern Europeans also experienced underdevelopment because of high rates of military spending; likewise, they are only beginning to comprehend the ecological damage caused by those same military activities. Even in Western Europe, certain groups remained relatively poor, proving that (white) Europeans in the North may also experience underdevelopment. In short, the East-West political system and the North-South economic system created wealth in some countries at the expense of others. Those systems also stratified societies internally by consuming enormous resources for military spending, profiting a small class of people while impoverishing many others.

This all suggests that while poverty in Africa seems to have little to do with ecological destruction in Russia or the war in former Yugoslavia, these actually constitute interrelated global problems. Unequal development is often enforced by armed intervention, and competition over scarce ecological resources often leads to war. Militarism causes environmental destruction, and both exacerbate development problems. Worldwide environmental problems are linked directly to the implementation of mainstream development models.

Most important, we argue in this book that these problems are not only interrelated; they are gendered. Ecological destruction, unequal development, and militarism disproportionately affect women, and women craft unique strategies in response. The current environmental crises, increasing global inequalities, and military conflicts worldwide can be understood only if we examine misguided development strategies, the militarization of global culture, *and* the persistent subordination of women as part of these processes. While previous studies have linked gender and development, gender and the environment, and gender and militarism, few works explore gender as the nexus for all three of these interrelated global problems. We aim in this book to explore these complex interrelationships. Studying one problem without con-

2

sidering the others can produce incomplete and artificial analyses. We can no longer think about women and development without considering both direct and structural violence, and these cannot be divorced from their impact on the environment. Examining the environment, development, and militarism through the lens of gender highlights the invisibility and marginalization of women. Consider the following examples.

WOMEN AND THE ENVIRONMENT

Ecological degradation affects women disproportionately. The increased burdens placed on women result not from environmental deterioration per se, but rather from a sexual division of labor that considers family sustenance to be women's work. Thus, fuel gathering, food preparing, water collecting, and subsistence farming are generally considered women's tasks. In much of Africa women produce 80 percent of the food. Women comprise 60 percent of the farmers in India, 64 percent in Zaire, and 98 percent in Nepal. Environmental degradation exacerbates women's burdens differently than for men. Deforestation and desertification, for example, increase the burden women bear in being responsible for finding fuel and food for their families. A rural woman in India may wake at dawn to search for fuel, food, and water. In Nepal, women and girls walk long distances to collect 84 percent of the fuel they need. In Bangladesh, rural women and children may spend three to five hours daily searching for firewood; in parts of the Himalayas it may exceed 7 hours (Rodda 1991:47). In El Salvador, 80 percent of the natural vegetation has been eliminated and 77 percent of the soil has eroded or lost its fertility, making it harder and harder for peasant women to find firewood and food. Given the 1.8 percent yearly loss of the world's rain forests, deforestation and declining soil fertility make women's lives increasingly difficult.

Obstacles to obtaining fuel, combined with fewer available plant foods, often leads to less nutritious diets for women. The long hours women work worldwide in finding food, fuel, and water often lead to health problems. As women struggle to find food for their families, their own needs are often denied. Insufficient food intake commonly affects poor women. The negative health effects of environmental degradation occur especially in poor rural areas of developing nations. A study of rural Sri Lankan women concluded that they suffered from persistent sleep deprivation due to their multiple roles. Women in Africa are 200 times more likely to die from pregnancy-related causes than are women in industrialized countries. As they struggle to care for their families, women's health often suffers from polluted rivers, depleted land, vanishing forests, and disappearing wild plants and animals.

Desertification and pollution have turned women's quest for safe water into one of their most pressing and difficult problems worldwide. Illnesses caused by a lack of potable water account for 34.6 percent of all child deaths in the Third World. As pollution increases, women must walk further to find

LORENTZEN AND TURPIN

3

safe water for their families. In some parts of Africa, women spend eight hours a day collecting water. In southern Nigeria, oil industry pollution in rivers and creeks means that women can no longer find fish and safe water in the increasingly polluted rivers and creeks (Rodda 1991:84). Urban women often face problems of poor housing as well as inadequate water supplies and sanitation, as more women and their families migrate from the countryside. Women also bear the brunt of caring for children and for the sick and elderly; thus, they are especially affected by contaminated water. There is little doubt that women bear most dramatically the burdens of a worldwide environmental crisis.

WOMEN AND DEVELOPMENT

Environmental deterioration, which hurts women the most, often emerges from mainstream development models. Development policies based on export-driven agriculture, increased mechanization, structural adjustment policies, and other forms of commercial development often affect women adversely. The destructiveness of mainstream development models that link agricultural development to capitalist-industrial development has been extensively documented. Movements such as the Green Revolution removed agriculture from the context of a nature/survival economy and placed it within the market economy. New technologies were created for agribusiness, and in the process soil fertility, pest control, and the growing and storing of seeds was no longer the work of peasants, especially peasant women.

Mainstream development models did not produce the food self-sufficiency that was promised. Africa now struggles to feed its people, yet it was relatively self-sufficient as late as 1970. This food scarcity occurred for several reasons. Monocultures often replaced a diversity of crops. This created surpluses at one level, as well as crops for sale. Yet, the poorer sections of rural society were often worse off. In India, the thousands of rice varieties found before 1980 were radically reduced. The crisis of desertification in Africa and elsewhere can be traced to aspects of the Green Revolution, such as the high water demand it created for the new crops, the water-logged deserts it produced from large water projects, and the water depletion it caused where rivers were dammed or diverted.

In short, mainstream development has been a disaster for much of the Third World. The stated goal of increasing local self-sufficiency was rarely met, and instead increased soil degradation, deforestation, and desertification generally resulted. Less examined has been the disproportionate impact of development models on women. Development often means the transfer of resources into men's hands, even where women do the bulk of the labor. In much of Africa, colonial laws and development policies generally allocate land only to men. Women have lost their traditional rights to the land, even though they do up to three quarters of the agricultural labor.

A gendered division of labor also means that women bear the brunt of misguided development policies. In rural India, for example, women's traditional work had been producing sustenance. With the Green Revolution's commodification of food production, the role of women shifted from farm producers to subsidiary workers. Deforestation (where trees were cut for profit), the creation of dams for water projects, and the shift to fertilizers and purchased seeds, all combined to make women's work as farm producers increasingly difficult. Women worked even longer hours to provide basic needs.

When the dairy industry grew during the White Revolution in India, women were again adversely affected. Traditionally women were experts in animal husbandry as well as in food processing. Women made curds, butter, ghee, and buttermilk for consumption by family and village members. When milk became a commodity for sale, basic rural needs were neglected. Currently, 70 percent of the milk in India is manufactured into products such as cheese, butter, and chocolate that are consumed by 2 percent of the population (Shiva 1989:172). Not surprisingly, rural Indian women have led protests resisting the sale of milk.

Recessions, debt crises, and structural adjustment programs initiated by the World Bank and the International Monetary Fund place the heaviest burdens on poor women. If food prices rise and wages fall, a woman must spend more time finding ways to feed and clothe her family. If she lives in a city she must search for cheaper markets, prepare cheaper food, and eat less in order to feed her family. Furthermore, as women in Central America discovered, traditional diets of beans and corn, rice, and tortillas are often undermined by the intensive marketing of processed foods such as bread and cola. If the family lacks income because of the monetization of local economies, a woman may join the increasing numbers of those who work in the informal economy, making goods for sale on the streets of large urban centers. Women comprise 91 percent of the informal economy in Haiti, 88 percent in Ghana, and 54 percent in Thailand, as they desperately seek to supplement dwindling family incomes (Vickers 1991:25). As competition in the informal economy becomes more difficult, women must find other ways to get cash. Increases in AIDS/HIV in Zimbabwe, Thailand, and other developing nations are linked to a marked growth in prostitution as women find no alternative means of generating income.

Structural adjustment programs typically reduce social services and safety nets. Health expenditure cuts in Sao Paulo State, Brazil, produced an outbreak of deadly communicable diseases among children. In Chile, the cancellation of a child-feeding program led to a significant increase in child mortality (Vickers 1991:26). Again, women's work and caretaking becomes increasingly difficult. Mainstream development models have placed unequal burdens on women worldwide as they struggle to care for their families, often at great cost to their own health and well-being.

WOMEN AND MILITARISM

We cannot understand the new world order without examining gender and militarism. Yet women's invisibility in military affairs and policymaking reflects taken-for-granted international assumptions about the maleness of war. Even though they are more likely than men to become war's casualties or refugees, women have little or no say in making military or security decisions.

War and militarism become increasingly dangerous with the advent of new technologies. The past century has witnessed the killing of about 104 million people in wars—more than three quarters of all war dead recorded since the year 1500 (Hauchler and Kennedy 1994:183). Most people killed in war are civilians. But while 50 percent of the casualties in World War II were civilians, in the 1980s this figure rose to 80 percent, and by 1990 it was a staggering 90 percent. Women and children constitute the vast majority of these civilian war casualties.

Women are also most likely to be uprooted by war; more than four-fifths of war refugees are women and young girls, who often experience additional violence during their flight. By the end of 1992 there were more than 46 million people who had lost their homes: about 36 million of these were women and girls. In Africa there were more than 23.6 external and internal refugees; more than 12.6 people fled their homes in the Middle East and in South and Central Asia. There are two million displaced persons in Latin America, and about 6 million refugees in Europe. About 2 million people fled the former Yugoslavia (Hauchler and Kennedy 1994:185). While stationed in camps and refugee settlements, as well as in their new societies of residence, women and girls suffer sexual abuse, abduction, and forced prostitution. During World War II the Japanese set up brothels in East and Southern Asia, forcing between 100,000 and 200,000 women into prostitution. In the former Yugoslavia, thousands of Muslim women have been forced into camps and raped by Serbian soldiers. Muslim and Croat soldiers have also committed mass rapes.

The continuing invisibility of women in war manifests itself, for example, in the fact that the widespread use of wartime rape is still not recognized as a war crime by international agencies. Violence is routinely used to control women's sexuality and reproduction. Soviet soldiers raped approximately two million women in eastern Germany in 1945, and in 1971 Pakistani soldiers raped more than 200,000 Bengali women in the Bangladesh war of independence. One estimate suggests that during the war against Kuwait, Iraqi troops raped as many as 3,200 women between August 1990 and February 1991 (Enloe 1994:186). Most recently, in Bosnia-Herzegovina, rape has been used as a weapon for ethnic cleansing, which uses attacks on women to humiliate another ethnic group and to inflict genocide.

Women also suffer from the economic, social, and ecological consequences

LORENTZEN AND TURPIN

of war. The Sudan provides a graphic example: there the government spent about $640 million in 1990 on the horrific war in the South. This constitutes 80 percent of Sudan's total development assistance for that year (Hauchler and Kennedy 1994:186). The war devastated the economy and the food supply, resulting in the starvation of over 5 million people. Because of their family roles, women are more likely to give up food so their children can eat. Women in the Sudan suffered not only their own and their children's starvation, but also the loss of their property, family, homes, and way of life.

TYING IT ALL TOGETHER

As we have seen, environmental crises, misguided development strategies, and the militarization of global culture all affect women disproportionately. In this book we argue, however, that militarism, the environment, and development are linked *and* gendered. War destroys the physical and social environment, consumes massive sums of money, and shatters development progress. All of this exacerbates the structural violence women experience. And both militarism and environmental deterioration are rooted in development models that emphasize capital accumulation for the few. The global forces of militarism, the accumulation of capital, and the exploitation of natural resources depend on a gendered order.

Examples from many of the world's regions demonstrate how development models, environmental crises, and militarism are inextricably linked. Take El Salvador, for instance. With every major ecosystem at risk, with two-thirds of the original rain forest destroyed, with its soil, water, and the food chain contaminated by pesticides, with the world's highest population growth rate, with its declining per capita food production, and with its ongoing increases in environmentally related infectious diseases, El Salvador truly constitutes an environmental disaster. This ecological crisis has resulted from both militarization and development models. Since World War II, the capitalist export sector, aided by the World Bank and the United States Agency for International Development, has pursued a development model that has pushed crops such as coffee for export. In the process, huge tracts of land were destroyed, forests were removed, and harmful pesticides were used. In addition, environmental problems were exacerbated by war and militarization. The military conflicts were battles over land and models of development, clashes between peasants, and the capitalist-export sector. The militaries of both El Salvador and Guatemala followed Vietnam-style "scorched earth" policies where entire regions were deforested and burned, thus hastening environmental decline. In the case of El Salvador, war, development, and the environmental crisis are clearly linked. And the links are gendered: the burden is borne primarily by women as family sustenance becomes increasingly impossible. As many men left rural lands either for war or to seek nonexistent jobs in the city, women

7

were left with more of the hard work of providing for their families. For many Salvadoran women activists, the violence done to the earth by war and development practices mirrors the violence done to women.

In the United States, militarism and development are linked by the state's maintenance of a permanent war economy, commonly called the military-industrial complex. This complex is gendered in many ways. The expenditures are enormous, diverting funding that could instead go to social programs. For every dollar spent on research and development in the United States, sixty-four cents are spent on the military, while only 1 percent goes toward protecting the environment (Sivard 1991). Five hours of U.S. military spending could fund 1,600 rape crisis centers and battered women's shelters for a year (Peterson and Sisson Runyan 1993:85). Given the low rates of female participation, most women get little of the direct proceeds of military spending. Yet, although few women are soldiers, many serve the military as defense industry workers. Eighty percent of the poorly paid assembly plant workers in Silicon Valley are women. Most of them are also Black, Latina or Asian (Peterson and Sisson Runyan 1993:90). In addition, the United States military has the dubious distinction of being the single greatest polluter in the country. Thus, militarization diverts funding from social and environmental programs while it finances environmentally damaging activities.

In Africa, war and maldevelopment have produced environmental disasters that have helped generate a near continent-wide food crisis. Military conflicts in Ethiopia, South Africa, West Africa, Sierra Leone, Uganda, Rwanda, Somalia, the Sudan, and elsewhere, have promoted great internal migrations throughout the continent as well as the inevitable environmental devastation caused by war. Conflicts often arise over land and natural resources in times of ecological scarcity. Since the early 1970s, the rate of growth in food production has lagged well behind the demand in most sub-Saharan countries. This food crisis results from the failure of export-based development, from the monetization of African economies, and from the deforestation and desertification caused by development projects such as damming and timber-clearing for market purposes. The increased scarcity often escalates military conflicts. Whether due to war or environmentally destructive development schemes, the food crisis especially harms women. In Kenya, women spend the same amount of time as men working to produce cash crops such as coffee. But they spend at least 18 times more time than men on basic life maintenance tasks such as collecting water and firewood, preparing food, caring for children, and cleaning the house. Providing for the family becomes more burdensome as war, environmental crises, and export-led development merge to make women's resource prospects bleaker and bleaker.

The Gulf War also illustrates how underdevelopment can foster war, and how war causes environmental and economic destruction. Both sides in the Gulf War deliberately destroyed the region's ecology as part of their war strategy. Iraq pumped oil into the sea, causing an oil slick approximately 80 miles long and 10 miles wide. About 600 oil wells were set afire in Kuwait. Likewise, as a result of U.S. ecological warfare—including the deliberate bombing of chemical and nuclear facilities—black rain fell as far away as Iran and the Himalayas. The economic and ecological bases of the region were devastated. Any improvements in living conditions for women and children that were achieved after the Iran/Iraq war were effectively obliterated by the Gulf War. Basic health and sanitation levels dropped drastically, and the devaluation of local currencies made it almost impossible for women to buy food (Vickers 1993:62).

These examples show that we can no longer think about women and development without considering both direct and structural violence. This violence, in turn, cannot be divorced from the impact on the environment. The case studies in this volume demonstrate that the links between gender and militarism, development, and the environment prove to be the critical problems in the new world order.

CONTRIBUTORS

The contributors to this book recognize the great price women pay when they confront the interlocking problems of militarism, underdevelopment, and environmental decay. Our writers come from around the globe and represent a wide range of disciplinary perspectives, including economics, sociology, education, conflict studies, environmental science, public health, social psychology, gender studies, development studies, political science, and religious studies. Their research examines geographical regions that are traditionally considered underdeveloped, such as Africa and India, as well as those typically excluded from development studies, such as the United States and Eastern Europe.

To begin with, Lorraine Elliott shows that what we think of as merely environmental problems are actually related in complex ways to gender. She analyzes the ways we pursue economic and territorial security, and their connection to environmental degradation. Thus, development and militarism, as well as environmental policy, must be addressed through the lens of gender. Elliott contends, however, that ungendering the language we use to discuss these problems is not enough. We must also undo the public/private dichotomy that underlies patriarchy, liberalism, and the domination of nature.

Democracy with a man's face in Russia and Eastern Europe has meant little for women's well-being and security. In her provocative article, Lenore Goldman shows that the emerging post-communist systems fail to address women's needs every bit as much as those of the communist era. She weaves together the issues of gender, violence, family, and environmental concerns, based on her work as a consultant to numerous grassroots women's groups. The strong pro-women's stances championed by some Russian and Eastern European women challenge liberal western definitions of feminism.

9

LORENTZEN AND TURPIN

Linda Forcey finds that when a First World woman lives in a Third World context, it transforms her ideas about feminism. Forcey's exploration of environmental and peace movements in India has convinced her that ecofeminist perspectives that integrate environmental security and gender concerns must also link development strategies with peace issues. Forcey argues that peace constitutes a prerequisite for global resource security.

Claire Van Zevern movingly portrays how the unique relationship between land and indigenous women in Hawaii has been shattered. With United States colonization, precious resources were destroyed by the U.S. military, and later exploited by corporations and tourism. The consequences, as Van Zevern argues, have been devastating. The fragile ecosystem of the islands has been irreversibly damaged, and patriarchal gender roles have emerged among indigenous peoples.

Shut out from traditional sources of power and funding, grassroots women's organizations practice sustainable development out of necessity. Julie Fisher's overview of such organizations shows how their analyses link poverty with population, the environment, and development. While debates rage at the international policy level, many Third World women face the daily need to survive and provide for their families.

Contrary to commonly held beliefs, the religious state of Iran continued the gender policies of the secular state that preceded it. Hamideh Sedghi demonstrates that both the secular and religious states have used violence, sexual control, and the regulation of women's work to pursue economic policies and development models that privilege men. Thus, development policies in Iran have maintained a patriarchal structure of relations, adversely affecting women.

The declining conditions in Nigeria and Zimbabwe in the 1980s were exacerbated by drought, regional military conflicts, and migration from rural to urban settings. Mary Osirim provides a gendered analysis of development paradigms based on interviews with women microentrepreneurs. State development policies, demanded by the International Monetary Fund and the World Bank, have forced women into the informal sector of the economy in their struggle to survive.

The gendered structure of power, especially in developing countries, puts women at special risk for contracting HIV/AIDS. Geeta Rao Gupta, Ellen Weiss, and Daniel Whelan demonstrate how the worldwide growth of HIV/AIDS among women relates to the violence, economic inequality, and sexual control experienced by women. A woman's risk-reducing behavior depends not only on her individual choices, but on macro-political constraints such as the gendered distribution of wealth and social power.

Wars, maldevelopment, and environmental disasters have all contributed to the African food crisis. Ruth Oniang'o examines women's efforts to survive in the worst conditions. As primary food providers, women craft unique strategies to feed their families, including sacrificing their own nutritional needs. These efforts, however, are generally invisible to international policy makers. Oniang'o argues that we must rethink economic policies to ensure sustainable development. Food security can be enhanced only by creating gender-specific programs.

Maternal mortality, more than any other health indicator, demonstrates the gap between more and less affluent nations. Kathleen Merchant argues that high maternal mortality rates result from maldevelopment and gender discrimination. Women in less-developed countries have particular social vulnerabilities that produce health consequences at each stage of the life cycle. A social context of gender and economic injustice contributes to poor health and malnutrition for women. Thus, unequal development policies foment structural violence against women.

Perhaps the most brutal recent example of violence against women—wartime rape in the former Yugoslavia—graphically illustrates the links between gender and militarism. Vesna Nikolić-Ristanović's interviews of refugee women in this war-torn region show how control over women's sexuality gets played out at different levels of violence. Both domestic violence and wartime rape stem from the militarization of men's and women's lives. Given dwindling economic and environmental resources, men turn to weapons to bolster their masculinity, rendering women the victims of both enemies and friends.

Our final article claims that women approach security issues quite differently than mainstream male policymakers. Betty Reardon argues that we must bring more women into the policymaking process. She proposes a feminist conception of authentic global security that includes four essential elements: sustainability, vulnerability, equity, and protection. Her vision, a fitting conclusion to the volume, constructively links gender to prospects for peace, environmental security, and sustainable development.

REFERENCES

Enloe, Cynthia. *The Morning After.* Berkeley: University of California Press, 1994.
Hauchler, Ingomar and Paul Kennedy. *Global Trends.* New York: Continuum, 1994.
Peterson, V. Spike and Anne Sisson Runyan. *Global Gender Issues.* Boulder: Westview Press, 1993.
Rodda, Annabel. *Women and the Environment.* London: Zed Books, 1991.
Shiva, Vandana. *Staying Alive: Women, Ecology and Development.* London: Zed Books, 1989.
Sivard, Ruth Leger. *World Military and Social Expenditures.* Washington, D.C.: World Priorities, Inc., 1991.
Vickers, Jeanne. *Women and the World Economic Crisis.* London: Zed Books, 1991.
Vickers, Jeanne. *Women and War.* London: Zed Books, 1993.

WOMEN, GENDER, FEMINISM, AND THE ENVIRONMENT

Lorraine Elliott

chapter 1

INTRODUCTION

EXPLORING THE connections between women and the environment is more than an exercise in "adding women" to the debate. Rather, it involves making women visible and examining the nature and basis of their invisibility. The debate about global environmental issues has proceeded for the most part on the assumption that environmental degradation or insecurity affects women and men equally and in the same way; in other words, that environmental insecurity is gender-neutral. Yet not only is environmental degradation gender-specific, at both a global and local level, but environmental policy debates have been gendered in a number of significant ways that have marginalized women and their expertise.

The asymmetries between the gender assumptions of environmental decisionmaking and the "reality" of environmental degradation are manifested in a gender blindness which disadvantages women even further but which also ensures that unless—and until—this lack of vision is recognized, we cannot adequately address or overcome environmental insecurity. The environment debate as a policy process is gendered in terms of where women are located, and in terms of what are considered appropriate forums for women's action and activity. This gendering derives from the public/private dichotomy which is a basic dualism within both the patriarchy and liberalism which have defined intra-state decisionmaking and inter-state politics. Women's marginalization into the private sphere means that they are often more closely connected with day-to-day ecosystem management. They are, therefore, more likely to be detrimentally affected by the impact of environmental degradation. But it is this very marginalization that ensures that this connection is often overlooked in debates on the pursuit of environmental security, that ensures that both women and women's experiences are disregarded or undervalued in the search for solutions, and that ensures that environmental security is frequently seen to be the lowest of low politics in the hierarchy of issues on the international agenda.

The term "global" is used in this paper in preference to "international," to signify concerns that are shared concerns (in the sense of world-wide) across peoples and the planet. The distinctions made between international (or transboundary) and local environmental concerns are marginally relevant when exploring connections between women and the environment. Women's location within international environmental insecurity and the related policy processes mirrors their location within local environmental insecurity. It is this location that is the focus of this paper. Further, the analysis presented here resists a compartmentalization of "environmental problems." Both the causes of environmental degradation and the nature of women's connection to that degradation cannot be adequately addressed without interrogating the ways in which economic and territorial security have been pursued and the mindset that determines how both should be approached and defined.

This paper begins with a brief summary of environmental insecurities. It then explores the impact of environmental degradation on women, considers where women are to be found (and not found) in environmental policy deliberations, and examines the nature of policy responses to the connection between women and the environment. The analysis then explores some of the arguments advanced within feminist scholarship about the basis of this gendering and marginalization.

ENVIRONMENTAL INSECURITY

Degradation of the environment as a result of human activities is no longer just a national or local issue. Issues such as depletion of the ozone layer, accumulation of greenhouse gases, desertification, deforestation, and the loss of species and genetic diversity are global problems with local and global sources and impacts. They are interconnected and complex issues, made more so because of the cumulative and potentially irreversible nature of their impact. Regardless of the source of the problem—which in many cases is the industrialized North—the effect will be felt globally and often inequitably. That impact is not just an environmental impact; these are not just technical or scientific problems requiring technical or scientific solutions. They arise out of particular economic, social, and political structures—in particular an emphasis on industrialization and the pursuit of economic security through growth—and they have economic, social, and political consequences.[1]

There is a strong degree of consensus among the scientific community that the accumulation of carbon dioxide, chlorofluorocarbons, methane, and nitrous oxide will enhance—and indeed quite possibly already is enhancing—the natural greenhouse effect with concomitant changes in climate, weather patterns, and sea levels.[2] The results of this will include coastal erosion, possible destruction of mangrove and coral reef ecosystems, and salt water intrusion into fresh waterways. As much as one-third of the world's croplands could be lost and up to 1 billion people could be affected by inundation of coastal and delta regions and low-lying island states.[3] Changes in climate zones, changes to flood and drought patterns, and possible increases in plant and animal diseases and pests will affect both plant and animal agriculture as well as contribute to the loss of biodiversity. Depletion of the ozone layer and the increase in ultraviolet B rays which result from the accumulation of anthropogenic chlorine and bromine gases will affect human, animal, and plant health through an increase in cancers and cataracts and a suppression of immune systems. Crop yields, animal husbandry, and the marine ecosystem will be affected.[4]

Over the last thirty years, 40 percent of the world's rain forests have disappeared, cleared for agricultural land (often large scale ranching or monocropping for export) or for commercial logging. On a local level, deforestation causes soil erosion and loss of soil fertility—and thus affects local ecosystem balance—as well as probably contributing to downstream flooding or siltation problems. It contributes to biodiversity loss and displaces indigenous forest dwellers. At a global level, deforestation is a contributor to the enhanced greenhouse effect, releasing stored carbon into the atmosphere and removing a potential carbon sink. While estimates vary, approximately 11 million hectares (or about 1.8 percent of the forest biome) is lost per annum. Partly as a result of this process, every year another 6 million hectares of productive land (where "productive" means sustaining rather than simply economically useful) becomes desert, threatening 35 percent of the earth's surface and 20 percent of its population. Both deforestation and desertification contribute to species loss. Estimates are uncertain, simply because we do not know the number of species on earth, but it is possible to estimate that between 5 and 15 percent of the world's species could disappear in the next thirty years, an average of up to, or perhaps more than, 150 per day. Not only are we losing species, but we are also losing genetic diversity, which will make plants and animals more susceptible to disease. Because we do not know the extent of genetic diversity, we cannot gauge the impact of species loss in terms of its inherent value, its impact on the ecosystem balance, or its potential "use" for the human species. We can add to this list of global problems environmental concerns that may have local causes and consequences, but which are also global in that they are replicated and shared across the planet. Such concerns would include air and water pollution (including acid rain), toxic and hazardous chemical use, waste disposal, and land degradation.

Lowering of agricultural yields, loss of croplands, diminishing of the marine ecosystem, rising sea levels, rapidly increasing health costs, and displacement of peoples will affect developing countries more heavily and more quickly. This arises because of the reliance of developing countries on primary exports, the importance of internal subsistence economies and their difficulty in meeting the costs of adjustment. While the impact of global environmental degradation will be felt first in developing countries which are least able to adjust, they are not the source of much of this degradation. The industrialized North, for example, accounts for 70 percent of CFC consumption. The United States uses six times the global average. China and India, with one-third of the world's population, account for only 2 percent of CFC consumption. The so-called Third World, with 75 percent of the world's population, contributes only 26 percent of fossil CO_2 emissions.

WOMEN AND THE ENVIRONMENT

Environmental Impact

To argue that women are differently situated in terms of environmental degradation is not to suggest that men are not affected by the environmental insecurity described above. Clearly they are, and more so in developing countries than in the economic North. However, women are affected disproportionately and in different ways, especially in developing countries where the link between poverty, women's status (or lack thereof), imposed development policies, and environmental degradation is a complex but intense one. This disproportionate impact is essentially a form of structural violence against women. Further, the nature of women's participation is both enforced and asymmetric. Women also disproportionately represent the world's poor and it is the world's poor who are hardest hit by environmental degradation.

There is a considerable amount of material available on women and environment in the Third World, arising from the Women in Development (WID) literature which acknowledges the connection between women, environment, and development. In developing countries especially, women are the key to the management of environmental systems. Women are the world's food producers as well as the world's food preparers. In some parts of Africa, for example, women produce 80 percent of the food. In India, about 60 percent of farmers are women. The impact of climate change and ozone depletion on agriculture will make food growing responsibilities more difficult and time consuming. Subsistence agriculture is also affected by changing patterns of flood and drought. Women manage the water supply as well as use it. Collecting water supplies is a major part of women's daily routine and one which is becoming more arduous as environmental degradation and the impacts of climate change and desertification alter the availability of water resources. Irene Dankelman and Joan Davidson note that in some parts of the developing world, women spend up to four hours per day collecting water (1988: 32). Women also provide fuel as well as burn it. In Africa, women collect about 80 percent of the fuel, often in the form of dead wood, which is required on a daily basis for cooking and for warmth. Deforestation removes a source of fuel, fodder, and food, all of which are the responsibility of women. There has also been a perception that the collection and burning of fuel is a significant contributor to the decrease in forest cover, which is connected to loss of biodiversity and to the accumulation of greenhouse gases. Yet women traditionally collect dead wood. The main contributor to deforestation is commercial harvesting and clearing of the land for large-scale agriculture. This economic activity has little benefit for women. Where it occurs, it frequently means that women have to devote a greater proportion of their time to collecting fuel (and therefore have less time to spend on food preparation and management) and that there is less land available for subsistence agriculture (in which women are predominantly engaged, often on poorer quality land).

Because of these connections, women in developing countries are, and will continue to be, more adversely affected by the impact of environmental degradation. Where energy, land and water—the key components of the ecosystem—are degraded and damaged, it is women's lives which are adversely and directly affected. However, they have little say over the practices that are environmentally damaging even though they are disproportionately affected by those changes. A gendered division of labor also ensures that women's work as providers of sustenance is undercounted and undervalued.[1] This makes it easy to target women as a *source* of environmental degradation, in a classic strategy of blaming the victim (one which is not unfamiliar to women living in a patriarchal society).

Yet, as Robyn Eckersley points out, women are less implicated in the major activities and centers of ecological destruction (1992: 67). Women in rural

17

[1]Women often do physically heavier work than men and work longer hours than men. They put in 66 percent of the world's working hours, earn 10 percent of the world's income and own 1 percent of the world's property.

ELLIOTT

and urban communities in the developing world are often forced unwillingly into unsustainable patterns of ecosystem management where the best land is taken for development projects (which are often unsustainable), and only small amounts of marginal land remain to provide food, fuel, and water.

The environmental impact on women's lives arises not just from global sources or the cumulative impact of industrialization in the North. Women, as Vandana Shiva notes, "bear the ecological costs of progress and development" (1989: 7). The responsibility for degradation lies not with women but with a narrow model of development. The result of much development activity in the economic South—imposed or encouraged through a Northern-inspired growth ideology and based on export-oriented industries and an influx of First World capital—has been a degradation and unbalancing of local ecosystems. The emphasis on a move away from multicrop agriculture to monocropping aimed at export markets has environmental consequences which affect women through their responsibility for food production. Monocrops are often unsuitable for the region; they affect the soil quality and require fertilizers which in turn require increased amounts of water. Their use can directly increase women's working hours as both agricultural laborers and providers of food. Women are still engaged in subsistence agriculture, but their task is made more difficult because of the reduced land resources to which they have access and over which they rarely have control, often forcing them to use marginal areas intensely. They also have to work harder to compensate for soil erosion and poor fertility. In the absence of fuelwood, women are forced to use substitutes such as dung and crop residues, which affect soil fertility.[5] So-called Green Revolution technologies contributed to erosion and desertification—ecological degradations which hit women hardest.[6] The Green Revolution also concentrated land ownership, thus further separating women from the land which they need to fulfill their sustenance responsibilities.

Population pressures are also often identified as a source of environmental degradation. This is often characterized as a Third World problem and the solutions most often proposed are simple numerical ones with a focus on family planning and birth control. The identification of the problem and the nature of the solution are both gendered and intimately tied to the status and role of women. It is, however, "false to blame global ecological degradation on the fertility of women in developing countries" (see National Women's Consultative Council, 1991: 44). The question of "how many people" cannot be separated from patterns of consumption which are inequitable in favor of people in developed countries. Further, lower birth rates, in *all* parts of the world, are more likely to result from the education and empowerment of women than they are from imposed birth control programs.

There is much less analysis available on the connection between women and the environment in the industrialized world. The relationship is, quite clearly, not the proximate one of women in the developing world. Neverthe-

18

Monocropping

ELLIOTT

less, so-called First World women are also predominantly responsible for household management and thus for decisions about energy, water use, and food preparation. In Australia, for example, a 1989 survey showed that women spent nine times as much time on laundry and 3.5 times as much time on cooking and childcare as men did on these activities (Instone, 1992: 525). Instone also cites a Swedish survey which suggested that 71 percent of Swedish men never clean the home, 52 percent never shop, 73 percent never wash clothes, and 64 percent never do the dishes. Environmental problems such as air pollution and the impact of industrial and hazardous wastes, which of course also afflict women in developing countries, affect women through their primary responsibility for health care of children and old people, responsibilities which make them more alert to and concerned for the impact of environmental pollution on the ecosystem.

Women's lives are also likely to be disproportionately affected by the nature of solutions proposed. Solutions based only on men's experiences are likely to contribute further to women's poverty, in both developed and developing countries. That in itself may enforce continuing environmental degradation. In developed countries, for example, a seemingly straightforward reduction in street lighting to save energy may have an adverse effect on women's safety. Stringent restrictions on the use of private cars, especially in the absence of extensive public transport policies, may affect women disproportionately in that much of women's use of cars is in support of household duties—taking children to school, the doctor, shopping—which cannot often be easily undertaken through public transport that is often geared, in its scheduling, to commercial working hours. Energy conservation measures, taxes on energy use, and changes to public transport need to take into account women's roles within the community and the extent of poverty among women. Chris Thomas (1983) suggests that alternative technologies that are argued to be more environmentally friendly may well increase women's loads or be inappropriate if their responsibilities do not change—e.g., the use of bicycles instead of cars makes shopping and child transportation difficult. Natural fibers may require longer washing and ironing times. The responsibility for making environmentally sound consumer choices is often placed on the household, which means that women will largely shoulder the burden of this responsibility. This reinforces the home as both the site of private and ecological morality, and as woman's domain. As Lesley Instone notes, "green-house-work" is couched in terms of extending a woman's labor of love for her family and home to the environment (1992: 525). In this way, the environment becomes part of the private domain of women.

Where is "Women and the Environment?"

There has been some response within the international community to the need to recognize connections between women and the environment. Nevertheless, the environmental debate has been gendered in the way women's connection with environmental insecurity has been acknowledged and addressed. It has, for the most part, been marginalized into special conferences. That is, "woman" as a category has been added *on*, not added *in*. These forums have, for the most part, also been mobilized by women. As Bella Abzug, former member of the U.S. Congress and Co-Chair of the Women's Environment and Development Organization observes, "everywhere women are catalysts and initiators of environmental activism. Yet policymakers continue to ignore the centrality of women's roles and needs" (see WorldWIDE Network 1992: 3). Maurice Strong, Secretary General of United Nations Conference on Environment and Development, has referred to the "pressing need to continue to *centralize* women's issues and to ensure the incorporation of their collective perspectives, experiences, and contributions to sustainable development" (UNIFEM, 1993: 3, emphasis added).

The 1985 Nairobi Forward-Looking Strategies for the Advancement of Women, adopted at the conference to review and appraise the United Nations Decade for Women, included environment in its plan of action and emphasized women's participation in national and international ecosystem management, although Annabel Rodda suggests that the link between women and environment was not a major theme (1991: 5). Nevertheless, the Strategies did note that "environmental degradation is . . . a contributing factor to deplorable conditions endured by many women" (see UNCED/UNICEF/UNFPA, 1991: 3). A series of "Women Nurture the World" workshops was convened by the Environment Liaison Centre at the non-govermental organisation forum held during the Nairobi conference. In 1986, a caucus on "Women, Environment and Sustainable Development" was held at the IUCN (the International Union for the Conservation of Nature)-sponsored 1986 international conference on conservation and development, which examined the implementation of the 1980 World Conservation Strategy. The same year UNEP (the United Nations Environment Program) established a committee of senior women advisors on sustainable development (Senior Women's Advisory Group on Sustainable Development). The IUCN set up a working group on women, environment, and sustainable development in 1987.

Between February 1989 and March 1991, four regional assemblies on women and the environment were convened as one of UNEP's programmatic responses to the Nairobi Forward-Looking Strategies. In November 1991, the Senior Women's Advisory Group (SWAG) to the Executive Director of UNEP convened a Global Assembly on Women and the Environment—the "Partners in Life" conference—with a particular focus on demonstrating women's capacities in environmental management. This meeting was followed immediately by the World Women's Congress for a Healthy Planet. In September 1992, INSTRAW (the U.N. International Research and Training Institute for the Advancement of Women) sponsored an inter-regional workshop on the role of women in environmentally sound and sustainable development in Beijing.

While there has, therefore, been growing attention paid to the connection between women and the environment in a number of women-centered forums, and some acknowledgment of the centrality of women's roles, knowledge, and experiences, little attention has been paid to women or questions of gender in the key texts. The 1987 report of the World Commission on Environment and Development, popularly known as the Brundtland Report after its chairperson Gro Harlem Brundtland, for example, makes almost no reference to the role of women or the consequences for women of global environmental degradation. The language of the environment debate is itself a gendered one, even where it pretends to be generic, and women have been silenced in this way. For example, the 1972 Stockholm Declaration on the Human Environment states, in its opening paragraph:

> *Man* is both creature and molder of *his* environment, which gives *him* physical sustenance and affords *him* the opportunity for intellectual, moral, social and spiritual growth.

Principle 8 of the Declaration suggests that:

> Economic and social development is essential to ensuring a favorable living and working condition for *man* and for creating conditions that are necessary for the improvement of the quality of life.

United Nations Conference on Economic Development (UNCED)

Gender issues were given little attention in the preparatory committees for UNCED and they were only taken up after intense lobbying by women. Filomina Chioma Steady, from Sierra Leone, was appointed as special advisor on women in environment and development to the UNCED Secretary General. The outcome of the Rio Conference was mixed in terms of its attention to women and to questions of gender. It must be acknowledged that the 1992 Rio Declaration was more sensitive to the gendering of language than its Stockholm counterpart. Principle 1 of the Declaration observes that:

> *Human beings* are the center of concerns for sustainable development. They are entitled to a healthy and productive life in harmony with nature.

More importantly, and again in contrast with the Stockholm Declaration, principle 21 specifically addresses the importance of women. Women, it says, "have a vital role in environmental management and development. Their full participation is therefore essential to achieve sustainable development."

Agenda 21, the global plan for action adopted at the Rio Summit, also addresses the women/environment connection. The Executive Director of UNIFEM (the United Nations Development Fund for Women), Sharon

21

Capeling-Alakija, went so far as to call it "a tribute to the solidarity of a global women's caucus which has played a strong role in helping to define a document which promises a world of better opportunities for women" (UNIFEM, 1993: 2). Nevertheless, Agenda 21 is a *non-binding* agreement among states. It emphasizes program action to be taken by governments, many of which have done little for women in the past. The references are a mix of participation-oriented statements and goals (a liberal agenda), along with more specific references to the ways in which women have been marginalized, emphasizing the importance of empowering women (for women and for achieving environmental security).[7]

Agenda 21 is something of a "wish list," both for the environment and for women. Joan Martin-Brown argues that "the events at UNCED did not succeed in fundamentally altering perceptions about either the roles and capacities of women or their relationship to the achievement of sustainable development" (1992: 706). Intergovernmental statements since then have at least continued to focus on Agenda 21 as a source of programmatic action on women and the environment. A resolution adopted at the 37th Session of the Commission for the Status of Women in March 1993 focused on the importance of giving *real* effect to Agenda 21, both within CSW, and at national and U.N. levels. The 1995 Fourth World Conference on Women in Beijing was identified as a forum for reviewing progress. The UNEP Governing Council has urged governments to involve women in all aspects and at all levels of decisionmaking on Agenda 21, and the Executive Director of UNEP has been asked to ensure that all UNEP programs take gender considerations into account.

Where are Women?

The Executive Director of the U.N. Population Fund has observed that if energy, land, and water are the keys to survival, the keys are held by the women of the world (WorldWIDE, 1992: 4). If women are detrimentally affected by environmental degradation, and if their activities in society as presently constructed are so important to the search for solutions, then it makes sense to ask, "where are women?" The question is more than a statistical one. It is a political one which, in exposing absences, also exposes the equally important question of where women are *not*. Making women visible reveals both absences and differential patterns of participation. Women's activity and participation in environmental politics (if we take that to include decisionmaking and management), is primarily confined to those areas which are marginalized or undervalued in their contribution to decisionmaking and debate. The connections between this marginalization and the devaluing of those activities makes a telling political statement about the nature of women's invisibility.

Just as women are underrepresented in the formal institutions of states, so too are they underrepresented in the formal international or interstate decisionmaking processes and forums where environmental issues are discussed and where decisions are made. As former Minister for Natural Resources and Tourism in Zimbabwe, Victoria Chitepo, has remarked "international agencies and governments have everywhere ignored the vital part that women play in caring for the environment. Their voice, like their knowledge and experience, is simply not heard" (Dankelman and Davidson, 1988: ix). Women's voices are silenced. As Sharon Capeling-Alakija, Director of UNIFEM, notes: "women have been central in the international effort to inscribe environment and development on the global agenda. Yet women are conspicuously absent from decisionmaking processes of all kinds" (WorldWIDE, 1992: 3). For example, at the UNCED, most of those making the decisions were men. There was only one woman head of state—President Finnbogadottir of Iceland. There was only one woman head of government—Prime Minister Gro Harlem Brundtland of Norway. There were few women among senior government negotiators. Since UNCED there has been some increase in the appointment of women to high profile environmental positions. The new executive director of UNEP is a woman (Elizabeth Dowdeswell). The Executive Director of the Earth Council, a nongovernmental organization established after Rio, is a woman, and the Council is making determined efforts to ensure gender balance in its membership and to "complement efforts of women's organizations and networks . . . to enable a better participation of women" (WorldWIDE, 1993: 8).

This absence from or marginalization within formal decisionmaking (or, in liberal terms, the public arena) does not mean that women are not active on environmental issues. Women are active and effective participants in nongovernmental organizations and in grassroots movements. Much of the organizational energy for environmental work comes from women. Indeed, it is this activity which brings women into much closer contact with the realities of environmental management and which provides examples of women's empowerment and commitment to the environment. The best known grassroots movements are probably the Chipko movement in Northern India and the Greenbelt movement in Kenya both of which date to the 1970s.[8] In the Northern Indian state of Uttar Pradesh, women placed themselves between loggers and the trees as a protest against logging and its environmental impact. In Kenya, the tree-planting activity begun by the National Council of Women has resulted in over 1,000 public green belts and over 15,000 private green belts owned by small scale farmers. There are many other lesser known examples of women working together to protect and repair the environment. For example, women have worked to combat soil erosion in Ghana, to focus on pollution control in Lake Maruit in Egypt, and to resist toxic waste dumping in the Bay of Bengal in Bangladesh. Women have actively lobbied for organic farming practices in Barcelona, built NGO coalitions for environment

ELLIOTT

23

and development in the Netherlands, and encouraged sea-turtle conservation programs in Brazil. They have fostered alternative methods of waste collection in Peru and campaigned against hazardous waste in the United States.[9] Women were actively involved in the Global Forum, the NGO gathering which paralleled and connected with the intergovernmental summit, and the WorldWIDE Network organized a workshop on women's contribution to environmental management. The NGO treaties which were negotiated at the Global Forum include the "NGO Global Women's Treaty seeking a just and healthy planet."

However, the question of "where women are" is still relevant to an investigation of grassroots activity. While it would seem that women make up half or more of the membership of nongovernmental organizations, public figures within the environmental movement tend still to be men.[10] This itself responds to and reinforces the idea of the public domain as men's domain. As Vandana Shiva notes, even the public face of the Chipko movement has been presented by men (1989: 67). Irene Dankelman and Joan Davidson surveyed 46 environmental NGOs in developing countries. In 31 of them women made up less than half the professional staff; 42 were headed by men, and 18 had no working relationship with women's organizations at all (1988: 117).

Women's visibility in grassroots movements and nongovernmental organizations contrasts strongly with their invisibility and absence in formal decisionmaking arenas. However, that very visibility is itself connected to the marginalization of grassroots activity in the global environment debate. The structural factors which have prevented women from becoming involved in the formal process have ensured that they will seek avenues for participation in those areas which are located at the margins. This participation, coupled with the view of women's activities as inherently less valuable, also ensures that these areas will continue to be marginalized. Women's contribution to environmental management through this activity is undervalued and not seen as crucial or important in the state-based decisionmaking apparatus. In a constructed world view which values scientific rationality, women's lived experience of managing and living and working in close proximity with the environment is seen as unscientific—and therefore of little value. However, women's participation in informal and cooperative movements must not be seen as simply or even necessarily a result of their marginalization or invisibility in formal processes. Such a view would define women not as agents but only as passive respondents to the inclusive or exclusive nature of state-based and male-dominated decisionmaking processes.

Women's participation in social movements and grassroots organizations may also be interpreted as a positive exercise of agency. Vandana Shiva identifies women not as victims but as "voices of liberation and transformation" (1989: 47). New social movements are based on values which are more amenable to women's lived experiences, but which may be unfamiliar in mas-

ELLIOTT

culinist institutions. They have horizontal rather than vertical links and emphasize cooperative rather than competitive action. Momentum is provided
by collective or group energy. Women's environmental experience is a direct
and proximate one, and is matched by activity and participation that is also
direct and proximate. It is, then, something of a dilemma that such activity
should be marginalized and undervalued.

The "more women" strategy identified in Agenda 21 is, for the most part, a
liberal feminist exercise, although it is likely that equity of representation will
change both the dynamics and the agenda of the environmental debate.[11]
Nevertheless, while full participation is clearly required on equity and democratic grounds, it does not necessarily address the connection between
women and environmental degradation. Nor does it address the other underlying gender inequities in the debate. The questions asked, the nature of the
debate, and the solutions proposed are gendered. Incorporation and participation is not enough and may well even be counterproductive to women if the
gendered nature of the institutional framework and the definition of concepts
such as sustainable development are not acknowledged and transformed at
the same time. These are shaped by masculinist institutions which take their
inherent terms of reference from men's lived experiences, which are then
adopted as the norm and treated as value and gender free.

FEMINISM AND THE ENVIRONMENT

Environmental degradation is both a woman's concern and a feminist concern. Feminist scholarship provides an analysis of environmental destruction
which locates the domination—and subsequent degradation—of nature in a
masculinist world view and identifies parallels and connections with the oppression of women. Current patterns of development and the use and management of natural resources are in line with male values which see the relationship with nature as one of control. There is a predominance of masculinist ways of seeing and doing, which replicates both the language and practice
of control. Solutions proposed have for the most part been predicated on
men's lived experiences rather than on those of women and are argued to be
found within rational and scientific knowledge which marginalizes women's
knowledge (which is defined as emotive). Indigenous women are especially
marginalized in this context. Such solutions are identified in terms of managing resources more efficiently and are frequently sought in the realm of the
economy, measured always in terms of the formal (male) economy. The
metaphors of environmental politics invoke images of the domestic space traditionally populated by women and children, and link environmental management to women's experiences not in a positive way, but in a way that continues to support the marginalization of both the women/environment connection and the participation of women in environmental decisionmaking.
The idea of the pursuit of ecological security as planetary "housekeeping" in-

25

ELLIOTT

vokes an image of the devalued and private domain of women, rather than the public statecraft of men. Ecofeminist analysis argues that in the search for solutions to the environmental crisis, the burden of ecological morality is placed upon women within the private domain (see Ruether, 1975: 200), whereas ecological immorality belongs to the activities of business and decision-makers within the formal and public sphere. Environmental responsibility increasingly falls on women and women are made consumers, not decisionmakers (Instone, 1992: 525).

Carolyn Merchant (1983) argues that this mechanistic view of nature, as something to be used, dates to the scientific revolution and the Enlightenment of the 17th century—a world view (indeed, a paradigm shift) written for and by men. As an emancipatory project, the Enlightenment was limited; it was *for* men and *from* nature. Both women and nature, then, became objects to be used and controlled. It emphasized and privileged rational thought and scientific processes as the only basis of human (or male?) progress—values which were then argued to be found in men but not in women. In *The Masculine Birth of Time*, Francis Bacon's metaphors are explicitly those of domination—nature is to be bound to service and made a slave (see Merchant, 1983: 114). Thus women's knowledge and women as knowers were undervalued and discounted.[12] Progress was to be found through and was connected with industrialization and the advancement of capitalism, which could only be achieved through the control and management of nature.[13] This epistemological transformation was gendered—control, rationality, and the metaphors of domination over nature were more appropriate to a masculinized society. The Enlightenment and the development of liberal theory emphasized a consciously constructed distinction between public and private domains. The latter was increasingly the sphere of women and women's work, both of which were made invisible, and were marginalized from the economy and the polity in industrialized societies. There were, at the very least, parallels between this marginalization and construction of dualisms, and the oppression of women and the domination of nature.

Domination over nature was also essential for and connected to control over geographic spaces and the process of state-making. It provided a basis and rationalization for the expansion of state power through imperialism. New sources of resources were necessary to maintain the economic and military strength of the state (vis-a-vis other states) in a mercantilist world. The expansion of the European state system in this way globalized the mechanistic view of nature. In many ways, non-western ecological traditions were lost in a hierarchy which now extended a God-man-woman hierarchy to include nature and non-European men and women.

Both the discipline and practice of international relations has taken as its primary unit of analysis the state, the geopolitical space, defined through boundaries drawn to ensure and enhance control over natural resources,

26

rather than ecopolitical space. However, ecosystems cannot be protected by such boundaries and, indeed, may be destroyed by the drawing of such boundaries. Traditional and masculinist notions of security in international relations are state-centric and conflictive. Territorial and political security is measured in part by control over geopolitical spaces and the natural resources of a state. Security is acquired and maintained against an "other" and includes undermining of the other's control over resources and space. This perspective also supports, and indeed emphasizes, military and territorial definitions of security, which is to be achieved through masculinist models of power balancing, power seeking, and self-help through military security. This competitive, security-seeking behavior of states, which realist international relations scholars normalized, and which itself drew from an analysis of human nature as competitive, self-interested and individualistic, presents dangers to the security of the natural environment and has engendered a mindset which is inappropriate to the pursuit of ecological security.

The masculinist project of militarism is also a cause of environmental insecurity, and compounds further the structural violence against women through environmental degradation. The mindset which underpins militarism is incompatible with both women's lived experiences and the search for ecological security.[14] Military power, the traditional instrument of security in a masculinist state-system, is not only incapable of achieving environmental security, but it may well be counterproductive. Warfare and the preparation for war imposes burdens on the environment, and negatively affects women both through the damaging of the environment upon which they rely for food, energy, and water, and directly upon them as targets of aggression and as objects through which to demoralize the enemy. Environmental degradation is frequently an "unintended consequence" of war. The environment is often used as an instrument of war to deny the "enemy" access to land or other valued resources. Further, the preparation for war also consumes resources and degrades local environments. Maintenance of militaries, whether in war or peace time, diverts resources. Military spending accounts for an estimated 1 trillion per annum (in U. S. dollars). Not only does this divert funding from social and environmental programs, but it also finances activities which are damaging to the environment.

This view of security contradicts and marginalizes the pursuit of ecological security. It offers no solutions for the security of the natural environment nor for the environmental security of the earth's inhabitants, human and non-human. Traditional state-centric notions of security in international relations argue that secure states make for a secure world and, by extension, for secure people or, in realist discourse, citizens. Environmental security, however, understands that it is only a secure ecosystem, which recognizes interdependencies and connections, which can ensure security for people. Yet ecological security is often associated (consciously or otherwise) with the devalued realm of women, and is not taken seriously on the foreign policy agenda of states nor in the mainstream discipline of international relations. As a "global issue that defies national boundaries and calls for collective action, caring for the environment does not fit well with the power-seeking, instrumental behavior of states" (Tickner, 1992: 97).

These connections between women/woman and environment/nature, and between feminism and ecology, have been most critically explored within that body of feminist scholarship which has been labeled ecofeminism. As a political project, ecofeminism calls simultaneously for a review of man's relationship to nature and man's relationship to woman (Salleh, 1992: 197). While there is as much diversity within ecofeminist scholarship as there is within feminism generally, ecofeminism takes as its starting point the parallels between the domination of women and the domination of nature identified above. It acknowledges that women's lives as they are lived are closer to nature than men, and therefore women are—or at least ought to be—in the vanguard of developing sustainable responses to the environment. There is, therefore, an acknowledgment that the experience of women and men with nature is different. It is the basis for that difference, and the political strategy that is then advanced, that is the cause of some debate within ecofeminism, feminism generally, and ecophilosophy.

Two main strands of ecofeminism can be identified. Robyn Eckersley identifies them as biologically based and socially based (1992: 66). Val Plumwood refers to cultural ecofeminism and social ecofeminism (1992: 10). Biological or cultural ecofeminism portrays women's identification with nature as connected with and arising from women's reproductive and nurturing roles and capabilities in a way that is inherent and which provides a superior (rather than simply a different) insight. In this view, this insight is one that men cannot have. Biological ecofeminism also emphasizes women's spirituality and life affirming sensuousness, both of which are set against masculine competition and power. The metaphors of nature as female and the Earth as nurturing mother are powerful in cultural or biological ecofeminism. The ecological crisis, in this view, requires acknowledging the value and superior insight of women and the feminine, a strategy Plumwood criticizes as the "feminism of uncritical reversal" (1992: 11). As Joan Griscom points out, simply because women are able to bear children does not mean that doing so is essential to their nature (cited in Eckersley, 1992: 67). Biological or cultural ecofeminism does raise problems associated with seeking to replace one set of dualisms with another, especially when those dualisms arise from within a patriarchal society. Further, this kind of biological determinism is itself the source of much of women's oppression and there are dangers in adopting it in order to privilege feminine values over masculine ones. Indeed, asking questions about who is closer to nature is problematic, because it derives from and perpetuates dualisms. Nevertheless, the extent of essentialism in ecofeminism

ELLIOTT

is unclear. Stephanie Leland does say, for example, that the "essential nature of man is masculine and the essential nature of woman feminine," and that the urge to separate, divide, and individuate is a masculine impulse (1983: 68). Nevertheless, she also goes on to argue that each of us is a reflection of the interrelatedness of the dynamic energies of both principles. Indeed, when Vandana Shiva talks about the feminine principle, she does so not in an essentialist way, but rather one which may arise from women's lived experiences as they have been lived in the past, but which is not necessarily applicable to women only.

It is, however, a different matter to acknowledge that women may experience their lives in closer proximity to nature. It is not necessary to argue that this essentializes women's experiences. As Ariel Salleh points out, "it is nonsense to assume that women are [inherently] any closer to nature than men" (1992: 208–9). What is more pertinent, she suggests, is that "the language that typifies a woman's experience situates her along with nature itself." Women's connection with nature, then, is to be found in the social construction of dualisms and hierarchies: women's access to the sustaining principle has an historical and cultural basis (Shiva, 1989: 42). Social ecofeminism acknowledges the basis of the dualisms and the gendered nature of women's experiences of nature under patriarchy, but seeks to move beyond those dualisms. In the same way, ecofeminists are resistant to the liberal feminist project of "more women" within a masculinist world, which seeks to sever the women/nature connection but does not challenge the basis of the dualism. Indeed, in this view, dualisms and hierarchies are inappropriate to an ecological life which must emphasize diversity and interconnectedness. Social ecofeminism uses the connection between women and nature as a "vantage point for creating a different kind of culture and politics that would . . . transform the nature/culture distinction itself and to envision and create a free ecological society" (King, 1983: 123).

The oppression and domination of women, and the construction of the feminine within patriarchal society, has engendered women's disproportionate disadvantage in environmental degradation. Yet it is that more proximate experience of nature, and the values that arise from that experience and that stem from the "feminine," which are a source (or a potential source) of women's strength and of the solutions to environmental insecurity. Vandana Shiva identifies the ecological crisis—the death of and violence against nature—as the death of the feminine principle (1989: 42). In contrast with the masculine, the undervalued feminine is holistic, caring, cooperative, intuitive, non-hierarchical, welcoming, and acknowledging of diversity. Women and nature, Shiva suggests, "are connected not in passivity but in creativity and the maintenance of life" (1989: 47).

While ecofeminism is a political project and activity which supports women's ecological activism, and seeks to explain and understand the connections between women and nature within a broader debate about ecological security, it is also engaged in a critical project within ecophilosophy. While ecology as a science is an holistic science which takes account of long-term views, few ecologists raise the issue of gender relations either within their discipline or in terms of rethinking its assumptions and propositions. Social ecologist Janet Biehl characterizes ecofeminism as a "disquieting tendency" within feminist thought (1991: 1). Ariel Salleh retorts that without feminism, the "radical potential of social ecology remains blunted" (1992: 199). Deep ecologist Warwick Fox argues that "feminism has nothing to add to the concept of environmental ethics" (cited in Plumwood, 1992b: 64). Freya Mathews suggests that women who subscribe to deep ecology invite the charge of exemplifying a masculine philosophy (1992: 489). Janis Birkeland refers to other forms of ecophilosophy or environmental ethics as "Manstream" green thought (1992).[15]

RE-GENDERING/RE-VISIONING

What is required to re-gender the global environment debate, to overcome what is both an explicit and an implicit gender bias? More women, or adopting gender-neutral language along the lines of the Rio Declaration, is not enough. The argument is not just about numbers or language, although both are clearly symptomatic of the gendered nature of the problem. It is also about the feminization of the institutional framework and issues. Feminization, in this context, is not a negative concept (as it is often used, for example, in the concept of the feminization of poverty). It is about valuing women's contributions and taking them seriously. Women must also be seen not just as victims of environmental degradation, but also as agents who must participate equally in the solution to these problems. Women's knowledge, experience, and potential are untapped at policy levels because their crucial roles are not recognized. What is required is a transformation of the institutions of global governance, not only to acknowledge the centrality of women's roles, needs, and experiences—itself an exercise which goes further than simply inscribing women's issues on the agenda—but in a way which ensures that women are able to participate fully as decisionmakers and agenda setters at all levels, and in a way which explores solutions and processes that fully reflect women's lived experiences and their values. The voices of women need to be heard. *Gender* issues—rather than *"women's"* issues—have to be integrated into environmental debates at the same time as the connections between environment and development, and environment and militarism, are acknowledged. These connections have yet to be adequately acknowledged in debates about rethinking our relationship with the environment and with nature. Without this recognition and the participation of women, environmental security is not possible.

Feminist international relations theory is more than a project of decon-

ELLIOTT

struction. It seeks to build a model of the world that starts at the bottom and emphasizes connections and interdependencies. It supports an interpretation of power as cooperation and empowerment rather than domination and subjugation. It also supports a view of security which speaks to the security of individuals. It emphasizes shared and common interests, accountability and responsibility, mutual support and trust— values that are not common to a masculinist international relations and which are often dismissed as irrational and, therefore, illogical. Yet it is this view of security which supports the achievement of environmental security. This pursuit of ecological security, based on women's lived experiences and feminist insights and values, includes a holistic approach which emphasizes the long-term needs of the ecosystem and of people, intergenerational equity, respect for nature and the environment, and a recognition of caretaker and stewardship roles.

The required strategy is neither a masculinization of women (a liberal feminist strategy), nor a feminization of men. Rather, it points to a nongendered humanity which recognizes and respects diversity without hierarchy or "otherness," which transcends gender. Vandana Shiva calls for a "recovery of the feminine principle which will allow a transcendence and transformation of the patriarchal foundations of maldevelopment" (1989: 13). In spite of its apparent location within dualism, the feminine principle recognizes neither dualisms nor an ontological divide (Shiva, 1989: 40). As Shiva points out, "the existence of the feminine principle is linked with diversity and sharing" and is "not exclusively embodied in women but is the principle of activity and creativity in nature, women, and men" (1989: 45, 52).

31

NOTES

1. For more detailed information on environmental issues, see, for example, Rodda, 1991; Thomas, 1992; and Porter and Brown, 1991.

2. The IPCC estimates are that if no action is taken to halt the emission of greenhouse gases, there will be an increase in average surface temperature of approximately 1 degree Celsius by the year 2030, and perhaps 3 degrees Celsius by the end of the next century. Those temperature changes will be uneven and are more likely to be higher nearer the polar latitudes. The melting of non-polar glacial ice and the expansion of water with thermal heating means that sea levels will rise (although the degree of that rise is contested). The estimated range suggests a rise of between 20 and 50 cm by 2030 and between 65 cm and one meter by the end of the 21st century.

3. Low-lying island countries which are likely to be inundated include the Maldives, the Marshall Islands, Tokelau, Tuvalu, Kiribati, and Tonga—states which have contributed nothing to global warming. Other countries at risk because of their high coastal population density include Bangladesh, Egypt, Gambia, Indonesia, Mozambique, Pakistan, Senegal, Surinam, and Thailand.

4. An increase in UVB rays decreases phytoplankton activity. Not only does this affect the robustness of the marine ecosystem (already often affected by over-fishing), but it also removes an important CO_2 fixer from the oceans.

ELLIOTT

5. The use of these fuel substitutes may also be damaging to health in that the smoke they produce can be toxic. They are also less efficient sources of energy and may require a move to foodstuffs that require less cooking time, but which are also less nutritious.

6. Green Revolution technologies often used seeds that were supposedly genetically superior, but which often stored poorly, required increased fertilizers, and had to be bought anew each year, rather than germinating from last year's crop. All of this meant that the poor—frequently women—were unable to take advantage of such technology as well as being further marginalized from the land.

7. In spite of the references to women and their connection with the environment and role in ecosystem security in the Rio Declaration and Agenda 21, neither the Climate Change Convention, the Biodiversity Convention, nor the Statement of Forest Principles refer explicitly to the impact of environmental degradation on women or the imperatives for involving women in decisionmaking.

8. For further details on the Chipko movement, see Shiva (1989) and Rodda (1991). Both also provide further information on the Greenbelt Movement in Kenya. The women of Chipko and Wangari Maathai and the women of the Greenbelt Movement have received the Alternative Nobel Prizes for their work.

9. These examples are taken from the list of women's environment and development projects presented as success stories at the Partners in Life Conference in 1991.

10. See NWCC (1991: 44).

11. Plumwood refers to this as the "feminism of uncritical equality" (1992a: 11).

12. In this context, several feminist writers have drawn attention to specific references to masculine science in the work of Francis Bacon. See, for example, Shiva (1989: 14).

13. Simone de Beauvoir argues, as others have done, that "men seek to dominate women and nature for reasons which are not simply economic" (cited in King, 1983a: 121). This kind of analysis links men's domination to their fear of the "other," in particular women, and to their identification of women with nature.

14. Jean Freer sees the space program as an extension of the militaristic assumption of conquering which has "forcibly turned our attention away from the earth and her needs" (1983: 132).

15. Ariel Salleh has been engaged in a debate with both deep ecology and social ecology. Environmental ethics, she argues, reflects "for the most part, endeavors of academic men and middle-class nature lovers" (1992: 196). She identifies deep ecology as a "basically male defined environmental ethic" (1992: 199).

REFERENCES

Biehl, Janet. *Rethinking Ecofeminist Politics*. Boston: South End Press, 1991.

Birkeland, Janis. "Ecofeminism and Ecopolitics." In *Ecopolitics V; Proceedings,* ed. Ronnie Harding. Kensington: Centre for Liberal and General Studies, University of New South Wales: 546–554, 1992.

Brewer, Pat. "Women and Ecopolitics," In *Ecopolitics V; Proceedings,* ed. Ronnie Harding. Kensington: Centre for Liberal and General Studies, University of New South Wales: 540–545, 1992.

Brown, Valerie A. and Margaret A. Switzer. "Victims, Vicars and Visionaries: A Critique

ELLIOTT

of Women's Role in Ecologically Sustainable Development." In *Ecopolitics V; Proceedings*, ed. Ronnie Harding. Kensington: Centre for Liberal and General Studies, University of New South Wales: 531–539, 1992.

Caldecott, Leonie and Stephanie Leland, eds. *Reclaim the Earth: Women Speak Out for Life on Earth*. London: The Women's Press, 1983.

Cheney, Jim. "Ecofeminism and Deep Ecology," *Environmental Ethics*, 9 (2), Summer: 115–145, 1987.

Dankelman, Irene and Joan Davidson. *Women and the Environment in the Third World: Alliance for the Future*. London: Earthscan, 1988.

Dobson, Andrew. *Green Political Thought*. London: Harper Collins, 1990.

Eckersley, Robyn. *Environmentalism and Political Theory*. London: UCL Press, 1992.

ECOSOC. *UN Economic and Social Council, Commission on the Status of Women, Resolution E/CN.6/1993/L.12*. 12, 22 March, 37th Session, Vienna, March 17–26, 1993.

Freer, Jean. "Gaia: The Earth as Our Spiritual Heritage." In *Reclaim the Earth: Women Speak Out for Life on Earth*, ed. Leonie Caldecott and Stephanie Leland. London: The Women's Press, 1983.

Global Assembly of Women and the Environment. *Partners in Life*. July, 1992. Collection of unpublished papers presented at the assembly.

Instone, Lesley. "Green-House-Work." In *Ecopolitics V; Proceedings*, ed. Ronnie Harding. Kensington: Centre for Liberal and General Studies, University of New South Wales: 524–530, 1992.

King, Ynestra. "Towards an Ecological Feminism and a Feminist Ecology." In *Machina ex Dea: Feminist Perspectives on Technology*, ed. Joan Rothschild. New York: Pergammon Press, 1983a.

———. "The Eco-Feminist Imperative." In *Reclaim the Earth: Women Speak out for Life on Earth*, ed. Leonie Caldecott and Stephanie Leland. London: The Women's Press, 1983b.

Leland, Stephanie. "Feminism and Ecology: Theoretical Connections." In *Reclaim The Earth: Women Speak Out for Life on Earth*, ed. Leonie Caldecott and Stephanie Leland. London: The Women's Press, 1983.

Martin-Brown, Joan. "Women in the Ecological Mainstream." *International Journal*, XLVII, Autumn: 706–722, 1992.

Mathews, Freya. "Relating to Nature." In *Ecopolitics V; Proceedings*, ed. Ronnie Harding. Kensington: Centre for Liberal and General Studies, University of New South Wales: 489–496, 1992.

Merchant, Carolyn. "Mining the Earth's Womb." In *Machina ex Dea: Feminist Perspectives on Technology*, ed. Joan Rothschild. New York: Pergammon Press, 1983.

———. "The Global Ecological Revolution: An Ecofeminist Perspective." In *Ecopolitics V; Proceedings*, ed. Ronnie Harding. Kensington: Centre for Liberal and General Studies, University of New South Wales: 505 (Abstract only), 1992.

Merryfinch, Lesley. "Invisible Casualties: Women Servicing Militarism." In *Reclaim the Earth: Women Speak Out for Life on Earth*, Leonie Caldecott and Stephanie Leland. London: The Women's Press, 1983.

Moma, Fatma E. *Statement by the Representative of International Council of Women*. Nairobi: International Council of Women to United Nations Environment Programme Governing Council, 1993.

ELLIOTT

33

National Women's Consultative Council. *A Question of Balance: Australian Women's Priorities for Environmental Action.* Canberra: Australian Government Printing Service, 1991.

Office of the Status of Women. *Women and the Environment.* Canberra: Australian Government Publishing Service, 1992.

Plumwood, Val. "Feminism and Ecofeminism: Beyond the Dualist Assumptions of Women, Men and Nature." *The Ecologist* 22(1), January/February: 8–13, 1992.

_____. "Ecosocial Feminism as a General Theory of Oppression: Towards a New Synthesis." In *Ecopolitics V; Proceedings*, ed. Ronnie Harding. Kensington: Centre for Liberal and General Studies, University of New South Wales: 63–72, 1992b.

Porter, Gareth and Janet Welsh Brown. *Global Environmental Politics.* Boulder: Westview, 1991.

Rodda, Annabel. *Women and the Environment.* London: Zed Books, 1991.

Ruether, Rosemary Radford. *New Woman/New Earth: Sexist Ideologies and Human Liberation.* New York: Seabury Press, 1975.

Salleh, Ariel. "The Ecofeminism/Deep Ecology Debate: A Reply to Patriarchal Reason." *Environmental Ethics* 14(3), Fall: 195–216, 1992.

Shiva, Vandana. *Staying Alive: Women, Ecology and Development.* London: Zed Books, 1989.

Sontheimer, Sally, ed. *Women and the Environment: Crisis and Development in the Third World.* London: Earthscan, 1991.

Simmons, Pam. "The Challenge of Feminism," *The Ecologist* 22(1), January/February: 2–3, 1992.

Thomas, Caroline. *The Environment in International Relations.* London: Royal Institute of International Affairs, 1992.

Thomas, Chris. "Alternative Technology: A Feminist Technology?" In *Reclaim the Earth: Women Speak Out for Life on Earth*, ed. Leonie Caldecott and Stephanie Leland. London: The Women's Press: 160–165, 1983.

Tickner, J. Ann. *Gender in International Relations: Feminist Perspectives on Achieving Global Security.* New York: Columbia University Press, 1992.

UNCED/UNICEF/UNFPA. *Women and Children First.* Report of the symposium on the impact of poverty and environmental degradation on women and children. Geneva: May 27–30, 1991, 1991.

UNEP. *The United Nations Environment Programme and the Role of Women in Environment and Development.* Para 17.4, UNEP/GC.17/32: 58–59,

UNIFEM. *Agenda 21: An Easy Reference To the Specific Recommendations on Women*, 1993.

Warren, Karen J. "The Power and the Promise of Ecological Feminism," *Environmental Ethics* 12(2), Summer: 125–146, 1990.

Women's Environmental Network *Ecofeminism.* London: Women's Environmental Network, n.d..

Women's Working Group on Seveso. "Seveso is Everywhere." In *Reclaim the Earth: Women Speak Out for Life on Earth*, trans. Frances Howard-Gordon, ed. Leonie Caldecott and Stephanie Leland. London: The Women's Press, 1983.

WorldWIDE Network. "Gender and Environment: Beyond UNCED." *Partners in Life.* Issue 4, July, 1992.

WorldWIDE Network. "Nourishing Grassroots Participation in the Post-UNCED Period." *WorldWIDE News*, Summer: 4:8, 1993.

ELLIOTT

TO ACT WITHOUT "ISMS":

Women in East Central Europe and Russia

Lenore B. Goldman

IN 1991, I began work as an organizational consultant in East Central Europe with women's groups, ranging from reproductive rights to environmental groups to business. What I found was wildly ironic humor, formed through surviving Nazism, enduring communism, reeling through capitalism, dying over nationalism, and confronting feminism. These people could smell an "ism" long before any fire.

I will describe in these pages characteristics of women's lives under communism and major impacts of the post-communist transition on women. Women's responses, including organizing activities and their relationship to western feminism, will be highlighted. The geographic focus will be on Hungary, Poland, the Czech and Slovak Republics, the former Yugoslavia, and Russia. But first, a story.

Hungarian videographer Marta Elbert, founder of the dissident filmmakers' group Black Box, documented the officially nonexistent poverty, mental illness, environmental disaster, and illiteracy. Elbert met with me in 1992 to discuss her work and Hungary's abortion rights campaign. Lunch and autobiographical narrative were over. As coffee was served, Elbert folded her arms. "Now I have my question for you," she said and spat out her challenge. "What makes you think women need to be emancipated?"

Layers of meaning underlie that one question. On its face, Elbert displayed the fashionable antifeminist banter fostered by the worldwide trivialization of women's oppression. Yet she opted to break through Central European politesse into real investigation, conveying her seriousness about the subject.

The word "emancipated" locates the questioner (since she is in the 1990s and not the 1920s) firmly in the communist and post-communist world. The challenges Elbert poses are multiple. Do I understand the difference between communist propaganda about women's emancipation and the reality of life during those decades? Do I know Hungary's unique history? And, am I imposing cultural imperialism, bringing a western formula for enlightening the backward East Central European women? Learning to answer Marta, through the land mines of her spoken and unspoken inquiry, is our entry point.

DOUBLE BURDEN, DOUBLE LIVES: STRANGLING
UNDER COMMUNISM

Work

Female labor was essential to post-war industrialization, replacing men lost to war, fueling the Cold War military buildup, and manufacturing to meet basic needs. "Worker" was one's primary identity in communist society. Propaganda campaigns partnered rosy men and women sporting hammers or riding tractors. Legal abortion and state-supported childcare reinforced women's full workforce participation. Low wages that precluded one-income households enforced it. While the West spent nearly twenty years emulating June Cleaver, women in the East were working and well educated.

Educational and employment opportunities for women were real, but unequal. Men had first choice in graduate education, professional specialization, and jobs. Women were clustered in lower-paid, lower-prestige professions. In Poland, for example, women earned two-thirds of men's wages between 1982 and 1991 (Titkow, 1994). Similarly, nearly half of Russia's working women are in industry, construction, and transportation; they perform nearly double the unskilled manual labor as men. Food, garment, and textile industries pay 25–30 percent below average and employ over 80 percent women (Mirovitskaya, 1993). In Russia, where doctors can earn less than subway janitors, women comprise the majority of physicians.

Just because women worked didn't mean the state or one's husband offered a hand once they got home. Communist rhetoric about women's emancipation cynically served the state's economic needs. Maternity leave, childcare, abortion, employment, and academic opportunities were accessible to women

GOLDMAN

for decades on a scale unknown in the United States. Yet access fluctuated, determined by the Party's economic policies. No mass grassroots women's movement existed, so top-down policy and Party-controlled institutions left traditional family roles unchallenged. Expectations of women as mother and wife persisted. Most women, married and with children by their mid-twenties, worked, tended children, cooked and cleaned without labor-saving devices, and often spent hours in food lines.

Constraints on professional advancement hit women who took advantage of paid maternity leave. Needed social services were tied to one's job, so they were often unavailable to women who didn't work for the state (Ferge, 1992). Working women, nearly the entire able-bodied population, depended on state-run childcare centers of inconsistent quality. Women felt themselves to be "unreliable" workers, "bad" mothers, and inattentive wives (Beres, 1992). In the absence of public dialogue about "superwomen" or support groups for emotional and logistical aid, most women bore hardship alone, often feeling like failures. Fantasies of eating bonbons and playing hausfrau went unvoiced until the 1990s. They represented what women missed most: a rest and a choice.

Politics

The Soviet Women's Committee maintained the state myth of the all-powerful Soviet woman. It was illegal for women to organize outside the official Communist Party women's councils. The councils were mechanisms whereby the Party controlled the female population; in some cases meeting attendance was compulsory. Job discrimination, genuine political underrepresentation, poor contraception, and the double burden of jobs and domestic work were systematically ignored. State images of motherhood reinforced women's responsibility to serve state and family, but carry none of the power.

Feminism was portrayed as the luxury of bored, whiny, bourgeois western women who could afford to burn bras, while women in East Central Europe lined up for hours to get them. Few knew feminist theory and taught, wrote, or organized as women, let alone as feminists. However, a handful of Russian women academics and dissidents, familiar with feminism, started meeting and writing about women's issues, forming groups such as Moscow's Center for Gender Studies. One group of women dissidents from Leningrad was punished for circulating a women's almanac, *samizdat*, as early as 1979 (Waters, 1993). The Polish Feminist Association began meeting in 1980 to read and discuss western feminist texts and do consciousness-raising. The changes enabled them to expand their work to include a hotline, a women's conference, support for the abortion rights campaign, and writing. Hungarian Zsuzsa Korosi launched a petition campaign in 1974, collecting 1,500 signatures against restricted access to abortion, a state policy designed to diminish the number of women in the workforce. She faced disciplinary action and eventually left the country.

GOLDMAN

37

Yugoslavia stood as the exception to women's activism under communism. Yugoslavia enjoyed a more relaxed political climate and easier contact with the West that facilitated the building of an autonomous independent women's movement beginning in the mid-1970s. The 1978 Belgrade International Feminist Meeting marked the formal beginning of Yugoslavian post-war feminism; the gathering spawned numerous women's groups (Mladjenovic and Litriin, 1992). Years before the change, women's hotlines for victims of violence, battered women's shelters, a women's lobby, professional associations, an open discussion forum, and women's studies courses were established. The few women activists in the region who were out lesbians before the change were also most likely to be Yugoslav.

Homosexuality was closeted throughout the region. A common medical response was to recommend sex-change operations, particularly for women. The former Czechoslovakia, former GDR, former Soviet Union, and Poland have the highest number of female-to-male sex changes in the world (ten times more frequent than male-to-female changes). The rate in Sweden is one-to-one, and the United States reports more male to female transsexuals (Mulholland, 1993). Czech gay men and female-to-male transsexuals cleverly subverted antigay organizing laws by founding Lambda as a support group for patients with "sexual disorders," even wrangling funding for an internal magazine. Shortly after the Velvet Revolution, they split from the government Institute of Sexology and formed separate groups for men and women (Trnka, 1993).

The Underground

The crucial locus for organizing against communism rested with the underground and dissident movements. When westerners think of resistance to communism, they generally think of Havel, Walensa, or even Gorbachev. Not many know of journalist Helena Luczywo, who rebuilt the underground Solidarity network and newspaper that linked workers and intellectuals throughout Poland after 10,000 members were imprisoned under martial law. There is also Jirina Siklova, forced out of her university professorship into cleaning subway toilets, who maintained Czechoslovakia's dangerous courier network and smuggled articles under male pseudonyms by night. Women played pivotal roles in the opposition movements of every country in the region. Luczywo and Siklova are but two of many women who received scant, if any, acknowledgment for their leadership in the revolutions.

Western journalists used female opposition leaders as direct sources for years, yet never reported their existence. How was it, then, that the Solidarity newspaper got written, produced, and distributed for years with most major male Solidarity leaders in prison? Who made decisions, aired radio communiqués, and raised money when Havel and other dissidents endured Czechoslovak prisons? Parliamentarian Barbara Labuda notes, "Men didn't have the skills to manage the underground. Women were the brainpower. I wrote all of Frasyniuk's speeches. I gave the *Washington Post* an interview in his name. . . . Why shouldn't I say that this legendary hero was watching soccer games on TV while I was doing all the work?" (Penn, 1994). Why did no one mention the women who risked their lives to maintain contact with reporters who built careers covering the region?

Environment

While dissident women were working underground, environmentalists combined their ecological commitments with opposition to the state. One spawning ground for women leaders came from environmental activists. Environmental issues mobilized women to action as they watched their children suffer from asthma and birth defects and their men die young of lung disease or cancer. Under communism, environmental problems did not officially exist. The subsequent absence of formal environmental ministries meant that work on environmental issues was not technically illegal, although independent organizing or criticism of the state was. Groups performing the more apolitical tasks akin to those of the U.S. National Park Service—clearing nature paths in wilderness areas or leading backpacking trips—were frequently left alone. The Slovak Union for Nature and Landscape Protection and the Polish Ecological Club are but two of the large national environmental groups that predated and continued under communism through the present time. I have met conservationists who have worked for these organizations as long as twenty-five years. While most of their chapters survived by limiting themselves to less political activity, controversial actions were occasionally ventured.

Bigger risks arose when fighting industrial toxins that belched relentlessly from factories. Women started grassroots initiatives under communism to protect their children's health. Major figures in the environmental movement include Hungarian Zsuzsa Foltanyi. A parent and a chemist, Foltanyi, like many other women, brought her technical skills to environmental activism. She and her colleagues used their expertise to conduct illicit environmental impact studies with limited equipment, to distribute exposes nationwide, and form the Danube Circle in 1982, which protested building of the Gabcikovo/Nagymaros Dam in Hungary and Czechoslovakia (Kiss, 1993). Foltanyi now directs the Environmental Partnership Program in Hungary, serving dozens of environmental groups that have arisen since the fall of communism.

In the late 1980s, mothers in Prague protested the critical air pollution levels in the capital city, first with petitions and then with street actions such as blocking major thoroughfares with baby carriages. The group Mama '86 formed in Kiev in response to children's needs as victims of the Chernobyl nuclear disaster. The Supreme Council of Ukraine has yet to recognize Kiev

39

GOLDMAN

as an environmental disaster zone, meaning that its 50,000 children cannot rely on government support for treating illnesses or other problems resulting from radiation poisoning (Syomina, 1993).

Women encountered more than governmental or industrial obstacles to a cleaner environment. In early 1993, as Czechs and Slovaks were mourning the split of their country, I conducted training for Slovakian environmentalists. Late one evening the women shared a retreat center sauna, the only time away from their male colleagues who tended to dominate group discussions. A different, but familiar, deterrent to women's activism concerned them. One organizer ironically ticked off the obstacles to women's environmental activism: "First you take care of your husband, then you take of your children, then you take care of your husband, then you clean the house, then you take care of your husband, then you do the shopping, then you take care of your husband, then you do the cooking, then you take care of your husband, then you take care of your job, then you take care of your husband . . ."

SLAPPED BY DEMOCRACY: THE TRANSITION TO CAPITALISM

Disappointments follow the first breath of freedom. Gorbachev promised to revitalize the women's movement, support more women in political life, and create visibility for women's issues. Yet his talk of a "truly female destiny" and stronger traditional families foreshadowed post-1989 policies toward women that Russian feminist Anastasia Posadskaya dubs the "post-socialist patriarchal renaissance" (Posadskaya, 1992). I have not met women who want to return to the communist system, but I have met many who are no fans of capitalism. The transition to free elections and the free market has been a rude awakening to democracy "with a man's face" and the feminization of poverty.

Economics and Employment

Bilateral and multilateral banks, foreign and multinational corporations, and western government aid programs have exported capitalism in its most raw form. New governments were ill-equipped to question economic models and transition strategies like shock therapy, let alone create their own. Replicating ancient skirmishes between imperialist powers vying for a new piece of real estate, the western countries scrabble for position, each exporting their own brand of democracy, each expecting payoffs for their investments. Some argue that East Central Europe is being systematically underdeveloped by the West to preclude competition. The region is delivering new consumer markets to multinational corporations. However, it may be primarily as producer markets that the former eastern bloc interests the west, offering a cheap, educated, white manufacturing alternative to Asia and the southern hemisphere.

Post-communist governments had been sold on a "free" market. The first years were fraught with disbelief at how little, particularly in terms of social policy, could be solved by the invisible hand. The labyrinth of laws, regula-

GOLDMAN

tions, administrative infrastructure, and underlying mores required to control capitalism was shocking news to most East Central Europeans.

Western aid and lending programs have pressured new governments to demonstrate attempts to establish balanced budgets. In some cases they have made financing contingent upon reduction in government spending. Social programs have been dismantled or privatized in order to comply with external budgetary mandates. The governments of East Central Europe have, in many cases, slashed the very social services for which western feminists continue to fight in their own countries. State-supported services that people had relied upon under communism became suspect. Governments, internally motivated to distance themselves from benefits associated with the recent communist past, designed policies under western tutelage that are proving successful in emulating the problems that capitalism has not solved—inadequate health care, economic inequity, homelessness, crime, and structural unemployment. Unemployment, the worsening economic situation in several countries, resurgence of institutionalized sex discrimination, restriction of abortion, cutbacks in services to the elderly (who are disproportionately female), and mass closure of free childcare and healthcare facilities have combined to produce the harshest impact on women.

Women's double burden has not ceased. Women in Russia sleep and participate in entertainment less than men, work 76.3 hours to men's 59.5 hours, and contribute 2.5 times more than men to domestic chores (Mirovitskaya, 1993). The first generation without job security in over forty years feels creative excitement if they have been successful entrepreneurs, and endures fear if not—both options known by few under communism. The initial wave of unemployment in several countries hit predominantly male industrial workers, when the most inefficient state-owned factories closed. Subsequent layoffs have targeted women. Millions are unemployed in countries throughout the region. By late 1992, 83 percent of Russia's unemployed were women, most between the ages of 36 and 45 and college educated (Mirovitskaya, 1993). In Poland, over half of the unemployed are women; the number of job openings is seven times greater for men than women (Titkow, 1994). The majority of jobs offered women are in massage parlors, gambling casinos, as secretaries, and as domestics for the growing elite. Advertisements often explicitly state that only young (under 30), attractive ("shapely," "blonde") women need apply.

Most job retraining in Russia is available to men, diminishing women's options during "economic readjustment" even though women are usually better educated. Job retraining programs offered to female graduate engineers and scientists permanently laid off from Russia's crumbling defense industry have focused on sewing and maidservant skills. Russia's 95 percent male legislature, media, and churches widen the gender divide. The Minister of Labor in February 1993 argued, "Why should we try to find jobs for women when men

41

GOLDMAN

are idle and on unemployment benefits? Let men work and women take care of the homes and children" (Haan-de Vogel and van de Zande, 1993). Were it only that simple. Few can afford it.

The communist world prided itself as being comprised of cultured societies in which a worker could attend opera. Literacy rates were higher than in the United States. Few cars, bad teeth, and shortages of consumer goods were the most visible signs of want; not so today. Before prices were liberalized, Russian women spent half their income on food. By the end of 1992, the figure was 80 percent, and 60 percent of Russia's children suffer diseases related to malnutrition (de Haan-de Vogeland and van de Zande, 1993). Seventy-five percent of Russia's pregnant women suffer anemia (Gaidarenko, 1994). Male life expectancy has sunk to 59 years, female to 63.

Politics

Women swallowed a bitter pill in the 1989 transfer of power. Men took all the credit, with the collusion of western journalists, giving virtually no acknowledgment to the revolutionary roles played by women. They also usurped almost every formal government position. Half of Solidarity's membership and core leaders were women, particularly during the dangerous period of martial law. Yet of the sixty participants in the 1989 roundtable negotiations between Solidarity and the Communist Party, only one was a woman. In 1990, only four women participated on the 96-member National Solidarity Committee (Titkow, 1994). By 1993, not one political party in the Czech and Slovak Republics was headed or vice-chaired by a woman. Although several served under Havel, not one woman is a current member of the Czech government (Siklova, 1993).

Sex and the Family

Idealized notions of the pre-communist, pre-Nazi past have been resurrected, reinforcing nostalgic images of God, homeland, and family. In 1993 the Russian Parliament defeated the Draft Family Law for being too progressive; it is likely to re-emerge in a more conservative form. The Draft defended the rights of the family, with no reference to individual rights, defining the family as a union of two people raising children and as the basic unit not of society, but of the state. The Draft Law affirmed the rights of the unborn child and the equal right of a man to determine maternity. Marriage contracts would be required to establish businesses or farms or to join family social organizations (Ershova, 1993).

Under pressure from the Catholic Church, Poland created a tax structure that discriminated against single parents by eliminating tax deductions for their children. A single parent of one would pay the same taxes as a married, two-income, childless household. Most single parents and widowed are women, most children of divorce reside with their mothers, and women earn

66-67 cents to a man's dollar. Not surprisingly, the majority of the nation's poorest families were among the two million women affected. The debate revolved around what constitutes a family. Proponents argued deductions would encourage women to have children out of wedlock. A major lobbying and media effort was led by Joanna Szczesna, former underground Solidarity leader, editor of Poland's largest daily newspaper, and a single mother herself. Her exposé that single parents had a 1.2 million zlotys tax deduction for a child while car owners got a 6 million zlotys deduction struck the final blow. The single parent deduction was restored in December 1993 (Szczesna, 1994).

The influx of western pornography and MTV adds another burden to women's load: having to play the sexpot, according to a western aesthetic, in addition to being worker, wife, and mother. Pornography abounds, filling the vacuum left by now-defunct socialist morality (Beres, 1992). Considered a sign of liberated democratic culture, girlie pictures line walls in public offices in Hungary and are blazoned in Russia's mainstream newspapers. Within months after the first democratic elections in forty years, live sex shows were proliferating while factories closed. A 1991 survey of Russian technical high school girls found that 80 percent aspired to become hard currency prostitutes (Gaidarenko, 1994).

With little or no available contraception, sex education, or a women's movement encouraging shared responsibility for family planning, abortion had become women's primary form of birth control. Even today, Russian birth control pill production satisfies only 2 percent of the demand. Condoms are available only in urban centers, in quantities of three per man per year (Gaidarenko, 1994). Childbearing women throughout the region average as many as 9 abortions. Large Catholic populations in Poland and Hungary notwithstanding, the majority understandably continues to support abortion rights. In the Czech Republic, only 4 percent favored absolute prohibition and 93 percent of women 18 to 39 years old sought full freedom to choose (Buresova, 1993).

New markets for *Playboy* are paralleled by conversion campaigns drawing millions to fundamentalist Christianity and right-to-life groups. Evangelical Christians and the Catholic Church have colluded to restrict reproductive rights. The movie *Silent Scream* is shown in public schools and on television throughout the region. The international convention of the right-to-life movement was held in Bratislava, Czechoslovakia in May 1992 to bolster their East European evangelism. By January 1993, the Hungarian Parliament outlawed abortion except to protect the mother or child's health, for rape victims, or for appealed cases of extreme hardship.

Poland's Federation for Women and Family Planning, one of the few remaining coalitions, has demonstrated the possibility of combining women's groups, civil liberties groups, and professionals despite poor funding and limited organizational infrastructure. They have exemplified, as has the Campaign for a Free Choice in Hungary, growing skill and sophistication as organizers and lobbyists. The Federation collected 1.5 million signatures for a public referendum on abortion, one of the most remarkable feats of civic involvement anywhere in the region (Nowicka, 1994). Yet Catholic Church pressure on the government proved stronger. In February 1993, the reproductive rights of Polish women were virtually rescinded. The Federation has had to develop an underground network to aid women seeking abortions while continuing to lobby for change.

Violence

Violence against women has risen since the Wall fell. Gang rape now comprises 11 percent of all rapes in Russia. Only 6 percent of children treated by the Moscow Sexual Assault Recovery Center received parental support of any kind (Gaidarenko, 1994). Extreme distrust of the authorities by rape victims in most parts of the world is exacerbated in East Europe after decades, sometimes generations, of totalitarian rule. The housing shortage complicates the import of western strategies for rescuing women victimized by domestic violence; finding a separate apartment can take years, even a decade. Married couples frequently live with parents for years until limited housing becomes available. Some government offices have an entire statistical category for divorced couples who continue to live together. Under communism, housing for a single or divorced individual without children was often unavailable. Under post-communism, it may be unaffordable.

44

The war in the former Yugoslavia provides the most horrifying example of violence against women, with thousands of victims of imprisonment, torture, rape, murder, and genocide. The war has also placed enormous demands upon women activists. Women who recently identified as Yugoslavian must now maneuver through new national boundaries to aid Serbian, Croatian, Bosnian, and Herzegovinan women facing wartime violence, in addition to men's domestic battering and peacetime rape that continues to plague women. Some groups have sustained cooperation internally and with other groups despite extreme nationalist pressure to disband. Key figures in the women's movement played significant roles in the peace movement while working to sustain autonomous women's organizations. Overall, women comprise the majority of peace and antiwar groups, including the underground network helping Serbian men escape the country to avoid serving in the military. One woman claims to have smuggled as many as 30,000 men out of Serbia (Goldman, 1994). Women are resisting pressure from both the mainstream community and the peace movement to abandon autonomous women's groups, such as rape crisis centers and women's shelters. Several women's groups have already disbanded, unable to withstand the pressures. Everyone has endured or witnessed crushing personal loss.

GOLDMAN

Environment

Despite closing the most inefficient industrial plants, upgrading others, and investing millions of western dollars in pollution controls since 1989, extreme contamination by heavy metals, sulfur dioxide, and other industrial pollutants persists in such regions as Eastern Slovakia, southern Ukraine, and Poland's Upper Silesia. In Silesia, only 13 percent of grain produced can be eaten by humans and only 40 percent of potatoes can even be used as animal fodder (Sokolowska 1993). Erika, a Hungarian activist, has hairy sideburns from the hormone treatments she undergoes since her ovarian cancer treatment in 1992. Judit, twenty-one, suffers environmental disease, bearing cold extremities, severe fatigue, frequent illness, and multiple allergies. Judit buys produce directly from village women whom she interrogates about gardening practices in an effort to reduce her ingestion of pesticides. The lead in paint, the lead in gas, Chernobyl fallout—few talk about it.

FINDING HER VOICE: WOMEN RESPOND TO TRANSITION

During dramatic social transformation, the old and new are juxtaposed in unexpected ways until the next stage evolves its own language and rhythm and form and foundation. Seeming inconsistencies can stymie resident organizers and outside observers alike. To sing one's own song means creating chances to not just react, but to act on one's own terms.

Early in the transition, since the *nomenklatura* controlled capital, women's councils around the region succeeded in retaining offices, conference centers, palaces, and salaries. They claimed millions of members, mostly listing the names of women who had been compelled to join under communism, when repositioning themselves to their established international network of contacts. Women in fledgling grassroots groups that lacked facilities, funds, organization, mailing lists, and diplomatic connections were galled. Most of the nations' best women organizers went directly from opposition movements into the new governments or into rebuilding civil institutions. Post-communist women's groups were left with few seasoned leaders. Former dissident leaders now working in new governments considered the economy and employment to be higher priorities, leaving only a few women government insiders advocating for women's issues. Early post-communist parliaments avoided addressing women's concerns whenever possible, distancing themselves from benefits associated with the communist past and potential identification with feminism. These first few years were rocky before women's organizations achieved in-country credibility or garnered funds. They confronted the old councils, established their own groups and policies, learned to manage funds, and engaged in concrete organizing initiatives like retaining abortion rights or childcare benefits. They both learned from and suffered through a morass of western feminists telling them what to do. Many battled

GOLDMAN

internally over use of imported terminology, with several groups opting to use the neutral term "gender" untarnished by either Communist Party references to women's emancipation or westerners' feminism.

Why do women in post-communist countries often seem so allergic to feminism? Communist claims of women's emancipation were known propaganda, yet caricatures of feminism took hold. Men were your partners in revolution and family was your haven from the state. Feminism that suggests rejection of or separation from men is seen as disloyal, dangerous, counterproductive, and infantile. Furthermore, there is a propensity, reflected in language and behavior, to hide individual feelings, needs, and demands. Non-Americans, and East Central Europeans particularly, tend to protect personal spaces from public ones. Western feminism, on the other hand, emphasizes both the inherent value of sharing one's personal feelings, and as a vehicle to clarify how the personal is political. Women in the region experience enormous discomfort verbalizing and visualizing intimate domains before an audience of strangers. Discourse linking this to gender is almost nonexistent (Smejkalova-Strickland, 1993).

Susanna Trnka relates a Czech version. She explains that women rarely speak of their own lives in relation to some kind of common lesbian experience; any assumptions of lesbian commonality were undermined by women stressing the uniqueness of their own lesbian experience. Most of the women she knows are unconcerned with creating a common "lesbian identity" and instead are quite certain and proud of the fact that their way of being a lesbian is different from anybody else's. When she told a Czech friend about coming-out groups in San Francisco, she was clearly baffled and uninterested by the idea of so many people coming together to share their experiences of being gay, bisexual, or lesbian. "My problems are different from everybody else's—what could we possibly have to talk about?" she asked (Trnka, 1993).

The Marxism that often informs feminism or links it to other social struggles arouses further suspicion and misunderstanding between western feminists and women in the East. Proclamations of patriarchy under capitalism tend to evoke memories of political indoctrination. As Jirina Siklova, one of the region's preeminent feminists, notes:

> The ideological character of feminist trends makes us feel the same nausea, which, in the past, we used to experience with references to "class struggle". . . . We have unfortunately become certain that someone who has previously been exploited and oppressed is not necessarily the best leader of society. Socialism was a failure. . . . Party bosses who allegedly led the working class simply introduced ideology to it and spoke for it. Every now and then I have the impression that something like that is going on in today's feminism (Siklova, 1993).

East Central European women are articulating their own terms for engagement. "We are, beyond doubt, captives of our past. I am afraid, however, that at times West European and American feminist intellectuals are captives of their own ideology . . . our feminist movement is going to develop not on the basis of taking up some great ideologies, but rather on the basis of solving concrete, non-political, and primarily practical tasks" (Siklova, 1993). And practical they are. Within a few short years, a proliferation of women's organizations have sprung up in East Central Europe, against difficult financial odds and political obstacles. With the notable exception of small, feminist, grassroots funders like the Global Fund for Women, U.S. government aid and private foundations excluded non-social service women's groups until nearly 1994. Yet directories in Poland and Russia list well over a hundred women's groups.

Those providing counseling on rape prevention, seminars for women in business, assertiveness training, women's journals, exhibitions for women artists, and help for victims of violence almost universally profess antifeminism. Grazyna Kopinska, an influential leader in Poland, exemplifies this resistance to the term "feminism" while being stridently pro-women. At a February 1994 conference, I squirmed as Kopinska began her presentation with the typical statement, "I'm not one of those radical feminists," until I heard the blessed "but." She plunged into a strident and stunning speech. The heartbreaking story of her childhood "slavery" to the men in her family, details of the abuse and inequities women endure from men, and an eloquent plea for equal footing for Poland's children left few unmoved.

Prague Mothers, the environmental group, has built a national network of twenty Centers for Mothers, even though they reject feminism and refuse to discuss it (Satavova, 1993). One of their organizers, Jana Hradilkova, worked for years at the Gender Studies Center and writes on women's issues. Lesbians, who have played important leadership roles in western women's movements, are also disinclined to identify as feminists. They have found the luxury of privacy from state scrutiny to be a great relief. Coming out of the closet and mounting women's initiatives were priorities for few during the initial transition. Those few who have engaged in intensive organizing have managed, in several countries, to establish lesbian and gay conferences, summer camps, journals, meeting places, and political and social organizations.

Democratic practices cannot be taken for granted in East Central Europe. Communism was preceded by Nazism which was, in many cases, preceded by monarchy. Command-and-control authoritarianism is more familiar to men and women alike than the basics of setting an agenda, running a participatory meeting, discussing opposing viewpoints, making group decisions, or tolerating diverse opinions in the same group. The processes needed for successful women's organizing are similar to those needed by civil society in general. Siklova claims:

The small, politically uninterested women's organizations, which are established and dissolved in the course of a few months, frequently make West European women politicians smile. They have no ideology, they lack political profiles, and they defy all examination and sociological analysis. Their protagonists are not interested in the philosophy of feminism and will not play any role in future political elections. Yet now, right now, they are of extreme importance to us. Women, both as women and as citizens, learn through them to organize themselves and to become conscious of and stand up for their own interests. Through these activities people turn into citizens (1993).

Siklova also offers an analogy:

If there are large burns on the body, it is necessary to implant small bits of skin in the burned places, and then patiently wait and attend to the implants. Some implants wither away, others heal up and expand, giving rise to a substitute skin covering the burned area. In our Republic, and I think in the other countries of post-communist Europe, we are at the stage of developing a "new skin." That is, we are at the stage of forming citizens—citizens, for the present moment, irrespective of sex differences. Should we thwart this by impatience, the whole "healing" process would be delayed. This is why I ask you not to recommend that we fight for something. Do not ask us what political program we have. "We have none." We are suspicious of all "isms." At this stage of our development, feminism is no more than an ideology for us (Siklova, 1993).

Understanding the frame of reference brought by post-communist women mandates breaking out of categories. The opportunity to work closely with women in the region during this exhilarating and exasperating, promising and painful period of social transformation has changed me more than it has affected them. They have enabled me to question, understand, rejuvenate, and differentiate the core of my feminism from its rhetoric.

REFERENCES

Beres, Zsuzsa. "A Thousand Words on Hungarian Women." Budapest: Feminist Network, 1992.

Buresova, Alexandra. "Reproductive Rights Advocacy: Work in Dissent." In Susanna Trnka & Laura Busheikin, eds., *Bodies of Bread and Butter: Reconfiguring Women's Lives in the Post-Communist Czech Republic*. Prague: Gender Studies Center, 1993.

De Haan-de Vogel, Olga & Anne van de Zande. "Restore Hope: Coping Strategies in Time of Growing Contrasts." In *From Problems to Strategy: Materials of the Second Independent Women's Forum*. Hilversum Netherlands: Center for Gender Studies, 1993.

Einhorn, Barbara. *Cinderella Goes to Market*. New York: Verso, 1993.

Ershova, Elean. "The Draft Russian Family Law: A Step Backward for Women." *Surviving Together*, Summer, 1993.

Ferge, Zsuzsa. "Unemployment in Hungary: The Need for a New Ideology." In Bob Deacon, ed., *Social Policy, Social Justice and Citizenship in Eastern Europe*. Aldershot: Avebury, 1992.

Gaidarenko, Natalia. Untitled unpublished paper. Moscow, 1994.

GOLDMAN

Kiss, Ida Miro. "Women for Water, Hungary." In Judith Bucher and Ewa Charkiewicz, eds., *Women and Environment in Central and Eastern Europe.* Amsterdam: Mileukonakt Oost-Europa, 1993.

Mladjenovic, Lepa and Vera Litricin. "Beograde Feminists 1992: Separation, Guilt, and Identity Crisis." Beograd, Serbia, 1992.

Mirovitskaya, Natalia. "Women and the Post-Socialist Reversion to Patriarchy." *Surviving Together,* Summer, 1993.

Mulholland, Lisa. "Kissing on the Subway: Sexuality and Gender in the Czech Republic." In Susanna Trnka and Laura Busheikin, eds., *Bodies of Bread and Butter: Reconfiguring Women's Lives in the Post-Communist Czech Republic.* Prague: Gender Studies Center, 1993.

Nowicka, Wanda. "Two Steps Back: Poland's new Abortion Law." *Journal of Women's History,* Vol. 5(3): 151–55, 1994.

Penn, Shana. "The National Secret." *Journal of Women's History,* Vol. 5(3): 55–69, 1994.

Posadskaya, Anastasia. "The Women's Dimensions of the Social Transformation: from Forum to Forum." In *From Problems to Strategy: Materials of the Second Independent Women's Forum.* Hilversum Netherlands: Center for Gender Studies, 1993.

Reed, Carma. "Beyond Familiarity, or Tearing Down the Wall of Global Sisterhood: Gender Research on Post-Communist Eastern and Central Europe." In Susanna Trnka and Laura Busheikin, eds., *Bodies of Bread and Butter: Reconfiguring Women's Lives in the Post-Communist Czech Republic.* Prague: Gender Studies Center, 1992.

Regulska, Joanna. "Transition to Local Democracy: Do Polish Women Have a Chance? " In Marilyn Rueschemeyer, ed., *Women in the Politics of Postcommunist Eastern Europe.* Armonk and London: M.E. Sharpe, Inc., 1993.

Satavova, Monika. "Prague Mothers." In Judith Bucher and Ewa Charkiewicz, eds., *Women and Environment in Central Eastern Europe.* Amsterdam: Mileukontakt Oost-Europa, 1993.

Siklova, Jirina. "MacDonald's, Terminators, Coca-Cola Ads and Feminism: Imports from the West." In Susanna Trnka and Laura Busheikin, eds., *Bodies of Bread and Butter: Reconfiguring Women's Lives in the Post-Communist Czech Republic.* Prague: Gender Studies Center, 1993.

Smejkalova-Strickland, Jirina. "Do Czech Women need Feminism? Perspectives of Feminist Theories." In Susanna Trnka and Laura Busheikin, eds., *Bodies of Bread and Butter: Reconfiguring Women's Lives in the Post-Communist Czech Republic.* Prague: Gender Studies Center, 1993.

Sokolowska, Janina. "The Impact of Environmental Degradation on Human Health." In Judith Bucher and Ewa Charkiewicz, eds., *Women and Environment in Central and Eastern Europe.* Amsterdam: Mileukontakt Oost-Europa, 1993.

Syomina, Anna. "Presentation of the Activities of Mama '86, Ukraine." In Judith Bucher and Ewa Charkiewicz, eds., *Women and Environment in Central and Eastern Europe.* Amsterdam: Mileukontakt Oost-Europa, 1993.

Szcaesna, Joanna. Interview. Warsaw, 1994.

Titkow, Anna. "Polish Women in Politics: An Introduction to the Status of Women in Poland." In Mariyn Rueschemeyer, ed., *Women in the Politics of Postcommunist Eastern Europe.* Armonk and London: M.E. Sharpe, Inc, 1994.

Trnka, Susanna. "First, We Need a Room—Lesbian Activism in the Czech Republic."

GOLDMAN

49

In Susanna Trnka and Laura Busheikin, eds., *Bodies of Bread and Butter: Reconfiguring Women's Lives in the Post-Communist Czech Republic.* Prague: Gender Studies Center, 1993.

Waters, Elizabeth. "Finding a Voice: The Emergence of a Women's Movement." In Naneete Funk and Magda Mueller, eds., *Gender Politics and Post Communism.* New York: Routledge, 1993.

GENDER, CLASS, AND RACE IN ENVIRONMENTAL ACTIVISM:

Local Response to a Multinational Corporation's Land Development Plans

Claire McAdams

chapter 3

INTRODUCTION

THIS PAPER examines a critical political event involving the environmental movement in Central Texas. It examines the class, gender, and race/ethnicity of activists opposing a proposed land development which constitutes part of the global investment strategy of a multinational corporation. The development was and is believed to be a threat to the local underground and surface water resources of the community, and has brought unprecedented opposition.

Integrating gender into this analysis is essential as most theoretical positions in social movement research are based on the study of male-dominated movements (Wood and Jackson, 1982; Taylor and Rupp, 1991). Gender differences in environmental activism have been assumed, with women's activism seen as less frequent than men's because of women's absence of available time due to their multiple roles and responsibilities (Berk and Shih, 1980). This position ignores evidence that women's priorities lie with protection and maintenance of home and neighborhood (Boulding, 1981; Freuden-burg, 1981; and Markusen, 1980, among others). Work force participation gives women greater power in the family (Baca Zinn, 1980), and presumedly in both society and environmental activism (Logan and Molotch, 1987: 219). Shawn Burn and Alison Konrad (1987) see contact with political organizations, social group membership, and job autonomy as key preconditions to activism, but do not focus on gender differences in these attributes.

Surprisingly little focus is given to gender differences in environmental social movement organization (SMO) participation, despite gender differences in civil rights, antiwar, and New Left SMO participation which demonstrate that gender inequality structures the nature and style of women's participation in social movements (Barnett, 1993; Evans, 1979; Freeman, 1975; and Ferree and Hess, 1985) as well as the nature, style, and strategic choices of social movements. Thus, there remains a need for research which focuses on women's lives and interests as well as men's, so that more nonsexist theories of social movements can be built (Eichler, 1983; Taylor and Rupp, 1991: 122). Researchers must move beyond the traditional SMO research tendency to "accept 'official' definitions of social movement activity and to discredit the beliefs, ideas, and strategies of participants engaged in collective action" (Taylor and Rupp, 1991: 122). Verta Taylor and Leila Rupp note that the style of women's behavior in groups has rendered their SMO activities invisible to previous researchers:

> If group behavior does not conform to the stereotypes set forth, then it has often fallen outside the boundaries (of study). . . . Women have been much less likely to be aggressive and to use disruptive and confrontational tactics in pursuit of their aims. Instead, they have developed a style of participation in social movements—the temperence, abolition, child welfare, settlement house, and peace movements, for example—that can be seen as a natural extension of their traditional roles as nurturers and guardians of morality (Taylor and Rupp, 1991: 123).

Some literature on environmental SMOs describes activists' social differences (such as race, occupation, and region of residence, both in general and for women), but ignore how such differences shape organizational participation. Since the 1970s, environmental activism has been seen to represent "the selfish desires of the privileged at the expense of the working class" (Logan and Molotch, 1987: 220), with participants having "relatively high actual or potential educational status: scientists, teachers, governmental officials, professionals, and students" whose perceptions of long-term environmental crises stem from broader exposure to environmental phenomena, and who possess the leisure and conceptual tools to take a long-term view. By contrast, the less affluent public must "focus on the day-to-day problems of survival and comfort in, as well as escape from, environments that directly threaten their health, welfare, and security" (Morrison, Hornback, and Warner, 1972: 272).

A still commonly-held view is that the distributive effects of environmental policy work against the interests of the working classes and hamper working-class activism. Yet environmental protection directly benefits the poor, due to the proximity of their homes to industrial pollution sources (Berry, 1977; Buttel and Flinn, 1978; Bullard, 1990), the presence of toxins in their work settings, and their reliance on public open spaces for recreation (Logan and Molotch, 1987). With the majority of the poor being women, one would expect women's participation to be in their self interest, and to occur frequently. In the antitoxics movement in the United States, this is indeed the case, with working-class women and mothers forming a strong local/national leadership base in response to community threats from corporate pollution (Capek, 1993; Wellin, 1994).

John Logan and Harvey Molotch insist that affluent persons hold environmental SMO leadership (see Dunlap, 1975 and Lauber, 1978), reflecting their overall higher rate of participation in all movements (Milbrath, 1965; Verba and Nie, 1972; Warren, 1963). They see higher-status communities' greater likelihood of instituting growth controls (Dowall, 1980; Protash and Baldassare, 1983), as being part of a greater mobilization "on environmental issues generally" (Bridgeland and Sofranko, 1975; Eulau and Prewitt 1973), and as part of a lesser interest in promoting further development (Krannich and Humphrey, 1983; Maurer and Christenson, 1982). Affluent residents have the ability, based on " resources . . . to exercise control over their communities" (Logan and Molotch, 1987: 221).

Yet the body of research contains empirical inconsistencies: ignoring the impact of gender on participation; including differing issues under the term "environmentalism" (Calvert, 1979); using noncomparable items in surveys (Neiman and Loveridge, 1981); and not controlling for local and temporal differences in political and economic stimuli to activism. Many studies ignore that fact that "people recently threatened . . . are going to be more sensitive than those who have never been so threatened" (Freudenburg and Baxter, 1984), and that well-funded antienvironmentalist campaigns can make workers fear for their jobs (Neiman and Loveridge, 1981). Even studies showing the working class to have a tendency

> to be less environmentalist than other classes also show strong working-class environmentalist support . . . [T]he greatest cleavage seems to be between public opinion of all social classes . . . and urban growth machine elites (Logan and Molotch, 1987: 222).

As poorer and more affluent environmental SMOs form coalitions, they construct "the structural conditions that give (the environmental movement) strong cross-class appeal" (Logan and Molotch, 1987: 222–23). Yet womens' roles in coalition-building remain largely unexplored.

Regional differences exist in the class nature of environmental activism. In contrast to snowbelt activism, in which working-class opposition to factory-based pollution dominates, environmental activism in the sunbelt region is seen as focusing on regulation of new development (Frieden, 1979; Miller, 1981). Sunbelt communities draw migrants who are skilled and educated (Kasarda, 1983; Mollenkopf, 1983) and seeking a better living environment (Logan and Molotch, 1987). As Logan and Molotch note:

> Indeed, some of the high-tech colonies of California, Texas, and North Carolina are now concentrations of the most highly educated workers in the country. These people have strong organizational skills and high rates of political partici-pation, which they put to use in resisting the fiscal and social costs of develop-ment. Indeed, even a casual observer discovers that within the sunbelt, the cities with the largest numbers of high-tech migrants (Palo Alto, Santa Barbara, Austin) also have the strongest environmental movements (Logan and Molotch, 1987: 218).

It has not been shown, though, that the high-tech migrants themselves be-come environmental SMO activists in their adopted communities.

Austin's land development-related environmental activists may be similar to the activists described by Ronelle Paulsen (1991), who compares partici-pants in 1970s "community problem solving issues," such as local land use is-sues, with participants in protest activities. While both feel politically effica-cious, protest participants tended to come from families with moderate to high levels of socioeconomic status. Community problem solvers were more likely to be non-white, student leaders, and to have attended an urban school.

Environmental SMOs have long been noted as largely white in member-ship. Yet racial and ethnic minorities are at risk from environmental threat, suggesting the need for activism on environmental issues.

> Neighborhood-by-neighborhood comparisons of income level, race, and toxic waste site location reveal . . . The poorer the neighborhood, and the darker the skin of its residents, the more likely it is to be near a toxic waste dump (Brown, 1990; 148; see also United Church of Christ Commission for Racial Justice, 1987; Gould, 1986; Harrison, 1985.

Recent case studies of communities in the U.S. South show that African-American communities have acted against local environmental hazards through NIMBY campaigns ("not in my backyard") (Bullard, 1990; Bullard and Wright, 1992). These efforts involve grassroots environmental groups whose emphasis is on environmental justice, and which rely on preexisting grassroots organizations' leadership. As with most studies of the civil rights movement, these case studies ignore the gender of African-American ac-tivists. Re-analysis of secondary data sources and new personal interviews, such as the work performed by Bernice McNair Barnett on the civil rights movement (Barnett, 1993), would seem to be in order if women's roles in so-cial justice-framed environmental SMOs are to be known.

Other theoretical work on minority environmental activism calls for re-defining environmentalism to include concern for and reform of the social, political, economic, and built environment (urban, suburban, and rural) as well as the natural environment (Weston, 1986: 11–15). For example, ethnic cleavages around environmentalism are seen to be fewer in newly developing areas such as the sunbelt, due to an absence of strong non-Hispanic, white ethnic cohesiveness, so that "the opportunity for use values [is] more con-nected to the 'environment' . . . beyond the immediate milieu . . . [providing] the grounds for cross-class and cross-ethnic solidarity" (Logan and Molotch, 1987: 219–220). However, Kenneth A. Gould documents Native Ameri-can/white tensions around extractive industries on reservations, and Austin has experienced Mexican American/Anglo tensions over powerboat races on the in-town lake.

Urban land development and neighborhood empowerment issues are foci of grassroots environmental SMOs such as the National Congress of Neigh-borhood Women and the Mothers of East Los Angeles (Pardo, 1994), which are filled with and often led by women activists. These SMOs have received little research attention until recently. This research dearth is in contrast to the global reality in which women are the family members responsible for pro-tecting "household considerations in environmental management" (Kwitko, 1994); in other words, protecting the built, social, and cultural environments, as well as the natural environments, in which their families live. Better knowl-edge of the differences and intersections of mainstream environmental ac-tivism, grassroots social justice-framed activism on issues of the environment, and women's activities in each is lacking and needed, both for cases such as Austin and at higher (regional, national, global) organizational levels.

Theorists of both minority environmental activism and feminist environ-mental design now call for expanding the definition of environmentalism to include reform of the "built environment" and social/cultural environment, not just protection of the natural environment. They focus on creating envi-ronments which will provide safety, economic security, and adequate hous-ing, and which will allow the expansion of women's activities via neighbor-hood-level provision of employment, day care, educational facilities, infor-mation/resource centers, etc. (Wekerle, 1980: 29), meeting the needs of women as well as men. Because women in patriarchal society suffer from the lack of these elements of the built and social environment, their environ-mental agenda is potentially broader than that of existing environmental SMOs, and there might exist a tension between the need for protection of the natural environment and provision of the built and social environments which women now lack. Women and racial/ethnic actors share a similar dilemma: will scarce public resources go for natural environmental protec-tion before their own economic and social survival needs are met?

55

McADAMS

In Texas, as in much of the Southwest, population growth in the last several years has been so rapid (Orum, 1987) that the pressure on existing, finite water resources has become obvious to all citizens. In Austin, a key example is the six-year, ongoing effort of Barton Creek Properties to develop 4,000 acres as an exclusive golf community atop the Edwards aquifer recharge zone, some four miles upstream of Barton Springs, a natural spring which serves as recreational area, water source, and cultural symbol of Austin's relaxed lifestyle. The night-long City Council hearing in June 1990 on the proposed Barton Creek Planned Unit Development (PUD) at which more than 800 citizens appeared to oppose the PUD 1990, began unprecedented environmental SMO coalition tactics to strengthen local water quality regulation (via a revised Comprehensive Watersheds Ordinance; a successful citizen SOS [Save Our Springs] Initiative, and City Council election of sympathetic candidates). The PUD battle is but a highly visible part of a larger, longer conflict over the fate of the Edwards aquifer region as its water quality is threatened by land development. This conflict is being waged simultaneously within local, special district, regional, state, and national levels of government.

METHODOLOGY

To understand gender, class, and race/ethnicity in environmental activism, I have employed a case study, multimethod approach in order to gain in-depth and historical information not otherwise accessible. This includes the use of survey data from a questionnaire given to persons appearing at City Council hearings on the Barton Creek PUD and a development moratorium in the Barton Creek watershed on two dates in 1990. The study also uses a demographic and thematic content analysis of the public testimony given at these City Council hearings and recorded on videotape, demographic data on the entire Austin SMA collected by the U.S. Bureau of the Census and other agencies, newspaper coverage of the Barton Springs PUD issue and the SOS Initiative, and my own minutes of the Save Barton Creek Association (SBCA) meetings.

Through closed-end and open-end questions administered by written questionnaire to persons attending the above 1990 City Council hearings on the Barton Creek PUD and subsequent moratorium on development in the Barton Creek watershed,[1] and by content analysis of video tapes of public speakers at the former hearing,[2] the social characteristics of hearing participants are assessed. Statistical analysis includes only simple percentage comparisons due to the small number of cases in some categories of certain variables. Quotations from speakers at the PUD hearing and questionnaire responses are also provided.

Because much environmental activism involves decisionmaking at formal and informal group meetings and in interpersonal conversations, I have used a multimethod and/or flexible approach, which has let me change or choose aspects of the methodology during and after the data collection process so that I could better uncover unanticipated results (Klein, 1983; Jayaratne, 1983; Steurnagel, 1987; and Gadamer, 1975, all cited in Kathlene, 1990). As a use value-oriented actor in support of protecting the Barton Creek and associated watersheds from development, and as a life-long Austinite with a history of local use-value-oriented activism, I have combined activism and research. Here, this approach includes just under a year (1990-1991) of my weekly participant observation of the Save Barton Creek Association meetings, serving as co-secretary to the organization in order to make dual use (for my research and for the organization's files) of the written notes and audio tape recordings of each meeting.

FINDINGS AND CONCLUSIONS

Gender and Activism

My analysis provides no evidence that women's environmental activism is more limited than men's because of women's multiple roles. According to interview responses to a question in which respondents listed factors that made it difficult for them to attend Council hearings, however, 24 percent of women (to 16 percent of men) cited family responsibilities as a conflict; 24 percent of women and 32 percent of men cited "other responsibilities"; and 52 percent of both women and men cited work as a conflict. Overall, 66 percent of activists were male, a percentage which holds for both total and minority activism. Leaders and lobbyists, too, were often male (64 percent).

Women leaders exist in local groups (e.g., the Save Barton Creek Association) and extra-local organizations' chapters (e.g., Director at the Time of Clean Water Action); 36 percent of leaders and lobbyists on the PUD issue were women, and 64 percent were men. Within locally-based environmental SMOs such as SBCA, participant observation shows some gender differences in activist roles, with women more often fulfilling what some see as support roles such as bookkeeping, mailout production, membership chairperson, t-shirt sales coordination (i.e., fundraising), and attendance—but not necessarily speaking parts—at general SBCA functions and City Council hearings. There appear to be fewer women than men in roles such as SBCA policy committee member; SBCA attorney; paid fundraiser; or SBCA general meeting speaker—in short, those roles with more public visibility. Future research will pursue the reasons for and meanings of these differences. Do they imply sexism within the environmental movement, as was the case for the civil rights and antiwar movements, or are roles taken according to self-definition and choice? Are women defining "leadership" differently, including the less publicly visible roles as well as those usually considered political leadership roles?

57

McADAMS

Gender differences in environmental SMO participation emerge and reflect women's lives and interests. Listening to the "beliefs, ideas, and strategies of participants engaged in collective action" (Taylor and Rupp, 1991: 122), I find that female speakers tend to represent their own viewpoints, speaking independently of any environmental organization, more "as a natural extension of their traditional roles as nurturers and guardians of morality," broadly defined. These were unaffiliated persons who spoke of the protection of Barton Springs as an issue of secular morality, as an extension of personal spirituality and caretaking for one's home/locality.

Other women spoke on behalf of "radical" environmental SMOs such as Earth First! or local environmental SMOs such as the Save Barton Creek Association or the Hill Country Foundation. National environmental groups involved with the effort (e.g., the Sierra Club or the Audobon Society) more often featured male speakers.

Women cited various themes in opposition to the proposed PUD:

Barton Springs' cultural/symbolic/spiritual importance: "it is my church in times of need" (J. Clark, 1990); and arguments based in shallow ecological philosophy, in which the fight against pollution and resource depletion is necessary to protect health and/or affluence of humans in developed countries (Devall, 1992: 52). Speakers addressed the global importance of protecting a local nonrenewable resource:

> I have seen the Nile, the lifesource. Barton Springs is our lifesource; it nurtures us. The [economic] bust gave us a second chance. I hope it taught us not to let people come in from outside and make value judgments about what is important to us (Unidentified speaker, 1990).

Some speakers noted that profit from the development comes at the expense of future environmental quality.

Other women made the plea most frequently heard from males—the technical-based argument—citing changes over time in fecal coliform levels along various stretches of Barton Creek below development. But strikingly, women asked for enlargement of the scope of decisionmaking criteria from the usual rational-based choice, encouraging emotion-based action with messages such as "Let the place that you vote from be your heart" (P. Thompson, 1990).

Women spoke for protection of the social as well as physical environment, citing the PUD owner's record of being willing, in its Indonesia investments, to "work with a government with one of the worst human rights records in the world" (P. Bose, 1990). For the first time at a City Council hearing, ecofeminist statements were made:

> An idea of psychoanalyst Melanie Klein is that as every generation becomes more technologized, it becomes increasingly infantilized in its relationship to the earth- taking, not giving anything back. Often parents don't meet an infant's needs, and we become arrested in an infantile state our entire lives. Compound-

ed by the technology of our times, it's made us like two-year-olds with assault rifles—very dangerous people. . . . Mr. Moffet and Mr. Dedman (PUD owners): you are holding the creek hostage. . . . I just want to speak to the two-year-old in you that is hurting. I hope you have some grace in your life to heal that hurt. But I speak for Mother Earth and the people here to say: NO, NO, NO! [wags finger as does mother to child] (J. Thomas, 1990).

"Deep ecology" beliefs, stressing ecocentric identification, ecocentrism, and an ecosophy based variously in transpersonal pyschology, Eastern philosophies, ecofeminist theory, conservation biology, and concern with welfare of native peoples (Devall, 1992: 59–61), were also expressed:

Development strategy under capitalism is anthropocentric: "the Earth is ours to exploit. In 100 years, we will be alone without our animal friends" (Unidentified animal rights activist, 1990).

Clearly, women speakers extended the usual technical grounds for opposition, with discourse acknowledging varying strains of several ecofeminisms existent in the 1990s: liberal ecofeminism, radical ecofeminism (including Marxist and socialist ecofeminism), and conservative ecofeminism (e.g., cultural ecofeminism and essentialist ecofeminism) (Ozanne and Humphrey, 1994).

Class and Activism

One still commonly held belief is that the distributive effects of environmental policy work against the interests of the working classes and hamper working-class activism. Yet since the majority of the poor are women, one would expect women's participation in land development-related issues (as a subgroup of environmental issues) to be in their self-interest, and to occur frequently, as it does with "anti-toxics" issues (Capek, 1993; Wellin, 1994). Barton Creek PUD opponents were, by a slim majority, less than median income, but tended to be highly educated (at least two years of college level education, as is common in Austin). They were not urban growth-machine elites, but viewed themselves as having a stake in the community and its environment, and as feeling efficacious enough to interrupt their day and evening to speak at the televised City Council hearing. Most were individuals, not environmental SMO participants, who were sensitive to the perceived threat to Barton Springs posed by the PUD.

Unlike Logan and Molotch's predictions that activists are high-tech corporations' migrant professionals, I found that environmental activists in Austin are professionals who are rarely employed by high-technology corporations (9 percent); rarely, too, are they local newcomers in the employ of such firms (11 percent of activists). Most activists, instead, work in other than high-technology firms (89 percent).

While there is a highly educated, professional/technical presence in the lo-

59

McADAMS

cal environmental organizations, activist members tend to be retired, self-employed, and/or employed as lawyers (as opposed to high-technology firms' migrant employees). These persons had the contact with political organizations, the social group membership, and the job autonomy which characterize activism according to Burn and Konrad (1987). Like Paulsen's (1991) community problem solvers, these activists had strong political efficacy and educational backgrounds, but they were mostly white. However, the Barton Creek PUD activists resembled Paulsen's protest participants in their moderate to high socioeconomic status of birth family—not surprising, since the PUD hearing, while part of a land use issue, was also an event of strong community protest. The outstanding characteristic which PUD activists often share is lower income (in relation to those of prodevelopment lobbyist/attorneys and to the high-technology firms' migrant employees). Despite Logan and Molotch's assertion, few engineers or computer scientists who are employees of the large high-technology firms are environmental activists at the local level. Neither do they serve as public officials on boards, commissions, or other governmental bodies which help set land use-related, water quality-related, and thus urban growth-related policy.

Seventy-two percent of activists are 1- to 5-year local residents. Leaders have longer local residence. In 1990, Austin had the third-highest mobility rate in the nation, with 36.4 percent of residents in its 5-county area having moved in the last 18 months, due to a combination of high-technology employment, university attendence, and state government employment (Graves, 1994: A1). In local context, the 72 percent of activists who are 1- to 5-year residents have lived in Austin about as long or longer than the average population.

Family income of 49 percent of activists exceeds the 1990 $23,000 median income for Austin; leaders' income is less frequently (44 percent) in that category. The main cleavage on environmental issues such as the PUD tends to be between urban growth-machine elites and others, with elites favoring development over environmental protection (87 percent) more than do non-elites (4 percent).

Content analysis of the hearing videotapes demonstrates that a spectrum of environmental groups was present and active in opposing the PUD. Both before the hearing and during the hearing in waiting areas, groups as diverse as the Sierra Club, the Save Barton Creek Association, the Audobon Society, and Earth First! met, apportioning testimony topics and speaker order. The bulk of SMO testimony shared the theme that the PUD should be denied and the site purchased for a nature preserve, although the final speaker, a Sierra Club member, caused consternation by appearing "too accommodating." This camaraderie and coordination among the opposition emphasizes the split between elites and nonelites on PUD support. The coalition of poorer and more affluent groups provided, as Logan and Molotch (1987: 222–23) note, "the structural conditions that give [the environmental movement] strong cross-class appeal," which manifested itself fully in 1992 with the Save Our Springs (SOS) Coalition's successful SOS Initiative campaign to overhaul watershed protection legislation. Election returns showed support in almost all precincts except for the far northwest (more affluent, usually Republican) suburban areas, one small south/central area of working-class homes, and a working-class stretch in the suburban, less-populated eastern part of Austin. Cross-class SOS support was widespread, supporting Logan and Molotch's contention that urban growth machine elites stand in contrast to all other persons on issues of environmentally sensitive land development. Unfortunately, gender-based electoral results are not available, thus the cross-class support of women can only be surmised.

Race/Ethnicity and Activism

Thirty-three percent of minority activists were women and 66 percent were men. No racial or ethnic minority persons were leaders in the PUD opposition activism. The class background of minority activists appears consistent with the generally middle-class backgound (based on income) of non-minority activists.

Logan and Molotch (1987) and Bullard (1990) cite the alleged environment/jobs tradeoff as a deterrent to minority environmental activism. Minority environmental activism (6 percent of the total activist count of 203) in my analysis occurs regardless of whether minorities disbelieve the "urban growth brings jobs" rhetoric, as minorities were no more likely to refer to this theme in their hearing testimony than were whites.[3] Yet one African-American woman's testimony was a classic statement of the jobs/environment tradeoff (and of the economic invisibility of women):

> The Austin Black Contractors Association supports the PUD because . . . this project provides long-term business and economic development opportunities for our community; this project will create jobs for our community; and men who have jobs will be able to feed, clothe, house, and educate their children. I have empathy for the environment and endangered species, but it is clouded when I see on a day-to-day basis the hopelessness, homelessness, and joblessness in my community (C. Hadnot, 1990).

Was the PUD issue salient for racial and ethnic minorities, and especially for minority women? Austin's traditionally segregated minority neighborhoods are distant from the Barton Creek watershed, yet Barton Springs pool has seen frequent minority use since its desegregation in the 1950s. PUD hearing data suggests low salience of the issue, but the 1992 SOS Initiative election results show solid support in all but a few precincts, regardless of race or class. Comments of minority grassroots activists from the 1993 NAACP presidential race suggest a recognition of the tensions caused by organizations

61

McADAMS

such as the NAACP backing "well-off Anglos' environmental issues" before economic development issues are resolved. This environmental-justice frame transcends the view that a jobs/environment tradeoff could be beneficial, and shows a recognition of the growing political power of both traditionally male-led groups such as the NAACP and more recent local-level grassroots social justice organizations such as the East Austin Strategy Team (EAST), which have some women leaders.

Was social justice-framed environmental activism important in the Barton Creek PUD issue? Environmental activism appears still to be largely white-dominated (96 percent) as measured by appearances at local City Council meetings, and attendence at environmental organizations' meetings. The Barton Creek PUD protests included a handful of Mexican-American (7), African-American (2), and other minority (3) individuals.

Is environmental activism among racial and ethnic minorities growing? In Austin, African-American awareness of the need to act on local environmental issues (particularly NIMBY issues of hazardous facility siting and waste disposal) have led both the traditionally male-led civil rights groups such as the NAACP and the grassroots groups in which women are more apt to have more leadership roles, to embrace environmental issues. The local chapter of the NAACP supported the environmentalist position on the 1992 Save Our Springs initiative, but the tension regarding the legitimacy of the environment-jobs tradeoff manifested itself in the subsequent NAACP president's election (Banta 1993). Racial and ethnic minorities fear that mainstream environmental groups "gain the strength of minority support while doing little on other issues important to those communities," and that "limited minority resources are diverted to causes other than those traditionally important to the community: education, civil rights, and economic development" (Banta, 1993). Still, the legitimacy of the environment/jobs tradeoff, so common in past, is challenged as "concern about inequity—the inherent imbalance between localized costs and dispersed benefits—appears to be the driving force around which African-American communities are organizing" into grassroots organizations (Bullard and Wright, 1990 and 1992: 47) in which women find more voice.

Because the largest minority communities both (Mexican-American and African-American) are regular users of Barton Springs, they have been as able as have whites to observe the water quality degradation already occurring from land developments in the 1970s and 1980s in the Barton Creek watershed, such as a regional shopping mall some three miles upstream from the Springs (McAdams, 1980). In Austin, environmentally harmful projects such as large trash burners, creek channelization, gasoline tank farms, and noisy airports are often proposed for location in, or historically sited in, east-side ethnic neighborhoods. Those issues attract much grassroots social justice-framed activism. The Barton Creek PUD project, located across town from some ethnic residential neighborthoods, attracted less minority activism, as reflected in the paucity of minorities among environmentalist lobbyists and leaders, and the virtual absence (save one) of minority women activists. Austin's only Mexican-American member of the City Council described his support of environmentalist causes such as this PUD opposition as genuine and long-standing, but secondary to his concern for issues of racial/ethnic justice. He noted that his support brought forth surprise and concern among some Mexican-American supporters (Garcia, 1994).

THOUGHTS ON THE FUTURE: REFRAMING ENVIRONMENTALISM AND THE IMPACT OF WOMEN

If there is little overlap between environmental activism and social justice-framed activism to combat "environmental racism" in Austin, one can surmise that the separate foci are due to differences in worldview, with the former actors seeing environmentalism as primary and the latter seeing environmental protection as secondary to the achievement of social justice on issues involving environmental racism. The latter view reflects the global situation in which women, often lacking resources, are responsible for protecting "household consideration in environmental management" (Kwitko, 1994); in other words, protecting the built, social, and cultural environments, as well as the natural environment, in which their families live. Local, largely minority, grassroots groups continue to embrace social justice-framed issues in many U.S. cities, using the vast volunteer energies of women and occasionally according them leadership. Women activists fill and lead (although sometimes de facto, and as an outgrowth of disenchantment with male leadership) such environmental SMOs as National Congress of Neighborhood Women and Mothers of East Los Angeles (Pardo, 1994), which focus on urban development and neighborhood empowerment issues. In Austin, the social justice-framed SMO East Austin Strategy Team has provided environmental racism-based critiques of a gasoline tank farm and electric generation plant located in its minority community.

Such SMOs may not even label themselves as environmental SMOs, but their issues are indeed environmental, and the roles of their women are poorly understood and chronicled. Analysis of primary data sources and personal interviews are needed if women's roles in both social justice-framed organizations and other environmental SMOs are to be known.

The social justice-framed organizations' actors seem to be working on goals of interest to feminist as well as racial/ethnic theorists: they redefine environmentalism to include concern for and reform of the social, political, economic, and built environment as well as the natural environment (Weston, 1986: 11–15). They share a feminist focus on the creation of environments which will provide safety, economic security, and adequate housing and trans-

63

McADAMS

portation, and which will allow the expansion of women's activities via neighborhood-level provision of employment, day care, educational facilities, information/resource centers, etc. (Wekerle, 1980: 29), which would meet the needs of women as well as men. Because women, minorities, and the poor in patriarchal society suffer from the lack of these elements of the built and social environments, their environmental agendas are broader than those of existing environmental SMOs. Women, racial/ethnic minorities, and the poor (often the same people) have needs in tension with environmental SMOs, whose focus is the protection of the natural environment. Will public resources be earmarked for natural environmental protection before the economic and survival needs of women, racial/ethnic minorities, and the poor are met?

Texas state government is the locus of many environmental regulatory and legislative battles, as state agencies and the legislature resist "infringement" of state authority by municipalities such as Austin, with its more progressive environmental regulatory stances. Can environmentalist women look to state government for support of their agendas? Informal routes to state-level political influence appear as yet somewhat closed to women. The mixed appointment record of Governor Ann Richards (including a pro-development woman in the position of Texas Water Commissioner) and the pre-inaugural remarks of Governor George Bush, Jr. suggest that an officeholder's economic/political philosophy and funding networks may override gender-based environmental awareness in determining women politicians' helpfulness to women environmental activists' needs.

In January of 1993, Texas governor Ann Richards convened the first state task force to study environmental racism statewide (Ward, 1993). Yet it produced a watered-down report stemming from failure to even achieve consensus on the basic premise that a disproportionate number of Texas hazardous facilities are located in low-income and minority areas (Wright, 1993). One might expect this meager state response to spur social justice-framed SMO activism in the future.

I have learned much about interpersonal dynamics within and between groups, social structural constraints on group effectiveness, and the roles of key individuals as environmentalist allies attempt to reconcile their diverse political views while mobilizing to fight well-paid, well-organized, and politically influential private development interests. I have sought to understand as fully as I can the actions and voices I have observed and heard, and to gain a sense of the subjective as well as the objective realities of the environmentalist actors in the multiple situations in which the conflict to protect Barton Creek, Barton Springs, and the Edwards aquifer has been and continues to be fought. Future work to describe this, using multimethod data collection of ongoing group activism, will add to an understanding of the complicated intersection of gender, class, and race/ethnicity in environmental activism.

NOTES

The data collection and analysis for this paper was greatly aided by the support of Southwestern University, Georgetown, Texas, 78626, through its 1991 Cullen Faculty Development Grant program, which made possible the assistance of one of my fine students, Jon Brinkley (BA, May 1991, Southwestern University). My deepest thanks to Dr. Michael Rosenthal, Provost, for financial support; Drs. Ed Kain and Jesse Purdy, of the Human Subjects Research Review Committee, for helpful review of the questionnaire used within; Kathy Buchhorn, for clerical support on the questionnaire; and Drs. Gail Gemberling and Ronelle Paulsen for advice and humor regarding statistical procedures. Responsibility for any and all errors, of course, is my own.

1. First administration N = 53; second administration N = 34; combined N = 87; combined response rate = 25%.

2. N = 176.

3. N = 2; one pro and one con.

REFERENCES

Baca Zinn, Maxine. "Employment and education of Mexican-American Women: The Interplay of Modernity and Ethnicity in Eight Families." *Harvard Educational Review* 50 (1): 47–62, 1980.

Banta, Bob. "Minority Community Grappling with Goals, Environmental Agenda." *Austin American-Stateman*, January 4: A1, A7, 1993.

Barnett, Bernice McNair. "Invisible Southern Black Women Leaders in the Civil Rights Movement: The Triple Constraints of Gender, Race, and Class." *Gender and Society* Volume 7 (2): 162–182, 1993.

Berry, Brian J. L. *The Social Burdens of Environmental Pollution: A Comparative Metropolitan Data Source.* Cambridge, Massachusetts: Balinger, 1977.

Berk, Sarah F. and Anthony Shih. "Contribution to Household Labor: Comparing Wives' and Husbands' Reports." In *Women and Household Labor*, ed. Sarah F. Berk. Beverly Hills, CA: Sage, 1980.

Bernard, Jessie. *The Female World.* New York: The Free Press, 1981.

Bose, P. Austin City Council testimony, tape 1, June 7–8, 1990.

Boulding, Elise. "Women as Integrators and Stabilizers." In *Women and the Social Costs of Economic Development: Two Colorado Case Studies*, ed. Elizabeth Moen, Elise Boulding, Jane Lillydahl, and Risa Palm. Boulder, CO: Westview Press, 1981.

Bowles, Jennifer. Austin City Council testimony, tape 1, June 7–8, 1990.

Bridgeland, William M., and Andrew J. Sofranko. "Community Structure and Issue-Specific Influences; Community Mobilization Over Environmental Quality." *Urban Affairs Quarterly* 11: 186–214, 1975.

Brinkley, Phyllis. Austin City Council testimony, tape 1, June 7–8, 1990.

Brown, Lester R. *State of the World: A Worldwatch Institute Report on Progress Toward a Sustainable Society.* New York: W.W. Norton, 1990.

Bullard, Robert D. *Dumping in Dixie.* Boulder, CO: Westview Press, 1990.

Bullard, Robert. D. and Bevery H. Wright. "The Quest for Environmental Equity: Mobilizing the African-American Community for Social Change." In Riley E. Dunlap and Angela G. Mertig, eds. *American Environmentalism: The U.S. Environmental Movement 1970–1990.* Philadelphia: Taylor-Francis, 1992.

65

McADAMS

Burn, Shawn M. and Alison M. Konrad. "Political Participation: A Matter of Community, Stress, Job Autonomy, and Contact by Political Organizations." *Political Psychology*, Volume 8 (1): 125–138, 1987.

Buttel, Frederick, and William L. Flinn. "Social Class and Mass Environmental Beliefs: A Reconsideration." *Environmental Behavior* 10: 433–50, 1978.

Calvert, Jerry W. "Social and Ideological Bases of Support for Environmental Legislation: An Examination of Public Attitudes and Legislative Action." *Western Political Quarterly* 33: 327–337, 1979.

Capek, Stella M. "The Environmental Justice Frame: A Conceptual Discussion and an Application." *Social Problems*, Volume 40 (1): 5–24, 1993.

Clark, Jennifer. Austin City Council testimony, tape 2, June 7–8, 1990.

Criss, Ann. Austin City Council testmony, tape 1, June 7–8, 1990.

Devall, Bill. "Deep Ecology and Radical Environmentalism." In Riley E. Dunlap and Angela G. Mertig, eds. *American Environmentalism: The U.S. Environmental Movement 1970-1990*. New York: Taylor and Francis, 1992.

Dowall, David E. "An Examination of Population-Growth-Managing Communities." *Policy Studies Journal* 9: 414–427, 1980.

DRI/McGraw-Hill. "Spotlight on Austin, Texas." *Metro Insights: 5/13-5/18.* Austin: DRI/McGraw-Hill, 1990.

Dunlap, Riley E. "The Socioeconomic Basis of the Environmental Movement: Old Data, New Data, and Implications for the Movement's Future." Paper presented at the annual meeting of the American Sociological Association, San Francisico, August, 1975.

Eichler, Margrit. "The Relationship Between Sexist, Non-Sexist, Woman-Centered and Feminist Research." Paper presented at the National Women's Studies Association conference, Bloomington, Indiana, 1983.

Eulau, Heinz and Kenneth Prewitt. *Labyrinths of Democracy*. Indianapolis: Bobbs-Merrill, 1973.

Evans, Sara. *Personal Politics: The Roots of Women's Liberation in the Civil Rights Movement and the New Left.* New York: Alfred A. Knopf, 1979.

Ferree, Myra Marx and Beth B. Hess. *Controversy and Coalition: The New Feminist Movement.* Boston: Twayne, 1985.

Freeman, Jo. *The Politics of Women's Liberation*. New York: David McKay, 1975.

Freudenburg, William. "Women and Men in the Energy Boomtown: Adjustment, Alienation, and Adaptation." *Rural Sociology* 46 (2): 200–44, 1981.

Freudenburg, William and Rodney Baxter. "Public Attitudes Toward Nuclear Power Plants: A Reassessment." Paper presented at the annual meeting of the American Sociological Association, San Antonio, Texas, August, 1984.

Frieden, Bernard J. *The Environmental Protection Hustle*. Cambridge, MA: The MIT Press, 1979.

Gadamer, Hans-Georg. *Truth and Method*. Trans. G. Barden and J. Cumming. New York: Crossroad Publishing, 1975.

Garcia, Gustavo. Personal interview with Austin City Councilperson. July 28, 1994.

Gould, Jay M. *Quality of Life in American Neighborhoods: Levels of Affluence, Toxic Waste, and Cancer Mortality in Residential Zip Code Areas.* Boulder, CO: Westview Press, 1986.

McADAMS

Gould, Kenneth A. "Putting the RAPs on Public Participation: Remedial Action Planning and Working-Class Power in the Great Lakes." *Sociological Practice Review* 3 (3): 133–39, 1992.

Graves, Debbie. "Austin Ranks Third in U.S. Mobility Rate," *Austin American-Statesman: A1, A8,* December 13, 1994.

Hadnot, Carol. Austin City Council testimony, tape 1, June 7-8, 1990.

Harrison, Paul. *Inside the Inner City.* New York: Penguin, 1985.

Jayaratne, Toby Epstein. "The Value of Quantitative Methodology for Feminist Research." In *Theories of Women's Studies,* Gloria Bowles and Renate Duelli Klein, eds. Boston: Routledge and Kegan Paul, 1983.

Kasarda, John. "Entry Level Jobs, Mobility, and Minority Unemployment." *Urban Affairs Quarterly* 19 (1): 21–40, 1983 .

Kathlene, Lyn. "Uncovering the Political Impacts of Gender: An Exploratory Study," *Western Political Quarterly,* 42 (2): 397–421, 1989.

_____. "A New Approach to Understanding the Impact of Gender on the Legislative Process." In *Feminist Research Methods: Exemplary Readings in the Social Sciences,* Joyce McCarl Nielson, ed. Boulder, CO: Westview Press, 1990.

Kathlene, Lyn and John A. Martin. "Enhancing Citizen Participation: Panel Designs, Perspectives, and Policy Formation." *Journal of Policy Analysis,* 10 (1): 46–63, 1991.

Klein, Renate Duelli. "How to do What We Want to Do: Thoughts About Feminist Methodology." In *Theories of Women's Studies,* Gloria Bowles and Renate Duelli Klein, eds. Boston: Routledge and Kegan Paul, 1983.

Krannich, Richard S. and Craig R. Humphrey. "Local Mobilization and Community Growth: Toward an Assessment of the 'Growth Machine' Hypothesis." *Rural Sociology* 48 (1): 60–81, 1983.

Kwitko, Ludmilla. "Gender and Household Considerations in Environmental Management for Poor Urban Communities in Asia." Paper presented at the annual American Sociological Association meeting, Los Angeles, California: August 8, 1994.

Lauber, V. "Ecology and Elitism in American Society: The Fallacy of the Post-Materialist Hypothesis." Paper presented at the annual meeting of the Western Political Science Association, Los Angeles, California, March 16–18, 1978.

Logan, John and Harvey Molotch. *Urban Fortunes: The Political Economy of Place.* Berkeley: University of California Press, 1987.

McAdams, D. Claire. "A Power-Conflict Approach to Urban Land Use: Toward a New Human Ecology," *Urban Anthropology* Volume 9 (3): 295–318, 1980.

Markusen, Ann. "City Spatial Structure, Women's Household Work, and National Urban Policy." *Signs* 5 (3): 23–44, 1980.

Maurer, Richard, and James Christenson. "Growth and Non-Growth Orientations of Urban, Suburban and Rural Mayors: Reflections on the City as a Growth Machine," *Social Science Quarterly* 63: 350–58, 1982.

Milbrath, Lester W. *Political Participation: How and Why Do People Get Involved in Politics?* Skokie, IL: Rand McNally, 1965.

Miller, J. "Assessing Residential Land Price Inflation." *Urban Land* 40 (3): 16, 20, 1981.

Mollenkopf, John. *The Contested City.* Princeton, NJ: Princeton University Press, 1983.

67

McADAMS

Morrison, Denton E., Kenneth E. Hornback, and W. Keith Warner. "The Environmental Movement: Some Preliminary Observations and Predictions." In William R. Burch, Neil H. Cheek, and Lee Taylor, eds. *Social Behavior, Natural Resources, and the Environment*. New York: Harper and Row, 1972.

Neiman, Max, and Ronald O. Loveridge. "Environmentalism and Local Growth Control: A Probe into the Class Bias Thesis." *Environment and Behavior* 13 (6): 759–72, 1981.

Orum, Anthony. *The Making of Modern Austin: Power, Money and the People*. Austin: Texas Monthly Press, 1987.

Pardo, Mary. "The Dialectic of Tradition; Latina Grassroots Activists and the 'Mothers of East Los Angeles." Paper presented at the annual American Sociological Association meeting, Los Angeles, California, August 8, 1994.

Paulsen, Ronelle. "Education, Social Class, and Participation in Collective Action." *Sociology of Education* 64 (April): 96–110, 1991.

Protash, William, and Mark Baldasarre. "Growth Policies and Community Status: A Test and Modification of Logan's Theory." *Urban Affairs Quarterly* 18 (3): 397–412, 1983.

Richter, Dorothy. Austin City Council testimony, June 7–8, 1990.

Scanlan, Nancy. Austin City Council testimony, tape 1, June 7–8, 1990.

Steurnagel, Gertrude A. "Reflections on Women and Political Participation." *Women and Politics* 7:3–13, 1987.

Stevens, Christi. Austin City Council testimony, tape 2, June 7–8, 1990.

Taylor, Verta and Leila J. Rupp. "Researching the Women's Movement: We Make Our Own History, But Not Just As We Please." In Mary Margaret Fonow and Judith A. Cook, eds. *Beyond Methodology: Feminist Scholarship as Lived Research*. Bloomington, IN: Indiana University Press, 1991.

Texas Employment Commission. *Covered Employment and Wages by Industry and County: State of Texas, Third Quarter, 1990*. Austin: Texas Employment Commission Economic Research and Analysis Department. 11, 1990.

Thomas, Jacqueline. Austin City Council testimony, tape 2, June 7–8, 1990.

Thompson, Pam. Austin City Council testimony, tape 1, June 7–8, 1990.

United Church of Christ Commission for Racial Justice. *Toxic Wastes and Race in the United States: A National Report on the Racial and Socio-Economic Characteristics of Communities with Hazardous Waste Sites* (Public Data Access). New York, 1987.

U.S. Bureau of the Census. *County Business Pattterns 1988: Texas Employment and Payrolls, Number and Employment, Size of Establishments, by Detailed Industry*. Washington, D.C.: U.S. Government Printing Office, CBP-88-45 (October): 173–174, 319–326, 349–352, 1990.

_____. County/City Data, Census Tape PL94-171. Washington, D.C.: U.S. Government Printing Office, 1990.

Verba, Sidney, and Norman H. Nie. *Participation in America: Political Democracy and Social Equality*. New York: Harper and Row, 1972.

Ward, Mike. "Texas Panel to Study Environmental Racism." *Austin American Statesman*, January 7: A1, A12, 1993.

Warren, Roland. *The Community in America*. Chicago: Rand McNally, 1963.

Wekerle, Gerda R., Rebecca Peterson, and David Morley. "Introduction." In *New Space for Women,* Gerda R. Wekerle, ed. Boulder, CO: Westview Press, 1980.

Wellin, Elaine. "Breaking the Silence: The Social Construction of Women's Activism in Grassroots Environmental Groups." Paper presented at the annual American Sociological Association meeting, Los Angeles, California: August 8, 1994.

Weston, Joe. "The Greens, 'Nature', And The Social Environment." In Joe Weston, ed. *Red and Green: A New Politics of the Environment.* London and Wolfeboro, NH: Pluto Press, 1986.

Whitehead, Lisa. Austin City Council testimony, tape 1, June 7–8, 1990.

Wood, James L. and Maurice Jackson. *Social Movements: Development, Participation, and Dynamics.* Belmont, CA: Wadsworth Publishing Company, 1982.

Wright, Scott W. "Report on Ecological Racism Draws Fire." *Austin American-Statesman,* August 22: A1, A19, 1993.

THE INDIAN WOMEN'S MOVEMENT, ECOFEMINISM, AND THE POLITICS OF PEACE

Linda Rennie Forcey

ECOFEMINISTS RECOGNIZE that saving the environment is critical to economic survival. In India, as elsewhere, ecofeminists argue for a redefinition of development that is not destructive to the environment, and that increases women's access to resources and power. While ecofeminist politics are energizing and effective to some degree, I argue in this chapter that women's political action requires appreciation of the tension inherent in a gender-centered approach to global resources security.[1] Global turmoil, with its devastating environmental and human consequences, reflects a complex melange of economic, social, religious and gendered conflicts, precluding any simple gender-based explanation as to how we shape an environmentally sound and peaceable future.

I write about India as a novitiate and an outsider. A Fulbright assignment to India (Fall, 1992) found me lecturing on U.S. women's and peace studies at Banares Hindu University in Varanasi (Uttar Pradesh), and at Panjab University in Chandigarh. Further research took place at the Gandhi Institute for Study in Varanasi and in Delhi with Gandhian and women activists and scholars.

India in the fall and winter of '92 and '93 was in one of the more tumultuous and violent periods in its post independence history. The center of the storm was the destruction by Hindu fundamentalists of the 16th-century Babri mosque at Ayodhya on December 6, 1992. Almost three thousand people in the two months following the assault were killed in riots, demonstrations, and strikes. In the Punjab, Sikh and government terrorism and retribution continued. Approximately 20,000 Hindus and Sikhs have been killed since the 1982 Sikh militant rebellion (*New York Times,* 1993). Every day, five to a dozen men, women, and children are murdered, many banks and shops are robbed. At Punjab University, two sociology professors were murdered by militants in 1992; the campus resembles an armed camp. Nor has violence in the states of Kashmir and Jammu abated: since 1990, 5,000 have been killed and 120,000 people have fled Kashmir.

Amidst all the stories of violence, the media had also recently focused on violence against women, both physical and institutionalized. Newspapers carried a daily stream of stories of dowry deaths, rape, domestic violence, widow immolation, and female infanticide. They also frequently gave detailed descriptions depicting the deplorable condition of women and children due to poverty and lack of education. The women's movement, represented by university women's centers, research institutes, and a myriad of community activist organizations, was working hard to bring the plight of women to the public's attention.

THE WOMEN'S MOVEMENT

Elite Indian women grapple with issues of gender and peace which are the center of my work in the United States. V. Spike Peterson and Anne Sisson Runyan point out that while "how one becomes a feminist varies with each individual, the impetus for developing a feminist consciousness often arises when a person experiences a contradiction between who that person thinks she or he is and what society wants her or him to be" (Peterson and Runyan, 1993: 116). Among the most significant markers for modernization and feminization in India have been elite women's greater access to education and its consequent effects upon the worlds of kinship and family.[2] While many families continue to regard the education of girls as socially problematic, the trend in urban areas is clearly toward viewing women's education as enhancing their attractiveness, particularly given the increasing value placed on their earning potential (Mukhopadhyay and Seymour 1994). Recent ethnographic research confirms my own observations that female Indian students are expressing goals and aspirations that dramatically challenge their patrifocal heritage. They want more of an egalitarian relationship with their husbands and in-laws, and careers are often as important as marriage plans. These young women talk of "self-fulfillment" and "self-improvement" (Mukhopadhyay and Seymour, 1994).

Professional and academic women generally welcome discussion of U.S. perspectives on feminist theory and share concerns about child and aging parent care, divorce, family values, and changing roles of women and men. There are a growing number of two career families within the middle class, and educated women are in some instances better represented in the government and in professions than are women in the U.S. (Bumiller, 1991).[3] They are also concerned with educational and governmental reform. A widely shared cynicism exists about central and state governments' abilities to control violence and promote peace. Yet, among these cynics many find the legacy of Gandhian asceticism and Nehru's socialism equally distasteful.

A network of women's studies programs and women's centers with social action agendas at Indian universities and colleges enhances expectations for changed social roles. The centers are very different from women's studies programs in the United States. They grew out of an explosive 480-page governmental study in the mid 1970s entitled "Towards Equality," which documented the appalling living conditions for most of India's women and ways in which "development" often made conditions worse (Government of India 1974). Unlike most U.S. women's studies programs, these centers constitute a largely grassroots reform movement.

The energy, commitment, and creativity women scholars and activists exhibited in their reform projects pushed me toward rethinking the centrality of theory as opposed to action in most U.S. women's studies programs. Some of the Women's Centre's projects at Panjab University, for example, included week-long training sessions for village women to become more politically effective about women's issues on the grassroots level; instruction for police on issues of sexual harassment and violence against women; and training programs for women to educate others on preventive health, inoculation, and population control.

The women's movement in India outside the university is also alive and well. As Elisabeth Bumiller suggests, it is not easy for an outsider to understand because the movement's many approaches to theory and action have "spanned regions, political parties, class and caste, embraced both Mahatma Gandhi and Karl Marx, worked at often divergent purposes, encompassed elite groups and mass struggles , . . [while] not, in most cases, even thinking of itself as a collective movement" (1991: 128).

Two ideological tendencies exist within the broad array of the Indian movement—an equity and rights orientation and an emphasis on grassroots empowerment. Women's rights advocates locate the movement within the secular democracy that India's constitution proclaims. They see themselves as modernizers and social democrats seeking basic human rights, rather than as

73

"feminists" pressing a radical social agenda. Rights groups refrain from positing a conflict between women and men. Gender roles remain unchallenged, fearing that such an attack would mark the movement as overly influenced by the West and as attacking the family. They are determined to be in the mainstream of an attempt to modernize India without sacrificing essential Indian culture or values, except insofar as those values violate women's rights as human beings and as equal citizens (Calman, 1992).

The "empowerment" wing, as Leslie Calman names it, is also made up of educated, middle-class urban women. This wing, however, focuses on the empowerment of poor women from both rural and urban areas. "Rights" refer primarily to economic and social rights. As Calman notes:

> These require both political empowerment at the local level and access to the tools of economic well-being. The search is for empowerment from below, not the conferring of rights or economic development from above. Typically, the organizations mobilize poor women to seek expanded economic opportunity. In rural areas, this may involve seeking land ownership or improving agricultural wages. In both rural and urban areas, the creation of small cooperatives, sometimes linked together through a parent organization, is a staple of women's organizing (Calman, 1992: 15).

ECOFEMINISM

Efforts to save the environment reflect more recent forms of women's political activity. The Chipko movement of the Himalayan foothill regions in Uttar Pradesh is undoubtedly the most famous of India's new social movements. Widespread deforestation caused economic hardship for local people who drew their sustenance from forests. Deforestation hit women particularly hard due to their roles in gathering fodder, fuel and water. C.P. Bhatt and other male Sarvodaya workers initially organized the movement. The famous 1974 struggle developed when the forest department granted permission to fell ash trees and local people, mostly women influenced by Gandhian workers, turned to "tree-hugging" to prevent the felling.

Vandana Shiva argues that Chipko is part of the women's movement due to gender interests in the forest economy (Shiva, 1988). In the world view of the women of the Chipko movement, according to Shiva;

> Nature is Prakriti, the creator and source of wealth, and rural women, peasants and tribals who live in, and derive sustenance from nature, have a systematic and deep knowledge of nature's processes of reproducing wealth. Nature and women do not acquire value through domination by modern western man; they lose both through this process of subjugation. The domination of nature by western industrial culture, and the domination of women by western industrial man, is part of the same process of devaluation and destruction that has been characterized in masculinist history as the "enlightenment" (Shiva, 1988: 219).

FORCEY

Chipko, according to Calman, added a new dimension to ways in which the empowerment wing of the Indian women's movement conceptualizes "women's issues." She writes:

> The way in which economic development is to transpire so as to best fill human needs and the importance of environmental conservation were introduced as issues of central concern to women. While the movement created problems, particularly the sharpening of disagreements between women and the men of their communities, it also heightened women's participation in public forums and their awareness of their own potentialities (Calman, 1992: 94).

Ramachandra Guha, among others, contests these claims, arguing instead that the Chipko movement should be placed within the broader category of peasant movements beginning in the late 19th century (Guha, 1989). The intellectual debates about the Chipko movement's particular significance are still going on (Omvedt, 1993). Clearly, however, from the Chipko movement in India to the Greenbelt movement in Kenya, women are recognizing that a sustainable environment is crucial to their economic survival. Western ecofeminists have focused on the realization that there are connections among all living things.

Many women in India however, as in the United States, are deeply ambivalent about the social and political consequences of an essentialist approach to the woman/nature relationship. The ecofeminist debate as to whether women should be involved in environmental development policy because they are instinctively closer to nature or because they suffer ecological degradation most, brings the debate into focus.

In their personal lives as professionals and in their political lives as activists, Indian women often work to minimize differences between the sexes. They frequently refer to the more powerful of the goddesses and also to the all powerful mother-in-law as proof that women are not necessarily the weaker sex, nor necessarily nicer, kinder, or gentler. On the other hand, and sometimes almost in the same breath, they argue that of course there are differences. For most women's centers and activist groups, the task of empowering women by acknowledging their caring qualities while at the same time expanding their opportunities, is the very heart of their endeavors. Chadhri writes:

> Among the women associated with Gandhian studies in particular, many seemed to feel quite comfortable with Gandhi's essentialist views on the peaceable nature of women.[4] A female director of a Gandhian studies program writes that "Gandhi considered women as individual human beings with full and equal right to self development and blamed men for their inferior status" (Chadri, 1991: 8).

However, she explains, this did not mean that Gandhi found women to be like men. Rather, home life was to be the women's sphere and the outer world, the man's. Another female scholar writes:

75

FORCEY

> Women are by nature intended to be soft, tender-hearted, sympathetic to moth-
> er children. They, being women, are the natural preservers of life because life
> grows within them. They could make their influence felt if they would only be
> big enough to rise above the walls of narrow nationalism or subnationalism that
> confine us today.[5]

And a recent United Nations report by the International Labor Organization echoes both radical ecofeminists' and Gandhi's views: "Women tend to speak with a different voice, which as a rule lays stress on the social ethos of development, that is to say, education, dialogue and peace (Press and Sun Bulletin, 1993: 7A).

WOMEN AS PEACEMAKERS

My contacts within both wings of the women's movement were primarily young, highly articulate women in Delhi, many of whom had spent time in the United States. Most were well versed in ecofeminism and Western feminist theory, wrote for either *Manushi* (a feminist magazine similar to *Ms.*) or the more academic *Samya Shakti,* (much like *Signs*), and usually felt comfortable with the activities of both wings of the movement. For both these wings and the women's studies programs at universities, however, I had to define my uses of the word "peace" very carefully.

Difficulty arose because many find the word "peace" problematic. Peace, both in India and the United States, is generally interpreted narrowly to mean the absence of inter- and intra-state war or issues within traditionally defined national security. The relatively new field of peace studies calls this the "negative" approach, one that excludes issues of social justice and structural violence.[6]

As a feminist, I argued that peace studies can have no meaning unless placed in the context of feminist thought, particularly regarding the social construction of gender, especially in its caring/mothering aspect. Militarism in the United States, for example, has shaped economic priorities for the past forty years and more. I discussed how militarism's use of U.S. resources and capital depleted medical, educational and social programs, thus creating a new, primarily mother/child poverty class. Peace implies that every human being regardless of sex has the right to a life that includes fulfillment of basic human needs; thus, much of feminist research can also be considered peace research. And much of peace research *must* focus on the intrinsic value of caring, of mothering as we have come to understand it.

In the process of being forced to define my terms for Indian audiences, I found myself becoming even less sanguine about some basic assumptions in both fields. The issues raised by Indian women left me grappling with a number of tensions and questions for new social movement politics that incorporate issues of peace. Development discourse has undergone three major shifts in focus in the past decade, reflecting 1) an increased concern for protection

FORGEY

of the environment; 2) incorporation of gender concerns; and 3) an emphasis on people's participation in new social movements, especially in the protection, regeneration, and management of natural resources. Markedly missing from development discourse is a focus on peace issues.[7]

The major shifts listed above are to be celebrated; but why, with all the violent turmoil in the world today are peace and war as prerequisites for global resources security not among the major foci? Feminist peace researchers need to confront the dilemmas and paradoxes of social movements working for a sustainable environment in Third World countries (and first and second, too) in the context of a melange of complex international issues.

While in India, I sensed a fear among women activists that engagement with broader issues of war and peace might divert women's movement energy from the gender battle at hand. Women's center and activist audiences often seemed reluctant to think about including peace among their agenda items. Deliberately employing the language of war, they would only half teasingly argue, "the battle between the sexes is on and we have too many wars to wage before we can begin to consider thinking about peace." When, however, I would talk about the social costs of military spending in the United States and the price women pay, I would feel a greater understanding.

DIFFERENT ISSUES

As an outsider in India one must take care not to generalize. While my feelings of sisterhood and camaraderie were strong, so also were my perceptions of differences. First, no matter how receptive to other cultures a westerner might be, poverty and caste/class inequities in India cannot be dismissed. As Ruth Prawar Jhabvala points out: "The most salient fact about India is that it is very poor . . . [T]his must remain the basis of all [other things that might be said] (Jhabvala, 1986: 13). Eighty percent of the population still live in villages; life expectancy is 59 years; per capita income is $350; and the illiteracy rate is 66 percent for females and 52 percent overall.[8]

The implications of these statistics on how activist women in India think about peace is complex indeed. As I have noted, there is clearly a social transformation going on among a small but growing "middle class," who, in India, are in the top 10 percent income bracket. Indian women activists are frequently reminded of their status by the movement's critics; they are sensitive to criticism from the left, and they consciously try to overcome the impact of class as they work among the rural poor.

On some issues, however, like the government's "reservation" policy that seeks affirmative action for lower and lower-middle castes as well as for former untouchables and tribals, many women activists oppose the government's position. Most student organizations, upper-caste Hindus, and the active BJP (Bharatiya Janata Party) also oppose increased affirmative action. In addition, most women I worked with believed themselves oblivious to caste distinctions, yet most admit that such distinctions remained central in the arrangement of their children's marriages.

Second is the question of religion. As one learns quickly from a stay in Varanasi (Banares), reading Diana L. Eck's *Banares: City of Light,* (Eck, 1982), or visiting any of the sacred cities of India, there is no way to ignore the passionate absorption of the majority of Indian people in the myths, history, symbols, and literature of Hindu culture. The main effect of Hindu tradition is encapsulated in the term *dharma,* signifying a kind of natural law sustaining the universe and "the sense of right order and harmony within the individual heart." Within society, as Eck describes it, "dharma is the sense of social order and duty . . . different for the man and the woman. . . ." (Eck, 1982: 315). Much as I became enthralled by Hindu tolerance of a multiplicity of gods, goddesses, and ways to worship, the force of *dharma* seemed opposed to workable paradigms for social change. As Devaki Jain points out, in India, religion especially "tugs at women: it often hurts them" (Jain, 1986: 255).

Women, under the banner of Hindu nationalism, actively participated in violent disturbances in Bombay in 1993 following the destruction of the Babri Mosque at Ayodhya. The BJP's regional party in Maharashtra, *Shiva Sena,* orchestrated women in attacks on Muslim life and property, creating what Sikata Banerjee argues is a clever balance between tradition and change. "On the one hand, women are taught to stay within the bounds of Hindu womanhood as the *Sena* organizes traditional female rituals which emphasize women's primary role as wife and mother." And on the other hand, "women are committed to violence because they were organized, encouraged to transcend their domestic role and made a part of the political space." Banerjee asserts that the *Shiva Sena* (like the women's movement) encourages women to participate in the public sphere, shouting slogans which emphasize feminine power. But, Banerjee argues convincingly, "unlike the feminists, the *Sena* is harnessing this power not to challenge patriarchy but to foment communal hatred" (Banerjee, 1994: 9,13).

Many women with whom I spoke (both Hindu and Muslim) sense bitterly how traumatized their generation had been by the partition of India and Pakistan with its millions of families uprooted and often murdered. One young Indian woman who lost most of her family during the Jallianwala Bagh incident writes: "I have great envy of those who can talk about violence easily, for in India even after the Partition we were all taught that this was not a subject we could talk about. Women who had been raped, people who had lost their whole families—they did not talk" (Eck and Jain, 1986: 283). Many academics fear that this living memory, combined with continued hostilities with Pakistan, the BJP's militancy and popularity, continued violence in the Punjab, the nation's poor economic growth, and vast cynicism about politics, mean that India's communal problems have little chance for nonviolent solutions in the near future.

The religious issue becomes particularly acute as the leadership of the BJP, the main opposition to the governing Congress Party, calls for a new religious vision of India. The vision demands that Hindu values be propagated by the state, by violence if necessary. One BJP leader argued that India should "go nuclear and NPT as a nuclear state," so that, "the whole world will recognize us by our power" (*New York Times,* 1993: 3). In Uttar Pradesh, where the BJP ruled until the mosque assault, India textbooks were being rewritten to emphasize Hindu mythology, and family planning seemed to be encouraged only for Muslim families.

The appeal of the BJP clearly extends beyond religion. It reflects the issue of anti-U.S. and anti-Western sentiment, and free-market and anti-socialist sentiments. Women activists show strong resentment toward the United States' treatment of India, as did Gandhians. They see U.S. policy as "non-violent, non-cooperation against India to force [it] , . . . to do its bidding in the nuclear field" (Bhargava, 1992: 13). Historically, U.S. support of Pakistan has further fueled the anger.

On the other hand, however, with the collapse of the Soviet Union and the government's move toward free market economics and increased trade with the United States and Europe, many Indians exhibit enthusiasm for an unbridled market economy. Such Indians welcome the elimination of many existing governmental safety nets, and support a vast proliferation of MBA programs.

I sensed little difference in the attitudes of Indian women and men with respect to either the United States or the West, and as noted earlier, I found a particular mixture of Gandhian and Marxist allegiances within the women's movement. While many women argued forcefully against Western development projects that violated the economic lives of women and voiced strong support for the growth and development of small-scale rural economies where women could participate fully, few spoke against the Indian arms buildup that symbolizes India's place in the global military economy. In the wake of the growing communal violence stemming from the conflict over the Babri Mosque in Uttar Pradesh and the increasing popularity of the Bharatiya Janata Party, with its message of Hindu power, many women's rights activists did nevertheless emphasize the importance of preserving India's democratic secular state (Calman, 1992: 18).

CONCLUSIONS

India's present turmoil is reflective of a complex melange of economic, social, religious, and gender conflicts. This sojourn convinced me that among the challenges for feminist peace research and global resource security are identification with the real and potential empowering impact of women's move-

FORCEY

ment politics, along with relentless questioning of articulations that universal-ize the category of "woman."

The challenge for feminist peace researchers is to acknowledge the ten-sions among women and men in the context of tensions around global issues of poverty, class, race, ethnicity, and caste; religion and spirituality; and deeply entrenched anti-U.S. and anti-western sentiments among developing nations. Tensions among ordinary women in their daily lives to act as women who value mothering/caring labor, while also needing an identity not overdeter-mined by gender, must be acknowledged. To paraphrase Gandhi, we must ap-preciate the manyness of things and events.

NOTES

1. This paper was originally presented at the International Political Science Associ-ation XVI World Congress, Berlin, August 21–25, 1994.

2. It must be emphasized that only a fraction of Indians attend college—fewer than 2 percent in 1981 had college degrees. See Mukhopadhyaha and Seymour (1994: 8). Of those enrolled in universities and colleges in 1985, however, 43.6 percent in Delhi and 43.9 percent in Punjab were women. See Devasia and Devasia (1990:14–15).

3. The middle class, as used in India, refer to those in the top 10 percent and have standards of living not too dissimilar to western middle classes. See Bumiller (1991: 234).

4. Pushpa Joshi (1988: x) argues that Gandhi's views on women have been por-trayed either as "part of his humanism or a patriarchal compromise, which did not re-ally overcome the restricted views about women's roles which was widely prevalent in his generation." She believes that neither position is correct, and calls for an examina-tion of his ideas over time so that the "connection between shifts in his position with his understanding of the political imperatives of the India freedom struggle" can be better understood.

5. Ashok Rattan (1988: 216) references Rajkumari Amrit Kaur, *To Women* (Ahmedabad: Navajivan Publishing House, 1959: 30).

6. The general working definition of feminism with which I am comfortable takes as proven the historical oppression of women and stresses the interrelationship of the-ory and practice to eliminate it. Feminism, as I explained it, is both a way of viewing the world and an evolving social movement, embracing not one but rather several the-oretical approaches. See Sappiro (1986:440–41). Peace studies I defined as a relatively new, interdisciplinary academic field that, as Thomas and Klare (1987–5) put it, "ana-lyzes the causes of war, violence, and systemic oppression, and explores processes by which conflict and change can be managed so as to maximize justice while minimiz-ing violence." It includes "the study of economic, political, and social systems at the local, national, and global levels, and of ideology, culture, and technology as they relate to conflict and change."

7. The preliminary program for the International Political Science Association World Congress VI, held in Berlin, August 21-25, 1994, listed only three sessions with peace in the title.

8. U.S. Education Foundation in India Fact Sheet, distributed September, 1992, New Delhi.

REFERENCES

Banerjii, Sikata. "Hindu Nationalism and the Construction of Woman: The Shiva Sena Organizes Women in Bombay." Paper delivered at the Western Political Science Association Meeting, Albuquerque, New Mexico, March 10-12, 1994.

Bhargava, G.S. "India, US and NPT." *The Hindustan Times,* New Delhi, December 2, 1992.

Bumiller, Elizabeth. *May You Be the Mother of a Hundred Sons.* Calcutta: Penguin, 1991.

Caldecott, Leonie and Stephanie Leland, eds. *Reclaim the Earth: Women Speak Out for Life on Earth.* London: Women's Press, 1983.

Calman, Leslie J. *Toward Empowerment: Women and Movement Politics in India.* Boulder, CO: Westview Press, 1992.

Chadri, Sandhya. "Gandhi's Contribution to the Emancipation and Upliftment of Women." Unpublished paper, n.d. 1991 Chandigarh: Department of Gandhian Studies, Panjab University.

Devasia, Leelamma and V.V. Devasia. *Women in India: Equality, Social Justice and Development.* New Delhi: Indian Social Institute, 1990.

Eck, Diana L. *Banares: City of Light.* New York Alfred A. Knopf, 1982.

――― and Davaki Jain, eds. *Speaking of Faith: Cross-Cultural Perspectives on Women, Religion and Social Change.* New Delhi: Kali, 1986.

Forcey, Linda Rennie. "Women as Peacemakers: Contested Terrain for Feminist Peace Studies." *Peace & Change.* Vol. 16, (4): 331–354. October, 1991.

Government of India. *Toward Equality: Report of the Committee on the Status of Women in India.* New Delhi: Ministry of Education and Social Welfare, 1974.

Guha, Ramachandra. *The Unquiet Woods: Ecological Change and Peasant Resistance in the Himalaya.* Delhi: Oxford University Press, 1989.

Hill, Marvine. "Women's Group Seeks Environmental Role." *New York Times,* October 28, 1990. p. 16.

Jain, Devaki. "Gandhian Contributions Toward a Feminist Ethics." In *Speaking of Faith: Cross-Cultural Perspectives on Women, Religion and Social Change,* Diana L. Eck and Davaki Jain, eds. New Delhi: Kali, 1986.

Jhabvala, Ruth Prawer. *Out of India.* New York: William Morrow & Co, 1986.

Joshi, Pushpa. *Gandhi on Women.* Ahmedabad: Navajivan Publishing House, 1988.

Mukhopadhyay, Carol Chapnick and Susan Seymour, eds. *Women, Education, and Family Structure in India.* Boulder, CO: Westview Press, 1994.

Naipaul, V.S. *India.* New York: Penguin, 1990.

New York Times, January 24, February 7, 1993.

Omvedt, Gail. *Reinventing Revolution: New Social Movements and the Socialist Tradition in India.* London: M.E. Sharpe, 1993.

Peterson, V. Spike and Anne Sisson Runyan. *Global Gender Issues.* Boulder, CO: Westview Press, 1993.

Press & Sun-Bulletin, Binghamton, NY. February 5, 1993.

Rattan, Ashok R. "Role of Women in the Control of Social Violence." *Gandhi Marg,* July, 1988. (The author references Rajkumari Amrit Kaur, *To Women,* Ahmedabad: Navajivan Publishing, 1959.)

Runyan, Anne and V. Spike Peterson. "The Radical Future of Realism: Feminist Subversions of IR Theory." *Alternatives:* 16 (1): 67–1-6, 1991.

81

FORCEY

Said, Edward W. *Culture and Imperialism*. New York Alfred A. Knopf, 1993.

Sapiro, Virginia. *Women in American Society*. Palo Alto, CA: Mayfield, 1986.

Segal, Lynne. *Is the Future Female?* London: Virago, 1992.

Shiva, Vandana. *Staying Alive: Women, Ecology and Survival in India*. New Delhi: Kali for Women, 1988.

Singh, Khushwant. *My Bleeding Punjab*. New Delhi: UPS Publishers' Distributors Ltd, 1992.

US. Dept. of Commerce, Bureau of the Census. *Statistical Abstract of the United States, 1990*. Washington, DC.: U.S. Government Printing Office, 1990.

Thomas, Daniel C. ed. *Guide to Careers and Graduate Education in Peace Studies.*, MA: PAWSS, 1987.

Tong, Rosemary. "Feminist Thought: A Comprehensive Introduction." In J. Ann Ticknor, ed. *Gender in International Relations*. New York: Columbia University Press, 1992.

US. Education Foundation in India Fact Sheet. New Delhi: 1992.

LAND, ECOLOGY, AND WOMEN:

Global Implications for Hawaiian Sovereignty

Claire Van Zevern

We are the children of Papa-earth mother, and
Wakea-sky father who created the sacred lands of
Hawai'i Nei. From these lands came the taro, and
from the taro, came the Hawaiian people. As in all
of Polynesia, so in Hawai'i: younger sibling must
care for and honor elder sibling. Thus, Hawaiians
must nourish the land from whence we come. . . .
The land is our mother and we are her children
(Trask, 1993: xiii).

chapter 5

Lahui: *the People*

Native Hawaiians (*Kanaka Maoli*) have a reciprocal and familial relationship to
the land. Of the thousands of Native Hawaiian deities, many are symbols of
the earth, such as *Pele* (volcano), *Kane* and *Lono* (fertile valleys) and *Kanalua*
(ocean). The native language shows the centrality of land in Hawaiian culture;
the word *aina* means that which feeds (land) and a word for native born, *kama*
'aina, means child of the land.

Native Hawaiian culture specifies that land and resources are to be used
only to the extent that they are needed, therefore ownership of land is a violation of Hawaiian culture. The concept of ownership is in itself foreign and
contrary to the familial relationship between Native Hawaiians and the land.
Such a relationship is based on the concept *malama 'aina,* which means to care
for the land. Even the United States government, 102nd Congress 2nd Session, in offering a symbolic apology to the Native Hawaiians and admitting

the conspiracy involved in the initial annexation, recognized the importance of land in Native Hawaiian culture. Congress stated, "Whereas the health and well being of the Native Hawaiian people is intrinsically tied to their deep feelings and attachment to the land."

Haole: *White Foreigners*

Hawai'i is a land rich in natural resources, and is located strategically between mainland America and Asia. The United States, therefore, perceived the acquisition of Hawai'i to be in its best interest. The annexation was, however, somewhat fraudulent.

During the 1820s, American missionaries became involved with the production of sugar in the Hawaiian islands. These missionaries needed a permanent relationship with Hawai'i so that sugar would become a mainland U.S. domestic product. They also needed a way to legitimize their land holdings and facilitate business needs. With these as incentives, the foreigners began a process by which the Native Hawaiian government was replaced by an American one. The role of the missionaries is explained in *Ka Ho'okolokolonui Kanaka Maoli* in the following way,

> In 1891, the McKinley Tariff Act cancelled all duty fees on sugar imports and, instead, awarded 2 cents a pound subsidy to U.S. sugar producers to their advantage . . . Because the advantages sugar planters had were wiped out by the McKinley Tariff Act, they worked harder for annexation to the U.S. A two cents a pound sugar subsidy was indeed worthwhile, if they could just get Hawai'i annexed (1992: 4).

American authority manifested itself first in the Webster-Tyler Doctrine (1826) which declared Hawai'i to be within the U.S. sphere of influence. In attempts to gain a military foothold and because King Kamehameha V refused to sell any part of the Hawaiian archipelago, the United States seized Midway Island in 1867. Hawai'i was soon declared an American colony (1875). The existing leader, King Kalakaua, was forced to forego all power to American missionaries, who dominated the House of Nobles in the Native Hawaiian government. The document which caused this transition is known as the "Bayonet Constitution" because the King signed it under threat of death.

King Kalakua died in 1891 and was replaced by his sister, Queen Liliuokalani. The Queen, having received petitions from the majority of voters in Hawai'i who wanted the old constitution restored, made attempts to change the Bayonet Constitution. The U.S. government's view of her efforts was made clear by the arrival of 160 U.S. marines to Hawai'i, whose presence facilitated the creation of a provisional government by Mr. Henry Cooper. Queen Liliuokalani was then forced to surrender to this new government. Such blatant abuse of force alarmed President Cleveland and provoked from him some significant democratic rhetoric: "A substantial wrong has thus been done which a due regard for our national character as well as the rights of the injured people requires we should endeavor to repair" (Morse and Hamid, 1992: 416). Cleveland thus restored the Queen to her rightful position but did not remove the 160 marines—in order that a reminder be in place not to challenge American authority.

The Bayonet Constitution had succeeded in transferring power from the Native Hawaiian government to the House of Nobles. There was then a need to create an entirely new government giving all power to the United States Sanford Dole, the so-called acting president of Cooper's provisional government, therefore called a constitutional convention. The majority of the delegates to this convention were hand picked by Mr. Dole (19 out of 37). More than 80 percent of the Native Hawaiian voters were disqualified from voting to ratify or not ratify the constitution by virtue of their allegiance to the Queen and not to the Dole government.

The Dole constitution was thus ratified; following this Dole promptly ceded the sovereignty of Hawai'i to President McKinley in 1897. Hawai'i was annexed by the United States on July 7, 1898, via a resolution which required a simple majority, rather than by treaty which requires a two-thirds majority. Congress did not favor annexation because they did not want a large native population in a predominantly white union. The native population opposed annexation since they wanted self government. The annexation of Hawai'i guaranteed the United States a strategic location, sugar cane, sandalwood, and various other resources (Trask, 1993: 20).

Malama 'aina: *To Care for the Land*

Native Hawaiians are not only denied access to the land that was once theirs; their ability to practice *malama aina*, to care for the land as a family member, was also denied. Land in Hawai'i is not being cared for; it is being destroyed at an alarming rate. In the state of Hawai'i, only 10 percent of the original lowland rainforest remains intact. (D'Lemonick, 1990: 68). While in places like the Amazon, Sarawak, or Oregon, where the primary threat to the ecosystem and survival of inhabitants is deforestation, for the unique Hawaiian Islands, ecological degradation does not begin nor end with deforestation. Hawai'i is plagued by alien species and the effects of the development of geothermal energy. Given the uniqueness and small size of the Hawaiian Islands, the tiniest disruption creates a ripple effect throughout the ecosystem.

Hawai'i is the world's most remote archipelago (the nearest land mass is 2500 miles away). Ecologists estimate that a new species arrived in Hawai'i only once in every 10,000 years (Ezzell, 1992). Prior to 1,500 years ago when the first terrestrial mammal somehow found its way to Hawai'i, Hawai'i's only mammals were one species of bat and one species of seal. There were no snakes, no amphibians, and no mosquitoes.

VAN ZEVERN

Today, Hawaiian monk seals number fewer than 1,500. Half of the 140 original species of birds in Hawai'i are extinct. Of all endangered plant species in the United States about 20 percent are from Hawai'i (Harrigan, 1992). Most of the extinction or near extinction of the ecology of Hawai'i is attributable to the arrival of Europeans and the alien species they brought with them. Still today, snakes (currently Hawai'i has no snakes but the threat looms constantly) curl up in the wheels of airplanes full of tourists. Seeds and insects also find their way to Hawai'i by way of unknowing yet unrelenting tourists. (Surprisingly, agricultural restrictions are harsher for tourists entering mainland U.S. from Hawai'i.) Among the biggest threats to the ecology of Hawai'i are the alien species of Argentine ant, the cannibal snail, alien grasses, the feral pig, and a flowering vine called *banana poka*—these are taking over and destroying the native ecology at an alarming pace.

Alien species destroy the preexisting environment, in turn exacerbating the threat of extinction. The Argentine ant, which "eats every insect it can," is surpassing the higher-ups on the food chain such as the wolf spider and will soon "decimate the native fauna wherever it goes" if not controlled (Ezzell, 1992: 315). The cannibal snail was introduced intentionally to Hawai'i to control the population of another alien species, the African snail, and is now devouring the native O'ahu tree snail species of which 19 or 20 out of 41 species remain (Ezzell, 1992). Non-predatory grasses originating from North America and Africa also pose a threat to the native ecology as they change fundamental characteristics of the ecosystem. These alien grasses, which now constitute 93 percent of the standing biomass in Hawaiian dry forests, recover from fire more rapidly than native plant species and effectively overcome the latter (Ezzell, 1992). "This disruption, in turn, increases the ecosystems vulnerability to further alien invasion" (Ezzell, 1992: 316). The feral pig, also introduced by Europeans, tramples or eats native plant species and adds to the spread of the *banana poka* which is strangling the native rainforest. "The survival of tree-fern forest depended . . . on the integrity of the canopy of fronds . . . Pigs, in spreading the seeds of raspberry and *banana poka*, sent up vines that killed the canopy" (Brower, 1989: 24). Pigs also chew on the fallen trunks of tree ferns, creating cavities that collect rainwater, breeding mosquitoes and thus spreading avian malaria, the major cause of the decline of native forest birds.

The development of geothermal energy has added to the ecological crisis facing Hawai'i. The Hawaiian state government as well as energy conglomerates hope to replace imported foreign oil with geothermal energy by the year 2007. The drilling rigs, power plants, and transmission lines necessary to accomplish this already have destroyed (and continue to) parts of the Wao Kele O Puna rain forest. This forest is the largest low land rain forest left in Hawai'i and is legally set aside for use by the Native Hawaiians (D'Lemonick, 1990). So far, eight acres of land have been bulldozed and a plan exists to build a big-

VAN ZEVERN

ger plant which would require 350 acres (D'Lemonick, 1990). These figures themselves are somewhat misleading as the roads that connect cleared forest lands are equally destructive to the environment, disturbing the existing habitat and creating an immigration path for alien species to that habitat. Wao Kele O Puna is home to the Hawaiian Hawk, the Happy Face Spider and unique medicinal plants which do not reside elsewhere on the islands.

The destructive forces of development and militarism are magnified due to the small size and uniqueness of the islands. On the island of Kauai, for example, Nukolii, once a 60-acre piece of marshland, is now the Kauai Hilton and Beach Villas. This transition created an uproar from local and native residents especially because of the unethical means by which the land was sold (Conrow, 1988). According to activist John Pilkington, Nukolii is "not just another development, but a symbol of the people of Kauai loosing their right to self government" (Conrow, 1988: 11). Kauai is also home to a strategic target system which emits freon, liquid propellants, and exhaust—all of which affect human health, the marine food chain, and terrestrial and marine ecosystems. There is also a plan by Sandia National laboratories to engage in a "Brillant Pebbles" rocket program which involves an 800-meter-long coil gun that would create sonic booms every ten minutes and require as much electricity as Kauai's present generating capacity (Misrach, 1991).

The State of Hawai'i owns 36.5 percent of the land, much of which is ecological reserves; yet these reserves (900,000 acres, of which 270,000 are wildlife refuges) have been far from adequate. According to the Nature Conservatory of Hawai'i, of the 180 "natural communities" that presently exist, only 89 are represented in federal parks and wildlife refuges. Similarly, 141 (of the 180) are "rare," yet only 60 percent are protected by federal lands. Kauai, the habitat for much of Hawai'i's endangered birds, has only three small wildlife preserves (Brower, 1989).

The 41.2 percent of the land owned by large private landowners is blatantly abused with almost no private conservation efforts. Botanists have literally been banned from the two largest private estates, the McCandless Ranch and the Bishop Estate, despite the presence of endangered wildlife there.

> The owners of the McCandless Ranch on the Big Island, for example, have banned biologists from their land following the discovery there of the 'alala (the Hawaiian crow), only fifteen of which are known to exist. . . . The Bishop Estate, the biggest private land owner in Hawaii, is determined to log koa in Kilauea forest, one of the Big Island's few intact remnants of native forest. After botanists discovered an endangered plant in the forest, the Bishop estate banned botanists. (Brower, 1989: 25).

This dearth of private conservation efforts is an additional threat to the already existing ecological crisis in Hawai'i.

The colonization of Hawai'i and the destruction of its natural resources is a

87

form of direct violence against the Native Hawaiian people (Salmi, 1993). When James Cook arrived in the Hawaiian Islands in 1778, the native population numbered approximately 800,000. Today the Kanaka Maoli population is about 200,000 (or 19 percent) out of the total resident population of Hawai'i of one million (Blaisdell, 1992). The damage done by foreigners (including Americans) to the land is a threat to *Kanaka Maoli* (indigenous Hawaiians), the lives of other Hawaiian residents, and the millions of plants, animals, and insects that live on the islands. Today, the *Kanaka Maoli* have the worst health, social, economic, and educational status of all ethnic groups in Hawai'i. They have the shortest life expectancy and highest rates for major causes of death, the poorest academic performance, lowest median income, and highest rates of homelessness and family violence (U.S. Department of the Interior, 1983).

Aina: *Native Born*

Native Hawaiians are legally entitled to certain "ceded" lands in Hawai'i but have yet to receive them. The Great Mahele of 1848 divided up the land between the U.S. government and the *ali'i* (chiefs), thus introducing private ownership and displacing Native Hawaiians from their land. (The Great Mahele divided the land as follows: 36 percent to the U.S. government, 24 percent to Kamehameha III, 39 percent to 250 *ali'i* (chiefs) and 1 percent to the 80,000 commoners [U.S. Department of the Interior, 1983].) Despite the Kuleana Act of 1850, which authorized sales of government land to Kanaka peoples and included provisions to facilitate land claims by Kanaka farmers, a census taken in 1890 showed that out of a population of 90,000 only 5,000 owned land. (U.S. Department of the Interior 1983). The Hawaiian Homes Commission Act (1921) allotted 200,000 acres to those Kanaka with more than 50 percent native blood. Sixty percent of those lands were sold to non-Kanaka; the entire sacred island of Kaho 'olawe was taken over by the U.S. military. The military owns 30 percent of O'ahu with some 60,000 acres of trust lands taken by Executive order during World War II and the Vietnam conflict (Trask, 1993). According to Haunani Kay Trask of Ka Lahui Hawai'i, there are currently 20,000 families on the waiting list for land, while over 130,000 acres of trust lands are being used by non-natives. "Hawaiians do not have standing to sue for breach of trust on their lands" (Trask, 1993: 261). The New York Center for Constitutional Rights has since taken on the case of the Native Hawaiians (Koning, 1993).

The most fundamental aspect of cultural, social, economic, political, and human survival is land, without which these rights cannot be sustained (Churchill, 1993). By destroying the communal land base system, the capacity for self-sufficiency as well as people's ability to understand their relationship to the economic and social system is also eradicated (Wilmer, 1993). Land rights, therefore, are the basis for the Kanaka Maoli initiative for self government.

Kupa 'a 'aina: *hold fast to the land*

The movement for sovereignty was born out of the political activism of the 1970s surrounding land abuses in Hawai'i. Today, the largest of the sovereignty groups, Ka Lahui Hawai'i, has over 12,000 members (as of 1992). Sovereignty is defined by Ka Mana O Ka 'Aina (a pro Hawaiian sovereignty group) in the following way:

> Sovereignty is the right possessed by a culturally distinct people, inhibiting and controlling a definable territory to make all decisions regarding itself and its territory free from outside interference (Boggs and Akwai, 1992: 1).

Cultural survival is based upon the human right to develop self-sufficient economies which require a land base. The desecration and exploitation of land denies Native Hawaiians their survival and integrity as indigenous peoples. In the assertion for sovereignty, the Kanaka Maoli demand control of the land which was ceded to them (Homestead Act of 1921, Kuleana Act 1850, the Mahele 1848) and which is necessary to their survival.

Mana

Upon conquest, women and men lost social power along with their land. Western patriarchy introduced paternal blood lines and consequently displaced the traditional maternal lineage system which provided identity for Native Hawaiian women. The Native Hawaiian tradition of extended family diminished, thereby demoting women from life-givers to domestic servants (Trask, 1993) Industrial capitalism moved the source of production to outside the home, in turn reducing the family to a consumer unit and devaluing traditional forms of work. Women were forced into the labor market and now take jobs as domestic laborers, sales clerks and hula girls. Upon this transition to capitalism, women lost their traditional forms of work, social roles, and therefore respect, and entered the low-status, meaningless jobs shared by many of their mainland counterparts.

Post annexation and statehood, Hawaiian men were schooled in the American systems, and women were not (until much later). During this time, men began to believe that change could be made "the American way" (i.e., through the existing mechanisms). These men gradually lost their Hawaiian ways and began to internalize the patriarchal ideas which oppressed all Native Hawaiians. Women, on the other hand, were unable to enter the American political system and were therefore better maintained their traditions and customs.

Hawaiian women emerged during the 1970s. Articulate and culturally grounded, they took their place at the forefront of the sovereignty movement. Trask argues that the main reason for their strength and leadership is because they have not lost sight of *lahui,* the nation, and of caring for the nation which is an extension of family, land, and people (1993). Women such as

VAN ZEVERN

Mililani Trask (elected governor of Ka Lahui Hawai'i) and La France Kapaka (community activist) are characterized by their *mana*—their ability to speak for the people and the land and to command respect by virtue of this ability (Trask, 1993). In order to be a successful leader one must possess not only *mana*, but also *pono*, the traditional Hawaiian value of balance between people, land, and cosmos. According to Haunani Kay Trask, the reassertion of *mana* in the sovereignty movement is the defining trait for cultural and political leadership. Leaders only embody sovereignty if they are *pono* (believe in and work for the land and people): thus, political leadership is based on traditional cultural beliefs.

Hula

Tourism contributes much to the ecological destruction of Hawai'i, but it also degrades Native Hawaiians, their culture, and especially the women by way of the ideology of the tourist industry. The central role gender plays in the struggle over sovereignty can be seen in Hawai'i's tourism, which Haunani Kay Trask calls "cultural prostitution."

The islands of Hawai'i are gendered in the promotion of tourism: They are advertised as being beautiful, sexy, alluring, submissive—yours for the taking. Native Hawaiian women themselves are portrayed similarly, giving the illusion of a "sex paradise." Women who dance *hula* are objectified and made to wear lots of makeup, making hula profane where it was once sacred. This "cultural prostitution" is a manifestation of a male-dominated oppressive system. More specifically,

> "Prostitution" in this context refers to the entire institution which defines a woman (and by extension the "female") as an object of degraded and victimized sexual value for use and exchange through the medium of money. The "prostitute" is then a woman who sells her sexual capacities and is seen, thereby, to possess and reproduce them at will, that is, by her very "nature." The prostitute and the institution which created and maintains her are of course, of patriarchical origin (Trask, 1993: 185)

In fact, according to Cynthia Enloe, "The very structure of international tourism *needs* patriarchy to survive" (Enloe, 1989: 40) Hula in this form thus symbolizes the degradation of Native Hawaiian culture.

Currently, tourists outnumber residents of Hawai'i, six to one, Native Hawaiians thirty to one (Trask, 1993). Among the side effects of tourism are increased population and crime, depletion of water, and stunted growth of real income for Hawai'i's residents. Hawai'i's residents have the limited career options of unemployment, military work, or work in the tourist industry (which only grosses about $10,000–25,000); or they can leave Hawai'i. On O'ahu, where 80 percent of the population resides, the median cost of a home is $450,000. Families there spend almost 52 percent of their gross income on housing (Trask, 1993). O' ahu, only 607 square miles, serves five million tourists a year. The money from corporate tourism does not benefit the resident community. Multinationals based in Japan, Hong Kong, Canada, Australia, and the United States own the airlines, tour buses, hotels, restaurants, and golf courses used by tourists from those countries. The infrastructure is built by multinationals in exchange for county approval of more hotel units.

Tourism, a mere starting point to the discussion, itself connects various continents and nations, and specifically the women in them. The oppression of women that tourism creates (low status and low paying jobs, for example) and indeed thrives on, links women globally. The sexism that oppresses women from a rich nation manifests itself in the way men treat other women, for example on a business trip or vacation. In this way women from different nations and cultures are linked, in that all women are the object of sexist oppression. This statement is not essentialist, as Vandana Shiva's asserts: "Women acting together in spite of their diversity is not equivalent to the essentializing of women as a uniform category" (Shiva, 1994: 8).

The importance of women in Ka Lahui Hawai'i and the Native Hawaiian struggle for sovereignty threatens the men who have acquired and maintained power by oppressing all women, and particularly women of color in the existing patriarchical system. The leaders of the Hawaiian sovereignty movement are women of color, the lowest status according to current American social hierarchy. They are not submissive, passive, exotic sex goddesses ready and willing to be used and tossed aside. They are intelligent, articulate, nationalistic, and serious about their demand for sovereignty. In recognizing the legitimacy of their claim, we also deny the notion that one must be (at least) male to hold status and power.

IDEOLOGIES: DEVELOPMENT, MILITARISM, PATRIARCHY

Adjunct to this notion of male superiority is the patriarchical/industrial view that man is superior to the environment. It is precisely this attitude that has fed ecocide for centuries. Native Hawaiians, in their initiative for self government, demand an end to such an attitude. They, along with other indigenous groups world-wide, command a respect for the land that nurtures and protects us all. Those institutions that the patriarchical system has created and sustained, such as tourism and militarism, are by definition destroyers of the earth.

Native Hawaiian sovereignty poses a challenge to the power that enables the United States to claim land that is not theirs, in Hawai'i and elsewhere. Sovereignty movements are therefore a challenge to United States resource politics (Gedicks, 1993). Existing power structures have fought to protect the resources necessary for them to remain in power; resources such as those in Iroquis land, Lakota land, Kanaka Maoli land, the Persian Gulf, Somalia, and Central and South America, thereby engaging in a form of eco-genocidal vi-

VAN ZEVERN

olence against the peoples who possess such resources. The resource politics of the United States stem from the U.S. economic system. Specifically,

> Insofar as capitalism, as a historical form of economic activity, has not developed in a virgin natural environment freely available to all, the private appropriation of natural resources or their control by private interests has necessarily required . . . some form of "induced" renunciation on the part of the groups of people who were making use of them or controlled them before (Salmi, 1993: 35).

The nature of Western capitalism—and therefore U.S. resource politics—contradicts indigenous ways. Intrinsic to the notion of man's dominance over nature is a linear, industrial-oriented model of modernization. Progress, according to this view, is equivalent to economic growth and technological advancement, both of which create environmental destruction. Arguments for this type of progress suggest that modern land development benefits "everyone," including indigenous subsistence economies that are considered to be "inefficient and which take up too much land." The Western world view is profit-oriented and destructive to the environment; thus, it is based on values and material interests that contradict those of indigenous peoples, as well as of radical feminists (Wilmer, 1993; Enloe, 1989).

In the dominant theory of modernization, the state exists in order to facilitate economic growth and technological advancement. Consequently, it also shapes the distribution of rights and resources. While disagreement as to the shape and form of modernization may occur, the strategy of industrialization as a means of improving quality of life remains an ideology common to global elites. For this reason, quality of life is separated from cultural values. As Wilmer explains,

> Because modernization is believed to be a good in itself, a kind of moral community has developed in connection with its implementation, thereby rationalizing courses of action that promote modernization as well as those aimed at removing obstacles to modernization. The treatment of indigenous communities frequently falls into the latter category. Modernization represents the sum of attributes perceived by elites as endowing them with moral superiority, and nonmodern societies are therefore, by definition, morally inferior (Wilmer, 1993: 55).

This "moral community" has established itself in dominant international structures such as the World Bank and the United Nations. These institutions have shaped development policy for most of the Third World.

According to Joke Scrijvers, there is an inherent element of violence in "development" in itself. Scrijvers explains development in the following way:

> Development has always been intertwined with major economic and political interests, hence unavoidably also with (the threat of) violence. The dominant paradigm of "development," as a direct continuation of 500 years of colonial his-

92

SUSTAINABLE DEVELOPMENT AND WOMEN:

The Role of NGOs

Julie Fisher

IN 1987, Prime Minister Gro Brundtland of Norway headed an international commission that enhanced awareness of "sustainable development," defined as development in the present that does not destroy the resources needed for development in the future. The United Nations Conference on Environment and Development, held in Rio in 1992, further advanced international understanding of the connections between poverty and environmental degradation. But it took the Cairo Conference of 1994 to bring the third horseman of the global apocalypse—the projected doubling of global population by 2050—to center stage.[1] With population, inevitably, came the central role of women. Talk about the importance of women's productive activities to sustainable development existed before Cairo, but Cairo crystallized the dramatically positive connections between women's education, employment, and declining fertility as well as the need for reproductive health services, including family planning.

Although most Third World women are unaware of this international debate, many, faced with the daily need to survive and provide for the next generation, are actually implementing sustainable development. As they recycle waste, learn to build more efficient cook stoves, plant fruit trees in deforested areas, or visit family planning clinics, they become environmental activists. The nongovernmental movement increasingly supports these endeavors, reaching an estimated 500 million of the 4.2 billion people in the Third World.[2]

The global challenge described by the poverty/environment/population nexus is daunting at best. Only if the global community understands, appreciates and takes account of already existing institutional and human resources in the Third World can there be any hope of meeting the sustainable development challenge. Indigenous nongovernmental organizations (NGOs), emerging about 25 years ago, now serve as principal institutional resources for sustainable development in the Third World, due to their own activities and impact on governments. As the author of a recent book about the nongovernmental movement in the Third World, both the dramatic growth of the movement and the disproportionate and increasingly important role of women in creating, maintaining, and acting within NGOs, continually strikes me (Fisher, 1993).

A partnership between two types of NGOs—grassroots organizations (GROs) and grassroots support organizations (GRSOs)—increasingly accounts for the rapid growth of the independent or voluntary sector in the Third World. Grassroots organizations (GROs) are locally based groups that work to improve and develop their own communities through community-wide or more specific memberships, such as women. Although many have been promoted and stimulated by GRSOs, they have also become more active on their own. Over 200,000 GROs exist in Asia, Africa, and Latin America, more than half of them organized by women.[3] Faced with environmental deterioration and the increasing impoverishment of the 1980s, both traditional and newly created GROs began to organize horizontal networks among themselves. In some cases they have created grassroots support organizations from below by hiring their own expertise (Fisher, 1993).

GRSOs are nationally or regionally based development assistance organizations, usually staffed by professionals, that channel international funds to grassroots organizations and help communities other than their own to develop. At least 30,000 to 35,000 grassroots support organizations are active in the Third World.[4] Although some GRSOs are "counterparts" to international NGOs (INGOs) or NGOs from the developed countries, the vast majority of GRSOs are indigenous. GRSOs build umbrella organizations and network with each other, in addition to providing linkages with GROs.

The next two sections describe the general role of women GRO and GRSO activists in more detail. The third section concentrates on their role in confronting the interrelated barriers to sustainable development—population, poverty, and environmental degradation. The national advocacy role of women in NGOs, their role in international NGO networking, and the impact of donor relationships are explored in the fourth and fifth sections. The final section contains conclusions and recommendations.

GRASSROOTS ORGANIZATIONS

Pressures for survival both now and for the next generation cause women to organize in much of the Third World. Yet, having to walk further and further for food, water, and fuel motivates women to do more than survive. In Kangoussema, Senegal, women in a local GRO walk 70 kilometers round-trip to sell their vegetables for a net profit of 5–10 French francs. The male president of a mixed GRO in Senegal was quoted as saying that "Women organize themselves better, because they have more determination" (Pradervand, 1988: 7). The *Naams* groups in Burkina Faso led to a virtual revolution in relations between the sexes, with activist women organizing microenterprises.

Women are also organizing themselves in Latin America. In Lima, Peru, over 100,000 people, mostly mothers, form 7,000 *Vaso de Leche* (glass of milk) committees that work through 1,500 community kitchens. The community kitchens are also organized into barrio, zonal, and district organizations that undertake fundraising projects for sustainable development activities. The committees acquired considerable immunity from local politics, precisely because few men participate.[5]

Women also organize "Mother's Clubs," in South Korea and Indonesia, as well as in Latin America. Despite their adherence to traditional familial norms, such groups often radically change the way women think about themselves and the way they act in their own communities. In rural Colombia, women afraid to leave their houses hung their heads in shyness during the first women's clubs meetings organized by Save the Children. Within a few years, however, the women became valued contributors to family income and were actively involved in community activities and local development associations (Fisher, 1986). Brazilian mother's clubs, created by the Roman Catholic church in the 1960s, now mobilize politically on family planning and women's rights. Men generally do not organize as fathers. Yet for women, what begins as familial becomes political (Logan, 1990).

In South Asia, lower class women are active in GROs that promote women's issues. Indian women have mobilized around a number of notorious rape cases, dowry deaths, and bride burnings, for example, strengthened by GRSOs such as the Grameen Bank and the Bangladesh Rural Advancement Committee (BRAC) and the Working Women's Forum in India. In Pakistan, lower class women actively oppose the introduction of *sharia* law, which halves the value of women's legal testimony, and the Hadood Ordinance, which does not differentiate between rape and adultery.

FISHER

GRASSROOTS SUPPORT ORGANIZATIONS

Most GRSOs work directly through grassroots organizations. A survey of 60 Peruvian NGOs that work with women found that 77 percent of them work through women's GROs. Indeed, the authors of the survey argue that active GROs are both a prerequisite for assistance and an achievement in themselves (Delpino and Pasara, 1991).

The growth of GRSOs concerned explicitly with women in development has been the most dramatic component of their overall proliferation. *Mahila Parishad,* the largest women's organization in Bangladesh, staged a national meeting of 30,000 participants on democracy and development. Out of 1,141 GRSOs (and some charities) in a Brazilian directory, 251 work primarily with women (Fausto 1988).

Women's GRSOs tend to view themselves as part of a broader grassroots movement. The Muslim Women's Conference in Sri Lanka attracts both middle class and poor women, has 34 member organizations, and concentrates on employment training as well as the health of women and children. In the Philippines, *Katipunan ng Bagong Pilipina* provides educational materials for training and organizing to 28,000 rural members.

Not all GRSO organizers come from the educated middle class. Some are organized by women who leave their villages to obtain an education and then return to found a GRSO. In Tamil Nadu, India, six young *Harijan* (formerly untouchable) women college graduates returned to their village and trained fifteen "animators." Each animator was placed in charge of a landless laborers' association of several thousand covering five districts. The movement has built clinics and trained widows as paraprofessional health workers. After an eleven-year-old girl was raped by a landowner, the group staged a mass protest, forcing the government to arrest the perpetrator.

In addition to the preceding characteristics, the distinction between middle class feminist issues and the survival concerns of poor women blurs for many GRSOs. *Peru Mujer,* for example, grew out of the middle class feminist movement, but now works for legal changes benefiting women in general. It also promotes urban gardens to improve nutrition, operates training in weaving, marketing and administration, and promotes a participatory methodology for women who work in labor unions or in fields such as health education.

In Bangladesh a national association of women lawyers initiated a project that traveled to 68,000 villages, teaching millions of women (and men) basic legal rights. They later organized a women's health coalition patterned on international family planning programs and coordinated their efforts with other development agencies.

With few exceptions, such as in parts of the Caribbean where charitable approaches still predominate, a majority of Third World women's organizations focus on sustainable development. More specifically, they promote the message that development will fail without the full involvement of women. The initial shift from "women's projects" involving housekeeping skills or handicrafts to microenterprise development is now being supplemented by the broader conviction, backed by overwhelming evidence, that declines in infant mortality, family planning, environmental preservation, and income generation all depend on educating and involving women. There is also evidence that the changes in gender roles that accompany this involvement may enhance the productive and human potential of men.

In Bolivia, for example, CIMCA (Capacitacion Integral de la Mujer Campesina) uses innovative educational techniques to change gender relationships in rural areas. Men are sharing responsibility for gathering firewood in communitites where CIMCA works. In Querarani, each office of the local *Associacion Familiar Campesina* is jointly filled by husband and wife teams. Four *campesinas* were elected to the Executive Committee of the departmental federation, which represents several hundred thousand small farmers due to this activity.[6]

When donors or GRSOs lump male farmers with landless women in organizing GROs they "virtually guarantee that the men will reap the bulk of rewards" (Durning, 1989: 19). Yet GROs organized as strictly women's groups seem able to include men at a later stage without being dominated by them. Arguments for mixed groups make more sense once women have had the chance to strengthen their own autonomy and self confidence. Gram Vikas, a GRSO in Karnataka, recognizes this by organizing separate women's and men's *sanghas* (GROs) and then encouraging them to cooperate with each other and, in some cases, merge into mixed groups (Viswanath, 1991).

Many GRSOs founded by men have also come to depend on the central involvement of women. The Nigeria Society for the Improvement of Rural People works with women's groups to plant trees, develop pine nursery businesses, and maintain biodiversity in southern Nigeria. Coordinator Christopher Ugwu says "No environmental crusade has even the slimmest chance of succeeding without women being pivotal in its execution" (WorldWIDE News, 1994: 5).

Not surprisingly, however, the NGO movement still reflects the professional barriers faced by many Third World women. Elizabeth Moen, in her study of NGOs in Tamil Nadu, India, notes that male development workers have trouble relating to women as professionals, and women professionals are usually not very assertive (1991). Irene Dankelman and Joan Davidson surveyed 46 environmental NGOs in the Third World and found that women constituted less than half of the professional staff in 31 organizations and more than half in only nine (1988). Forty-two organizations sampled were headed by men and only four by women. Even more serious, eighteen organizations had no working relationships with any women's organizations, although twenty-seven collaborated with women's groups.

The difficulties that women face in coming to the attention of international donors who fund NGOs place a premium on resourcefulness, fundraising, and volunteering. Tototo Homes Industries in Kenya provides training and consulting to other development agencies, runs a profitable retail shop and charges modest fees for vocational training workshops to support their work with women's GROs (Leach, et al., 1988). *Rede Mulher* in Brazil, which concentrates on educating women about their rights through popular theater, has eleven paid staff members, but over 2,000 volunteers. The Family Planning Association of Sri Lanka has over 40,000 grassroots volunteers (Population Institute, 1988).

WOMEN AND SUSTAINABLE DEVELOPMENT

Population

Except in a few countries such as Thailand, Indonesia, Ghana, and Mexico, Third World NGOs have been less likely to focus on population than on other sustainable development issues.[7] The Cairo Conference, however, enhanced the role of women NGO activists on the population issue everywhere. NGOs at Cairo—80 percent of them represented by women–literally pushed governments towards coming to terms with the connections between fertility and the advancement of women. A considerable body of research indicating that family planning and health assistance dramatically affect fertility (more than projects that merely provide contraceptives) buttressed their efforts.

What needs to emerge in the post-Cairo environment is a concerted international effort to utilize the growing women's movement, and to integrate concern about family planning into broader programs that educate women and promote sustainable development. Not only would this be a more powerful sustainable development strategy than ad hoc attempts to increase family planning services, it would also build on existing institutional resources. GRSO umbrella organizations in Nepal and Ghana, for example, have used their member organizations with expertise in population to train other member organizations. The Planned Parenthood Association of Ghana has also organized a GRO network of "Daddies Clubs."

Knowledge about family planning and reproductive health also spreads more easily through existing women's organizations than through creating new organizations. The overburdened Zimbabwean Family Planning Council, for example, trained 20,000 members of the Association of Women's Clubs in family planning. Moreover, women's GRSOs, generally unable to afford investment in health infrastructure, need to be linked to and supported by primary health care facilities.[8] Hospitals or clinics initiating grassroots support activities would, in turn, benefit from already established linkages between women's GRSOs and GROs.

The networking activities of Family Care International (FCI) in Africa show that even a small U.S. NGO can facilitate linkages and have a major impact on the process of institutionalization. FCI focuses on women's health, family planning, and safe motherhood by working through both governments and NGOs in Ghana, Nigeria, Uganda, Tanzania, and Zimbabwe.

Poverty

Third World NGOs form part of the broader independent or nonprofit sector that includes traditional charities, arts organizations, and hospitals. Yet the *raison d'etre* of many NGOs is to combat poverty through promoting the for-profit sector at the grassroots level, often among women. The well-known Grameen Bank in Bangladesh would never have been able to spread its message to 35,000 villages without the high participation and repayment rates of women borrowers (Crossette, 1995). As of 1995 the Grameen Bank had two million shareholders, double the number in 1990 (Fisher, 1993; Crossette, 1995). In addition to the Grameen Bank, there are literally thousands of NGOs throughout Asia, Africa, and Latin America that use revolving credit funds and lend disproportionately to women. The Organizations for the Development of Women's Enterprise in Honduras, for example, is working in 27 villages. Their village banking program provides women with loans of one hundred to two hundred dollars.[9]

Although borrowers' groups are not always linked through networks, word about the availability of credit tends to spread rapidly among neighboring villages or neighborhoods. Membership in the Working Women's Forum in Madras, founded in 1978 by social worker and activist Jaya Arunachalam, reached 40,000 women in the city and 12,000 in the nearby countryside by 1983 (Tendler, 1987):

> The most astonishing aspect of borrowers' groups has been the ability of illiterate and extremely poor women to pass the word and extend their movement to other districts, towns and states in India. . . . Leaders rose, set up groups able to raise money, built up savings, negotiated bank loans, and provided for some welfare needs (Lecomte, 1986).

Grassroots enterprise development has been remarkably successful in reaching millions of people. Yet this process of "scaling out" must be matched by an equal ability to "scale up" to the economic institutions of society. In many countries commercial credit is still denied to women, even after they have already created successful microenterprises through access to revolving loan funds. And marketing beyond one's own village remains a formidable challenge.

It may be that scaling out will eventually, under conditions of increasing scarcity or emergency, lead to scaling up. Women's GROs, the backbone of horizontal networking during crises such as the 1985 earthquake in Mexico City, are also involved in regional and national enterprise development. Green

Zones, a cooperative movement organized by women in the midst of the civil war in Mozambique, grows and markets food near provincial capitals and
works with government, traders, transport systems, and other farmers (Ahsah
Ayisi, 1990).

Microenterprise strategies also have a spinoff effect on women's empowerment. A woman, living on an agrarian reform cooperative that benefited from
Technoserve-Peru's technical assistance, told me that she used to be at the
mercy of the truck drivers who carted her produce to Lima. "Now I negotiate with several of them to get the best price. I grow so many fruits and vegetables on this plot that they all want to sign up with me" (personal interview,
Peru, 1989).

Environment

Some GRSOs run by women use environmental issues as an anti-poverty
strategy:

> In Zimbabwe, the Women's Institute actively promotes forestry to raise
> the standard of living for their 1,000 local groups (Williams, 1989).
> In Kenya, the Greenbelt Movement involves more than 15,000 farmers
> and a half million school children in establishing 670 local tree nurseries
> and in planting more than 2 million trees for fuel and fruit (Postel and
> Heise, 1988; Rodda, 1991). Seedlings are sold to the movement and re-
> distributed at no charge. Local individuals or women's groups must first
> prepare available land (often roadsides or wasteland) to meet the move-
> ment specifications. Extensive follow up is provided through Greenbelt
> rangers, who check progress and care of the trees and offer advice.
> The Women and Energy Project of *Maendeleo Ya Wanawake* in Kenya
> trains women to build improved cookstoves built around clay liners, at a
> cost of 25–30 shillings. Leaders of women's GROs pay project officials
> who release a liner of the right size and shape. A trained worker then
> helps the community build a stove. As of 1988, over 1,000 of the fuel ef-
> ficient stoves had been constructed (Dankelman and Davidson, 1988).
> Women in Trinidad and Tobago organized Nature Seekers to patrol
> beaches early each morning and to protect endangered sea turtles from
> illegal poaching. Fishermen have cooperated and the community now
> realizes the financial benefits of the turtles' attraction for visiting natural-
> ists (WorldWIDE News, 1994).
> Other GRSOs integrate credit with poverty-focused and environmental
> strategies. In Lima, garbage trucks cannot enter many low income urban
> areas because the roads are too poor. One women's GRSO developed a
> system of collection by women on large tricycles and motorbikes to car-
> ry garbage to a central area. In the process 150 microenterprises were
> created (Ofosu-Amaah and Philleo, 1992).

Other GRSOs see environmental issues as the wedge with which to address larger social issues. In 1986 Lingkog Tao Kalikasan a "small but feisty"

FISHER

GRSO led by Sister Aida Velasquez, set up a Secretariat for an Ecologically Sound Philippines to address environmental problems affecting women, farmers, youth, and minorities. This organization became the "cutting edge" of environmental dialogue within the Philippines, according to Rush (1990).

The Chipko Movement was founded in Gadkharkh, Uttar Pradesh after a huge landslide led to renewed interest in reforestation. Chipko, organized around caring for tree seedlings, reached 25 villages by 1988. Chipko spreads its message through sustainable development camps that meet twice a year and through the political tactic of "hugging trees" threatened by bulldozers. Women's shared interests as primary users of the forest account for the spread of this and environmental movements such as the Appiko Movement in the Western Ghats (Dankelman and Davidson, 1988; Fisher, 1993; Viswanath, 1991).

Although the strength and visibility of women in this global nongovernmental movement grows out of extensive grassroots activism, Lorraine Elliott reminds us that this visibility "is itself connected to the marginalization of grass-roots activity in the global environment debate" (1996: 11). Whether woman activists live in poverty and are barely literate or regularly jet to international conferences, they share an understanding that this dilemma can only be challenged through local, national, or global networking.

Women not only network locally through community kitchens or environmental movements, they also take increasingly active roles within national NGO networks, sometimes in ways that can bring grassroots women into the dialogue. KENGO, a Kenyan umbrella organization of NGOs, hosted the Kenya Assembly of Women and the Environment in May, 1993. The 235 participants from Kenya and neighboring countries visited a fisheries project managed by women and heard environmental success stories from each other. Many participants had no formal education, yet they were "innovative, eloquent, and assertive, and very concerned with environmental issues such as pollution and desertification. They were all familiar with tree planting, but wanted to learn about tree species and wood lots for household fuel. They were concerned about . . . agroforestry and harvesting, and had considerable knowledge about drought resistant trees and famine foods" (Bhardwaj, 1993: 1,3).

103

IMPACT ON GOVERNMENT

The transition from organizing women to organizing women for development also includes the need to become "difficult" citizens. An organizer for The Society for Rural Education and Development of Tamil Nadu found that:

> When a revenue inspector visited the village to mark the route for a new link road, the men agreed to his proposed sketch. But the women did not agree and wanted it to be redrawn to fit the peoples needs . . . (Fisher, 1993).

GRSO leaders often become political advocates for sustainable development. In response to the campaign against the Narmada dam led by Medha Patkar, the Indian government recently announced that it would not use the unused portion of a World Bank loan for the dam. *Ação Democratica Feminina Gaucha* in Brazil lobbies for stronger environmental legislation and sees the mobilization of public opinion as a key element forcing governments to act.[10] In Zimbabwe, local women's organizations use agrarian reform legislation to force the government to focus on farmers' needs.

Advocacy often grows out of activism at the community level. During the Pinochet dictatorship in Chile, poor urban women organized community kitchens to feed their families. The kitchens also functioned as a form of political protest. Since 1986 DISHA (sanskrit for "direction"), a GRSO with a tribal staff, has been training forest women in Gujarat India in financial skills and environmentally sensitive farming. This also led to legal action for improved wages and working conditions. A two-year campaign tripled the minimum daily wage and won compensation for women injured in falls from Tendu trees. The women have gone one step further and are demanding a voice in forming laws governing forest use (*Cultural Survival Quarterly*, 1992).

Interactions with individuals in governments can also help undermine destructive policies, particularly if they are part of a coherent political strategy. CEMUJER in El Salvador uses the legal system to advance women's rights by building coalitions of women's groups and developing relationships with top officials, especially in the Supreme Court. Strong media outreach, workshops to sensitize government employees to women's legal issues, and courting allies such as female legislators and judges, rounds out CEMUJER's political strategy (WorldWIDE News, 1994).

Collaboration does, of course, entail the risk of cooptation. Yet experience with government can increase autonomy rather than dependence, particularly when GRSOs train government personnel. Although the clinics of the Women's Health Coalition in Bangladesh serve 75,000 women and children annually at low cost, the Coalition, recognizing that this is only a tiny fraction of the need, places a strong emphasis on training others, especially government health and family planning workers (Germaine and Ordway, 1989).

INTERNATIONAL TIES

NGO proliferation and networking on women's issues has helped to expand the international role of Third World women. At the Copenhagen Conference in 1980, which focused specifically on women, only 100 NGOs were represented. Five thousand NGOs attended the Cairo Population Conference in 1994, 80 percent of them represented by women. In contrast, 80 percent of the 3,500 government delegates were men.[11]

Given this recent proliferation, international NGO networking on women and the environment is difficult to keep track of, let alone assess. In Africa alone there are many international NGO networks relevant to women and the environment. Among these are the African Women's Association for Research and Development (AWARD), the International Committee for African Women for Development (CIFAD), the Women, Environment and Development Network, and the Arab Women Solidarity Association, located in Egypt. Computer linkages between researchers in Africa are provided by WEDNET to document women's indigenous knowledge and coordination with outsiders such as York University in Toronto, the International Development Research Council (IDRC), and the Environmental Liaison Center International in Nairobi (Williams, 1989; *Brundtland Bulletin*, 1989; *IFDA Dossier*, 1990; *Brundtland Bulletin*, 1989a [supplement]).

Among the other international women's networks are:

> The International Women's Tribune Network, located in New York City, which links thousands of women's groups worldwide. Its small staff, working with women from the developing world, produces low cost information and training materials.
>
> ISIS, the Women's International Information and Communication Service, is located in Santiago and Rome. With over 10,000 contacts with women's groups in 150 countries, ISIS promotes South-South exchanges among women's groups.
>
> WorldWIDE (World Women Working for Women Dedicated to the Environment), founded in 1982, with an international advisory council of representatives from major regions, helps organize local Forums. It publishes a directory of women environmental activists.
>
> DAWN (Development Alternatives with Women for a New Era) was founded in 1984 in Bangalore, with representatives from women's groups in India, Bangladesh, Africa, Morocco, Brazil, Mexico, and the Caribbean. DAWN sponsors research centers, publications, and training.
>
> NGOs as well as universities and governments are represented in The Third World Organization for Women in Science (TWOWS). TWOWS, housed at the Third World Academy of Sciences in Trieste, Italy, held its inaugural conference in 1993. It focuses almost entirely on sustainable development topics such as food production, nutrition, resources, and environmental impact. Organized by leading women scientists, it seeks ways to enhance participatory computerized information exchange (Third World Organization for Women in Science, 1993).
>
> The International Women and Environment Network, was created in Managua in 1989 by 1,200 participants from 60 countries attending the Congress on the Fate and Hope of the Earth (DAWN Informs, 1989).
>
> The Earth Council, an international NGO formed after the Rio Conference, makes the local efforts of women a central programming focus (WorldWIDE Network, 1993).
>
> The YWCA is also a worldwide women's network. Environment and

105

energy have become priority issues for the YWCA, and more than 150 chapters were environmentally active as of 1988 (Dankelman and David-son, 1988).

Global networking has accelerated due to preparations for the Fourth World Conference on Women, held in Beijing in 1995. One of the regional preparatory conferences, held in 1994 in Mar del Plata, Uruguay, attracted 1,200 participants from 41 countries.

International travel, cyberspace, and email provide women with unprece-dented opportunities to learn from each other. But if grassroots connections are weak, new technologies may become ends in themselves. It is essential to understand how knowledge emerges from below. The case of the Gavien Women's Development Group is illustrative.

Matarina, an illiterate teenager in Papua New Guinea, founded the Gavien Women's Development Group in her village. At age 28 she became the coor-dinator for four GROs, trained leaders at the local government center, arranged transport and training for leaders from neighboring villages, pro-duced educational cassettes on development, and traveled to other provinces for similar activities. Recognized at the national level, Matarina now shares her ideas and training programs with universities, GRSOs, and the govern-ment. The Gavien Women's Development Group has created an informal in-ternational network on women in development. It includes a Fiji network, feminist journalists and academics from the University of the South Pacific, the Women and Development Network of Australia, the Australian Council of Churches, aboriginal communities in Australia, and women's development leaders in Fiji, Tonga, Samoa, and Vanuatu (Cox, 1987).

NGO activists, in addition to their increasing role in international net-working, continue to depend on bilateral ties to voluntary and official donors from the North. Although U.S.-based NGOs still struggle with the shift from solo implementation to partnership with Third World NGOs, their interest in women's issues is well established. Catholic Relief Services, for example, works directly through women's work groups in the Gambia. Smaller, cut-ting-edge organizations such as ASHOKA and Trickle Up actively try to em-power women. ASHOKA provides support for women who are "public sec-tor entrepreneurs," and active in social and environmental issues in their countries. Trickle Up, by providing $100 in start-up capital, has helped tens of thousands of businesses get started in the Third World, more than half women-owned.

Large international bureaucracies such as the World Bank change more slowly. Challenges to increase World Bank gender sensitivity came from in-creasingly outspoken international NGOs whose influence grew in the late 1980s as they became cofinanciers of Bank projects. Bank assistance to the Mutualist Guarantee Associations in Ghana, for example, was modeled on an approach pioneered by Women's World Banking of Ghana, which provides technical assistance to the government and assists women entrepreneurs in preparing feasibility studies.

The World Bank also confronts a worldwide shift in thinking about development. Those who challenge a narrow approach to structural adjustment are increasingly interacting with those who espouse it in the field and at international meetings. The new agenda—sustainable development, natural resource preservation, food security, debt for development swaps, empowerment of women, and microenterprise development - has been partially adopted in some World Bank projects. The question is whether the World Bank and other multilaterals can overcome bureaucratic inertia.

CONCLUSIONS AND RECOMMENDATIONS

GROs and GRSOs are increasingly providing women with opportunities for implementing sustainable development. Networking and political pressure, building on what happens at the local level, can scale out the impact of women's NGOs at the grassroots level, and scale up their impact on policy. The large scale impact of grassroots organizing is still in question, however. The following recommendations may help to accelerate the impact of the global women's movement.

1) More international support should be provided for basic education for women. Increasing women's enrollment in vocational schools and universities that train extension agents in sustainable development is needed. Scholarships could be provided to encourage more women to pursue degrees in agronomy, forestry, population, etc. This could be supplemented with internships in national and international NGOs and agencies for women (Yudelman, 1994).

2) Although microenterprise credits have reached millions of poor women, international pressure could help open commercial or second step credit for women who have already started businesses and who could expand them and thus increase employment. According to Noeleen Heyzer, a director of UNIFEM (United Nations Development Fund for Women) "The type of banks we have set up have put money in hands of the hardcore poor . . . But many other women . . . have to get access to credit through commercial banks, and the whole structure of banking is such that they will have great difficulty" (Crossette, 1995: A12).

3) Increase gender and sustainable development training for NGOs, governments, and international donors, with a focus on GRSO networks in the Third World. Innovative projects which could be studied for wider application include the International Union for the Conservation of Nature (IUCN) and the Inter-American Institute for Cooperation on Agriculture (IICA), located in Costa Rica. These organizations provide

FISHER

training in sustainable development with a gender perspective to staff of both NGOs and governments. Similar courses are planned for Nicaragua, El Salvador, Guatemala, and Honduras.[12]

4) A financial commitment to implementing the recommendations of the Cairo conference on educating women, increasing employment opportunities, and providing access to family health care including family planning, is critical. Northern willingness to provide financial support and Southern willingness to shift funds away from military expenditures, which consume 125 billion dollars per year of Third World government funds, is called for.

5) Strong efforts should be made to support women's NGOs that wish to expand or add family planning and family health to their existing programs, through linkages with existing hospitals, and GRSO networks.

Third World women, despite overwhelming odds, are active participants in sustainable development strategies which recognize the poverty/gender/population/environment nexus. The task of more affluent nations is to understand, appreciate and accompany them.

NOTES

1. A recent study provides evidence that the lowest of the three United Nations projections is more likely to be accurate and that the world's population may stabilize at eight rather than ten billion. However, it relies on the likelihood of below replacement fertility levels after 2025 in the developed countries and in some developing countries. The authors remain extremely concerned about the projections for Africa. (See Seckler and Cox, 1994.)

2. See Fisher, 1993: 95–6; Fisher, 1994: 6; and UNDP, 1993: 86.

3. See Durning, 1989.

4. Fisher, 1993: 7. The UNDP (1993: 86) has estimated that there may be as many as 50,000.

5. Friedmann, 1989: 12. For a more in-depth profile of the community kitchens see Delpino, 1991.

6. Healy, 1991: 26. Women activists from community kitchens in Peru are also being elected to city councils in many Lima municipalities. (See Delpino, 1991: 59.) On the other hand, a successful GRSO in Karnataka, Gram Vikas, expressly discourages members of women's groups from entering politics. (See Viswanath, 1991: 158.)

7. Fisher, 1994. NGOs in Thailand and Indonesia were providing governments with models for integrated health and family planning based on trained village midwives as long ago as the early 1970s.

8. An exception is Mexico, where women have organized most of the largest family planning NGOs, including FEMAP in Juarez, Mexfam in Mexico City, the Red de Grupos para la Salud de la Mujer (Network of Women's Health Groups), and the Rural Health Promoters in Tabasco. (See Lopezllera Mendez 1988.)

9. Interview with the late Francisca Escoto, May 1989. ODEF is part of a small international network that inclues BEST, another enterprise development organization in Belize and Katalysis, a U.S.-based NGO in Stockton, California.

FISHER

10. Dankelman and Davidson, 1988: 149. Other NGOs are more cautious. Gram Vikas in Karnataka, for exmple, limits itself to insuring that its clients receive government benefits, and discourages political activism among its beneficiaries. (See Viswanath, 1991: 81,88.)

11. Presentation by Margaret Catley-Carlson, Conference on Population, Consumption and the Environment, Yale University, November 1994.

12. Yudelman, 1994: 10. See also Parker, 1993, for an example of a manual on gender analysis training for grassroots workers.

REFERENCES

Ahsah Ayisi, Ruth. "Mozambique's Minister of Agriculture: Promoting Organization Amid Chaos." *African Farmer*, No. 5: 45, 1990.

Bhardwaj, Prabha. "Kenya WorldWIDE Forum Hosts First National Assembly of Women and the Environment." *WorldWIDE News* Special Edition, Summer: 1, 1993.

Barroso, Carmen. "Innovations in Reproductive Health and Child Survival." Address at the Conference of The Association for Women in Development, Washington, D.C., April 16, 1987.

Brundtland Bulletin. No. 4: p. 29, 1989.

Brundtland Bulletin. No. 5: p. 62, 1989.

Cox, Elizabeth. "Networking Among the Rural Women in the South Pacific." *Ideas and Action* No. 175: 18–23, 1987.

Crossette, Barbara. "U.S. to Help Girls in Poor Lands Stay in School." *The New York Times*, March 8: A12, 1995.

Dankelman, Irene and Joan Davidson. *Women and Environment in the Third World: Alliance for the Future.* London: Earthscan Publications, 1988.

DAWN Informs Nos. 7/8: 6, 1989.

Delpino, Nena. "Las organizaciones femininas por la alimentacion: un menu Sazonado." In Luis Pasara, Nena Delpino, Ricio Vandeavellano and Alonso Zarzar eds. *La Otra Cara de La Luna.* Buenos Aires: Manatial S.R.L., 1991.

———— and Luis Pasara. "El otro actor en escena: Las ONGDs." In Luis Pasara, Nena Delpino, Ricio Vandeavellano and Alonso Zarzar eds. *La Otra Cara de La Luna.* Buenos Aires: Manatial S.R.L., 1991.

Durning, Alan B. "Action at the Grassroots: Fighting Poverty and Environmental Decline." *Worldwatch Paper 88.* Washington, D.C.: The Worldwatch Institute, 1989.

Elliott, Lorraine. "Women, Gender, Feminism and the Environment." In Jennifer Turpin and Lois Lorentzen, eds. *The Gendered New World Order: Militarism, Development, and the Environment.* New York: Routledge, 1996.

Fausto, Ayrton. "La Cooperacion al Desarrollo en un Proceso de Fundacion Democratica: El Caso de Brasil." *Cooperacion Internacional al Desarrollo.* Santiago: 3, Taller de Cooperacion al Desarrollo, 1988.

Fisher, Julie. "Colombia: When Women are United." In *Already I Feel the Change: Lessons From the Field 1.* Westport, CT: Save the Children, 1986.

————. *The Road from Rio: Sustainable Development and the Nongovernmental Movement in the Third World.* Westport, CT: Praeger, 1993.

————. "NGOs: The Missing Piece to the Population Puzzle." *Environment* 36 (7): 6–11, 37–41, 1994.

109

FISHER

Friedmann, John. "Collective Self-Empowerment and Social Change." *IFDA Dossier* 69: 3–14 1989.

Germaine, Adrienne and Jane Ordway. "Population Control and Women's Health: Balancing the Scales." *International Women's Health Coalition.* in cooperation with the Overseas Development Council, New York, 1989.

Healy, Kevin. "Animating Grassroots Development," *Grassroots Development* 15(1): 26–34, 1991.

Leach, Mark, Jeanne McCormack, and Candace Nelson. The Tototo Home Industries Rural Development Project. New York: The Synergos Institute, 1988.

"India: Working Women's Forum" *IFDA Dossier* 1990. Nos. 75/76: 97, 1990.

Lecomte, Bernard J. Project Aid: Limitations and Alternatives. Paris: OECD Development Center Studies, 1986.

Logan, Kathleen. "Women's Participation in Urban Protest." In Joe Foweraker and Ann L. Craig, eds. *Popular Movements and Political Change in Mexico.* Boulder, CO: Lynne Reinner, 1990.

Lopezllera Mendez, Luis. *Sociedad Civil y Pueblos Emergentes: Las Organizaciones Autonomas de Promocion Social y Desarrollo en Mexico.* Mexico City: Promocion del Desarrollo Popular, 1988.

Moen, Elizabeth. *Voluntary Sector Grass Roots Development in Tamilnadu.* Tamilnadu, India: Gandhigram Rural Institute, Deemed University, 1991.

Ofosu-Amaah, Waafas and Wendy Philleo. "Women and the Environment: An Analytical Review of Success Stories." Presented at the United Nations Environment Programme, Global Assembly, Women and the Environment, November 4–8, 1992.

Parker, A. Rani. *Another Point of View: A Manual on Gender Analysis Training for Grassroots Workers.* New York: United Nations Development Fund for Women, 1993.

Pasara, Luis, Nena Delpino, Ricio Vandeavellano, and Alonso Zarzar. *La Otra Cara de la Luna.* Buenos Aires: Manatial S.R.L., 1991.

Postel, Sandra and Lori Heise. "Reforestation with a Human Touch." *Grassroots Development* 12 (3): 38–40, 1988.

Population Institute. *The Nairobi Challenge: Global Directory of Women's Organizations Implementing Population Strategies.* Washington, D.C., 1988.

Pradervand, Pierre. "Afrique Noire: La Victoire du Courage." *IFDA Dossier,* No. 64: 4–12, 1988.

Rodda, Annabel. "Women in Environment and Development." *Current World Leaders* 34 (6): 880–891, 1991.

Rush, James. *The Last Tree.* New York: The Asia Society, 1991.

Seckler, David and Gerald Cox. *Population Projections by the United Nations and the World Bank.* Washington, D.C.: Center for Economic Policy Studies, Winrock International, 1994.

Tendler, Judith. *What Ever Happened to Poverty Alleviation?* A Report Prepared for the Mid-Decade Review of the Ford Foundation's Programs on Livelihood, Employment and Income Generation. New York, 1987.

Third World Organization for Women in Science. General Information. Trieste, Italy, 1993.

United Nations Development Program. *Human Development Report.* New York, 1993.

Viswanath, Vanita. *NGOs and Women's Development in Rural South India: A Comparative Analysis*. Boulder, CO: Westview Press, 1991.

Williams, Paula. "Despite Many Voices, African Women Unite." *Letter to the Institute for Current World Affairs*, No. 13: 1–3, 1989.

WorldWIDE News. "Gender and Environment: Beyond UNCED." *Partners in Life* Issue No. 4: 1993.

WorldWIDE News. No. 2: 1994.

WorldWIDE News. No. 3: 1994.

Yudelman, Sally. "Women Farmers in Central America: Myths, Roles, Reality." *Grassroots Development* 17–18 (2–1): 1994.

111

FISHER

WOMEN, THE STATE, AND DEVELOPMENT:

APPRAISING SECULAR AND RELIGIOUS GENDER POLITICS IN IRAN

Hamideh Sedghi

chapter 7

INTRODUCTION

THE "Islamization" of gender relations and gender policies by the post-revo-lutionary state in Iran has been the object of significant attention (Azari, 1983; Tabari and Yeganeh, 1982; Haeri, 1989; Friedl, 1991; Ferows, 1983; Moghissi, 1994). Islamization measures aim at the implementation of the *Shari'ah* (Islamic Laws) and the *Fatva* (religious verdicts) to counter the cor-rupt and immoral influences of the monarchical era and its westernizing im-pact. Accordingly, the entire society must be "purified"—which every revolu-tion deems necessary—and women, as symbols of the purification policies, are to surrender to the new state's wishes. The secular Pahlavi state, attempt-ing to develop and "modernize" the society, undertook to emancipate women through civil codes, statutes and other reforms. Secular reforms were meant to liberalize gender relations, and increase economic and professional options for some women. Thus, in comparing the gender policies of the secular and the religious states, critics have invariably articulated a dark portrayal of the Islamic state, while depicting the Pahlavi state as the Golden Age, dismissing the limits of its reforms pertaining to women (Nashat, 1983; Afkhami, 1984).

Given the differential behavior of both secular and religious states toward women, my objective is to locate gender within the specific political context of each of the two contemporary states in Iran, for both have embodied gender interests and have constructed gender policies in their broader political projects and development.[1] I argue that the political projects are inextricably linked to economic models and development strategies and I reject the binary vision of the secular/religious dichotomy in the analysis and evaluation of gender policies of the state. By examining the two states in terms of their policies on women's sexuality, women's work, and political and economic mobilization of women in the context of development strategies, I suggest that both states have dramatically and adversely affected women's position, though in different ways and to different degrees.

Placing the state and gender policies at the center of women's studies, particularly in Middle Eastern studies and Iranian studies, requires some discussion. Many theoretical studies address the state's role in reproductive policies which aim at expanding or restricting women's rights and control over their sexuality (Petchesky, 1984; Gelb and Paley, 1982; Mies, 1986). In development studies, works concentrate on economic policies as they affect women's and men's work differently (Beneria and Sen, 1981, 1982) and on studies which examine mobilization policies with implications for gender relations and gender construction (Andors, 1983; Urdang, 1979; Massell, 1974; Molyneux, 1986). Within the regional studies of the Middle East, much of the literature focuses on the Arab world (Mernissi, 1991; Ahmed, 1992; Keddie and Baron, 1991; Tucker, 1993; Kandioyti, 1991; Ghoussoub, 1987, 1988; Hammami and Rieker, 1988), and with the exception of a few studies on Iran (Sedghi, 1976, 1980; Yeganeh and Keddie, 1986; Higgins and Golnar, 1989; Ramazani, 1993), a systematic comparative analysis of gender issues in both the secular and religious states remains largely neglected.

This study highlights specific gender policies of the state and analyzes the state through the lens of gender. It posits that regardless of its nature, the state acts in its own interests, not necessarily in the interests of women. In the Iranian case, I argue against the binary visions and suggest that state policies on women have a politico-historical context and cannot be simply reduced to a secular versus religious dichotomy. Second, both the secular and religious states, though in different ways and in different degrees, failed to articulate the interests of women at large. Third, a reciprocal relationship exists between the state and women, for women are *not* merely passive victims, but active and reactive agents (Harding, 1987, 1990). Women's responses to the state's enforcing of gender policies and the articulation of their own interests must be seen within the parameters of the cultural, socioeconomic and regional environments within which women are situated.

I focus on both the Iranian secular and religious states' policies and interests in sexuality, women's work, and the political mobilization of women in the context of particular development strategies. Utilizing a comparative historical approach, I concentrate on the Pahlavi state from the late 1960s to 1979, and on the Islamic state since the late 1970s in terms of their respective gender policies. Considering the diverse experiences of women in urban, rural and tribal Iran, and differences in their class and ethnic backgrounds, my focus is on urban Muslim women only.

STATE AND SEXUALITY

Sexuality, more than any other subject, has been at the center of Middle Eastern studies' discussion of women (Mernissi, 1985; Haeri, 1989; Ahmed, 1992; Badran and Cook, 1990). Despite methodological differences, a near consensus exists that sexuality and sexual control of women constitute an important part of the ideology and behavior in Islamic societies. Regardless of the political nature of the state, Iranian society has been marked by privatization of women as property and as sexual objects (Sedghi, 1976).

Control over women's sexuality has deep historical roots in Iran. The critic Reza Barahani suggests that the "masculine history" allows male sexuality to be defined in terms of its control over women and its violent appropriation of their bodies. Violence towards women and sex segregation, Baharani maintains, are not new to Iran; they construct the masculine culture and the history of the society in which massacres, drinking wine in the skulls of enemies, and the plucking out of eyes of thousands, have been common practices of kings, dignitaries, and power-holders. Within this context, male sexuality is defined through the negation and control of everything that is feminine, including women's bodies and sexual desires (Farhi, 1990).

On the other hand, feminists such as Farah Azari and Azar Tabari see the control and subjugation of women as linked to the *Shi'i* Islam, its tenets and cultural practices in Iran. Despite their differing approaches to sexuality and sexual control, these perspectives fail to contextualize historical changes. The secular westernizing Pahlavi state paid homage to its masculine history, although it redefined it, and the religious state of the Islamic Republic took that history to its "illogical" conclusion.

During the 1960s and 1970s, the Pahlavi state liberalized some of the sexual mores through civil and penal codes, and through social and cultural campaigns. Some women, particularly those of the middle and upper classes, welcomed these measures and enjoyed their newly-defined freedom. However, most of the Iranian women remained subordinated and society generally clung to traditional views and behavior toward sexuality. Virginity, modesty, chastity, fidelity, and subservience to men's sexual desires and male dominance in the family remained as legitimate cultural norms and practices. Paradoxically, the sexually pure and obedient woman/girl found protecting herself difficult. Growing up in the cities of the 1960s and 1970s, women and schoolgirls experienced routine forms of harassment, including pinching, cursing, or the praise and attempted physical contact of male bypassers in the streets. At home women might be referred to as *manzel* (the home), or *Za'ifeh* (the weak), or *mar-e khosh khat-o khal* (the beautiful but sneaky snake). The daily papers had extensive coverage and columns on wife-beating and wife-killing (Sedghi, forthcoming).

The abuse—verbal and physical—of women both in the public and private spheres continued throughout the Pahlavi's state liberalization policies and during the period of "reform from above." In fact, denigration of women in daily life differed little from the contemptuous attitude of the monarch himself. In his 1973 interview with Oriana Fallaci, the Shah stated that:

> [Women] may be equal in the eyes of the law, but not . . . in ability. [Women have] never produced a great cook . . . [they] have produced nothing great . . . When they are in power [women] are much harsher than men. Much more cruel. Much more blood thirsty. . . . [Women] when [they] are rulers [are] . . . schemers . . . [and] evil. Every one of [them]. . . (Fallaci, 1973).

Despite these remarks, the monarch received support from the official proponents of women's rights. For example, former Princess Ashraf, the head of the Women's Organization of Iran (WOI) praised her brother's "top-down" reforms on gender issues. In stating her support for her brother's role in promoting women's emancipation, she said that

> Equality between men and women has been truly realized under the laws of my King brother. . . . We expect the Shahanshah [to] provide the framework of social and economic activities of women by . . . his orders (Pahlavi 1974).

Supporters of the previous state argue that despite the monarch's misogynist attitude, the secular state reformed laws pertaining to marriage, divorce, polygamy, and child custody. As I have shown elsewhere, the family Protection Laws of 1967 and 1975 challenged some of the traditional and religious norms pertaining to women, yet the reforms were limited both in promulgation and implementation. In the absence of democratic structures, limited educational and employment opportunities, and the persistence of patriarchal values, it was difficult for most women to achieve emancipation and feminist consciousness.

On the other hand, "liberated" women experienced an ambivalent situation in the society. Furugh Farrokhzad, the most celebrated woman poet, dared to cross traditional sexual boundaries, yet could not find comfort in Iran. In her poem "The Windup Doll," she expresses her pain at wanting to control her own sexuality, yet not wanting to be rejected by society. From behind the window, she criticizes women for their passivity, yet she understands women's lives as objects at home and as individuals in the exile of their homes. Depicting the alienation of women, Farrokhzad discovers her own alienation as a liberated woman in a male-dominated society (Farrokhzad, 1971).

Under the post-revolutionary regime, however, a new concept of women's liberation emerged. Women are to achieve liberation under the tenets of Islam. Women serve as guardians of religion, state, and society. Women should follow the path of Fatima, the Prophet's daughter, symbol of motherhood and wifely virtues, and most of all, the heroine who was an authentic and devout Muslim, devoid of anything impure, foreign, and alien to Islam. In this way, the Islamization of women has had a triple purpose: it provided an alternative to the "immoral" West that had seized power and knowledge from the East; it created the illusion of an historical cultural authenticity, which in turn provides a model for the "purification" of the present; and it strengthened social-sexual controls over women through religious law and policy.

Islamization's effect upon women is evident in public policies aimed specifically at the control of their sexuality. For example, the state has instituted the *Hejab* (modesty) through the *Chador* (the all-covering veil), or through the combination of *Rupush* (long loose dress), the *Rusari* or *Maghna'eh* (long scarf), and *Shalvar* (long and loose trousers). The Ayotallah Khomeini vividly articulated the new dress code in his 1979 interview with Fallaci. He stated:

> The women who contributed to the revolution were, and are, women with the Islamic dress, not elegant women all made up like you, who go around all uncovered, dragging behind them a tail of men. The coquettes who put on make up and go into the street showing off their necks, their hair, their shapes, did not fight against the Shah. They never did anything good, not those. They do not know how to be useful, neither socially, nor politically, nor professionally. And this is so because, by uncovering themselves, they distract men, and upset them (Fallaci, 1979).

Additionally, *Mot'eh* (temporary marriage) and polygamy are encouraged and *Qisas* (the Bill of Retribution) has lowered the official value of a woman to half that of a man in adultery cases, involving death sentences. Other policies emphasize women's primary duties as wives and mothers, and establish sex-segregation in public spheres such as the job market, the educational system, and the transportation system.

Gender relations, transformed by religious ideologies at the service of the state, increased men's control over women's sexuality. While the secular state promoted some control by women over their sexuality and officially promoted their emancipation, its gender policies failed to reach the lives of the majority of Iranian women. The religious state, however, redefined women as the

117

SEDGHI

centerpiece of Islamization, and by so doing, achieved greater control over women's sexuality, and a more powerful patriarchal domination in both private and public spheres.

WOMEN, WORK, AND DEVELOPMENT

The study of women's work in the Middle East has been relatively neglected (Youssef, 1976; Afshar, 1985; Hijab, 1988). While studies explore women's work in rural and tribal Iran (Friedl, 1981, 1989), only a few studies in Persian (Plan and Budget Organization, 1974; Bagaerian, 1992) and in English (Moghadam, 1988, 1994; Sedghi, 1986 and forthcoming) look at the overall effect of change on women's labor force participation. It is imperative to analyze women's work, paid and unpaid, in relationship to the overall changes within the Iranian economy.

The capitalist tendencies of Iran under the Pahlavi state are well documented (Abrahamian 1982). By 1979, the unprecedented growth of the economy, along with heavy foreign investments, rapidly transformed Iran's economy and society. In the early 1960s, with the inauguration of the Land Reform and the granting of suffrage to women, the Shah temporarily defeated secular and religious opposition. In part, the Shah, like his father, manipulated women's issues in order to achieve victory over the religious opposition. However, unlike his father, the Shah's state promoted formal emancipation of women and their right to work within the capitalist structures.

Secular reforms increased some women's options, but in other cases they actually strengthened class bias. Reforms benefited a small group of elite Iranian women in high offices, both public and private. Based on my own interviews, I found that these women represented the interests of upper-class men in power, against the interests of other social classes. These women did not have female solidarity across class lines; rather, they held a contemptuous attitude toward women "who had not made it or those who could not make it" (Sedghi, forthcoming). Possibly the state's gender policies aimed only at integrating well-to-do women into the state structure. Admitting women of other classes would potentially disturb the power structure, family relations, and overall religious and cultural customs.

Women's labor force participation increased in the Pahlavi state. By 1978, women's employment reached 13 percent of the total employed population. Over 58 percent of these women, primarily from the middle and lower classes, were absorbed by the service sector (Sedghi, forthcoming). A small number of upper-class women occupied high-level positions in state organizations. On the whole, although the job market opened to women, the state's programs did not fundamentally alter the sexual division of labor in the market, and it did not interfere at all with the sexual division of labor in households, where men continued to be dominant.

As a result of these developments, employed women obtained a degree of financial and social autonomy, but were subordinated by hierarchies based on new relations to capital. Yet, one could argue that women's paid work not only provided a degree of material autonomy, but also a relaxation of sexual customs that had reinforced segregation and limited public mobility for women.

By integrating mostly urban women into the work force, and by relaxing traditional social mores, the state stripped the clergy of its patriarchal power. By tampering with gender relations, the state transferred patriarchal power from the clergy to the state. Thus, when the clergy regained power, it redefined women's position as one of the most important political projects of the new state. The religious state attempted, first and foremost, to regain control of female sexuality and women's paid work and autonomy, developments consistent with the state's efforts at economic change.

The post-revolutionary state attempted to build an "Islamic" political economy. Similar to its predecessor, it encouraged state intervention in the economy as well as privatization. However, unlike the previous regime, it promoted anti-westernism, economic self-sufficiency, and strict observation of Islamic conduct, particularly in the workplace.

Gender policies have been at the center of the new development strategies. The post-revolutionary state legislated new policies pertaining to labor force participation. The new legislation restricted employment opportunities for women, including passage of a law mandating part-time employment for women. As part of the "purification policies," women with high governmental positions during the Pahlavi era were forced to retire. Many educated and professional women resigned from their posts due to restrictions at work and/or harassment at the workplace (Sedghi, forthcoming). Later, during the Iran-Iraq war and the resulting deterioration of the economy, the state introduced massive layoffs in which women were often the first to go.

The religious state preferred women in the home. Labor force participation of women gave them greater autonomy, and potentially threatened the clergy's patriarchal power. It seemed logical to maintain and reproduce the masculine history of the society. However, the policy of restricting women's labor force participation of women created a number of contradictions for the new state.

One contradiction involved the interpretation of Islam concerning women's marketplace participation. Because Islam does not forbid women to work, the state does not have a strong religious and ideological argument against women working outside the home. However, the imposition of sex-segregation policies works against participation of women in many jobs, particularly in high governmental and other positions which involve significant interaction between women and men. Inconsistencies between religious interpretations and state policies have indeed created tension among employed women.

Women's labor force participation is further complicated due to the Islamic state's inheritance of an employment and educational situation shaped, in part, by the integration of women into the work force. Women's work outside the home had been accepted by society at large, and especially by women. Resistance to the state's restrictions comes from more secular and well-to-do women as well as from politically conscious and educated female supporters of the regime (Sciolino, 1992; Hedges, 1994; Bahrampour, 1994; Brooks, 1995). The Islamic state confronts resistance by both secular and religious women who support greater work participation of women.

The state encourages women's work in certain areas—nursing, teaching, and medicine (Iran, 1986, 1990). To enforce its sex-segregation policies it needs the labor of these women. The state resolves this contradiction by de-professionalizing these professions. With little training or advanced education, a new labor force of female quasiprofessionals labor in teaching, nursing, and medicine, focusing on the caring for women. Despite this trend, the absolute number of women in the labor force has declined dramatically since the revolution (Population Census, 1986, 1990).

Women's paid work needs to be evaluated in relation to women's unpaid work in the household. Segregation policies have increased women's work at home for a variety of reasons. The sexual division of labor in the household intensified due to state encouragement of male domination over both women's sexuality and women's work at home. In addition, the general decline in household income levels, the growing shortages of consumer goods, and the increasing rates of inflation and unemployment have all increased the time women spend on shopping and on household chores. These factors are further exacerbated by many years of the state's encouragement of population growth and the resulting increased burden of childbearing and childrearing by women. In short, women's unpaid activities have grown, while the sexual division of labor in the household has intensified.

Newly created occupations in state paramilitary organs have absorbed additional women's labor. This new category of women is active in the labor force for the first time. These women do not appear in the Census statistics nor in any other available data, yet they are visible in the streets of cities and towns. This paramilitary female force enforces the state's sex-segregation and modesty laws against women who do not properly observe the Islamic tradition and the state's mandated dress code. These women, though few in number, receive salaries from the state and act as guardians of the segregation policies of the state. The mobilization by the state of female paramilitary forces represents a new form of utilization of women's labor power, explored in more depth in the following section.

WOMEN AND MOBILIZATION

In Middle Eastern studies, the literature on mobilization of women by nationalist, socialist, and Islamicist forces are generally abundant (Jayawardena,

1986; Alexander, 1993; Parker, 1992; Shahidian, 1994; Sedghi, 1994). However, little information exists on state policies of mobilization, either secular or religious. My assumption is that, generally, states build alliances with different social classes, including women, and women's mobilization is a significant aspect of state-building. State-women alliances occur through state mobilization policies. In Iran, both the secular and religious states have alliances with different classes of women, reflecting disparate objectives.

The secular state assigned the task of mobilization of women to a state-sponsored organization, the Women's Organization of Iran. The Shah's twin sister, Ashraf Pahlavi, directed the organization in order to "achieve its progressive aims, [and] prepare women maximally for the advancement of Iran." Ashraf Pahlavi claimed that her aim was to "integrate Iranian women into every facet of society and to create the condition of equality our female ancestors had enjoyed centuries ago" (which has been lost under the influence of Islamic Arabs) (Pahlavi, 1974). Through the initiative of WOI, the Family Protection Laws and other legislation for the emancipation of women were introduced, and literacy classes and vocational training centers were established for women to develop marketable skills. Among other activities, the research organ of WOI produced a number of studies on the condition of women in Iran.

Some women benefited from WOI's version of top-down reform, but as a state-run organization it strictly regulated the activities of its membership and discouraged non-WOI women from articulating their concerns. This strategy was consonant with the tactics of the state, which had sought legitimacy through cooptation and repression (Bill, 1972). An elitist, hierarchical, and extremely insular organization, WOI acted as an arm of the state in the promotion of "feminism from above" and helped to neutralize or negate attempts by nonconformist women and feminists.

WOI's working methods were bound to be somewhat contradictory and schizophrenic. The organization was divided by its conflicting aims and loyalties. As an extension of the state involved in the promotion of modernization and feminism from above, the WOI occupied an ambivalent position in the modern history of women's politics in Iran. On the one hand, it represented the Pahlavi state and the elite women associated with the Court. On the other hand, through its research activities, though ideologically guarded, it managed to produce studies on women with the potential of forming a new consciousness regarding women's subordination. Such an historical ambivalence needs to be weighed against the memories of such outspoken women as Farrokhzad, Dehghani, Tabrizi, and many others who were ignored or silenced or tortured by the state. Needless to say, the former leaders of WOI who currently live in exile have not critically evaluated their role in women's politics in Iran. Those leaders continue to remain staunch advocates of the monarchical regime.

The current regime also mobilizes women. Mobilized women are generally composed of the "gender police" and the "gender auxilliaries". They come from middle class background and poor backgrounds. Women are recruited by various Islamic committees and associations, and organized into groups such as *Zanan-e Sarallah* (Mobile Security Women), *Zanan-e Hezbollah* (Women of the Party of God), and other *Khaharan* (sisters) organizations. The state empowers these organizations to police the public activities of women who fail to observe Islamic measures and mores, particularly those that relate to sex-segregation in public. In effect, the mobilized women have been inducted into a security agents' corps and paramilitary force, enforcing state law, while also instilling a new consciousness by educating nonconformist women on religious conduct. In so doing, the state has succeeded in setting the power of mobilized women against those who are nonconformists, but powerless.

Besides mobilizing women as security agents, the religious state has organized women for various social and political projects. One group of slum-dwelling women have been "bought by the regular provision of rations and modest food supplies provided by the government" (Afshar, 1987). Such distribution policies, however, perpetuate the victimization of poor women by "integrating" them into the orbit of the state, and in effect, insuring their economic and social dependency on the government. Another mobilized group consists of the "deprived" women who were socially and politically alienated by the Shah's regime. These women take pride in the wearing of the *Chador*, in participating in state-organized demonstrations, and, thereby, lending political support to the state.

The mobilization of women under the current regime is a complicated phenomenon. Sex-segregation policies require enforcement by women agents. Mobilization increases women's dependency on the state at the same time as it empowers women with a new sense of self, an identity that was repressed under the secular state. The mobilized women achieve recognition by the state, and the state, in turn, receives legitimation and consolidation from their support. However, the newly mobilized women face a contradiction. While they achieve a new identity, they experience a greater degree of subordination due to the intensification of patriarchal power both in the private and in the public domain.

CONCLUSION

The state, regardless of its nature, plays a critical role in the determination of women's position. It is the nature of the state and its development strategies that sets policies and agendas that define women's position. By comparing the gender policies of both the secular and religious states in terms of issues of women's sexuality, labor force participation of women, and political mobilization of women, I have suggested that within their specific contexts, both the

Iranian secular and religious states acted in their own interests and failed to articulate the interests of women at large. Women's sexuality, women's work, and mobilization of women underwent a shift in balance as the nature of the state and its development projects changed.

The modernization attempts of the secular state failed to reach a large portion of women, especially in rural areas. In theory, the transfer of patriarchal power to the state may have been achieved, but in practice, the state was unable to reach a large segment of the society. While the Pahlavi state eliminated the opposition, institutions secondary to the state—such as religion—still existed, with which people could identify. Under the religious state, however, religion lost being a refuge or balancing power vis-a-vis the state; it also lost much of its moral character (Friedl, 1983) and became the locus of the state's power. In that sense, the religious state took the state-building of the Pahlavi state to its logical conclusion. Both states, although in different ways, and to different degrees, subordinated women. The policies of the present state cannot be used as a means of glorification of the past which it inherited.

NOTES

1. I am grateful to Fatemeh Moghadam, Francine D'Amico, Judith-Maria Buechler, Peter Beckman, and my 1995 Women, Islam and Politics Seminar students for their helpful comments on an earlier draft of this paper. Different versions of this paper were presented at the 1990 Middle East Studies Association in San Antonio and at Tufts University in 1995.

2. The state is composed of a set of institutions and it is a site of contestation or an arena of struggle. I do not reify the state, for stakes can be changed as their organizations and leaders change. Similar to its class/group interest, the state's gender interest refers to the state's desires to articulate and maintain the support of gender in order to bolster its power base. In doing so, the state's gender interest arises from its need to expand its power base by drawing and/or mobilizing women, as well as representing them in political processes. (See Maxine Molyneux, 1986.)

REFERENCES

Abrahamian, Ervand. *Iran Between Two Revolutions.* Princeton, NJ: Princeton University Press., 1982.

Afkhami, Mahnaz. "Iran: A Future in the Past." In Robin Morgan, ed. *Sisterhood is Global.* New York: Anchor Books, 1984.

Afshar, Haleh. "Women, Marriage and the Shi'i State in Iran." In Haleh Afshar, ed. *Women, State, and Ideology: Studies from Africa and Asia.* Albany, NY: SUNY Press, 1987.

Afshar, Haleh, ed. *Women, Work and Ideology in the Third World.* London: Tavistock, 1985.

Ahmad, Leila. *Women and Gender in Islam: Historical Roots of a Modern Debate.* New Haven, CT: Yale University Press, 1992.

Akhavi, Shahrough. *Religion and Politics in Iran: Clergy-State Relations in the Pahlavi Period.* Albany, NY: SUNY Press, 1980.

Alexander, M. Jacqui, Lisa Albrecht, Sharon Day, and Mab Segres, eds. In press. *The Third World Feminist Perspectives on Racism.* New York: Kitchen Table Press.

Andors, Phyllis. *The Unfinished Liberation of Chinese Women, 1949–1980*. Bloomington: Indiana University Press, 1983.

Azari, Farah., ed. *Women of Iran: The Conflict with Fundamentalist Islam*. London: Ithaca Press, 1983.

Badran, Margot and Miriam Cook, eds. *Opening the Gates: A Century of Arab Feminist Writing*. Bloomington: Indiana University Press, 1990.

Bagherian, Mitra. *"Eshtegha va Bikari-ye Zanan as Didgah-e Tose'eh"* (Employment and Unemployment From the Developmental View). *Zanan* (Women) I: 157–76, [1371] 1992.

Bahrampou, Tara. "Hers: Under Wraps." *The New York Times Magazine*. July 10, 1994.

Banani, Amin. *The Modernization of Iran, 1921–1941*. Stanford, CA: Stanford University Press, 1961.

Beneria, Lourdes and Gita Sen. "Accumulation, Reproduction, and Women's Role in Economic Development: Boserup Revisited." *Signs* XII: 279–298, 1981.

Beneria, Lourdes and Gita Sen. "Class and Gender Inequalities and Women's Role in Economic Development—Theoretical and Practical Implications." *Feminist Studies* VIII: 157–176, 1982.

Bill, James. *The Politics of Iran: Groups, Classes and Modernization*. Columbus, OH: Charles E. Merrill Co., 1972.

Brooks, Geraldine. "Teen-Age Infidels Hanging Out in High Tops and Jeans: Iranian Youths are Quietly Subverting Their Parents' Revolution." *The New York Times Magazine*. April 30, 1995.

Ehsani, Kaveh. "Iran's Development and Reconstruction Dilemma." *Middle East Report* 191, November-December: 16–21, 1994.

Fallaci, Oriana. "A Shah's Eye View of the World." *New York Post*. December 29, 1973.

———. "An Interview With Khomeini." *The New York Times Magazine*. October 7, 1979.

Farhi, Farideh. "Sexuality and the Politics of Revolution in Iran." Paper delivered at the 1990 Annual Meeting of the American Political Association, San Francisco, California, 1990.

Ferdows, Adel. "Women and the Islamic Revolution." *International Journal of Middle East Studies*. XV: 283–298, 1983.

Friedl, Erika. *Women of Deh Koh: Lives in an Iranian Village*. New York: Penguin, 1991.

———. "Division of Labor in an Iranian Village." *MERIP Reports* 95 (March-April): 12–18, 31, 1981.

———. "State Ideology and Village Women," In Guity Nashat, ed. *Women and Revolution*. Boulder, CO: Westview Press, 1983.

Farrokhazad, Furugh. *Bargozideh-e Ash'ar-e Furugh Farrokhzad* (Selected Poems of Furugh Farrokhzad). Tehran: Morvarid, [1343] 1964, [1350] 1971.

Gelb, Joyce and Marian Paley. *The Politics of Women's Liberation*. Princeton, NJ: Princeton University Press, 1982.

Ghoussoub, Mai. "Feminism—or the External Masculine—in the Arab World." *New Left Review*. 161: 3–18, 1987.

———. "A Reply to Hammami and Reikder." *New Left Review* 170: 108–109, 1988.

Haeri, Shahla. *The Law of Desire: Temporary Marriage in Shi'i Iran*. New York: Syracuse University Press, 1989.

Hammami, Reza and Martina Rieker. "Feminist Orientalism and Oriental Marxism." *New Left Review* 170: 93–106, 1988.

Harding, Sandra. 1987. "Introduction: Is There a Feminist Method?" in Sandra Harding, ed. *Feminism and Methodology*. Bloomington: Indiana University Press.

———. "Feminism, Science, and the Anti-Enlightenment Critiques." In Linda Nicholson, ed. *Feminism/Postmodernism*. New York: Routledge, 1990.

Hedges, Chris. "Darakeh Journal: With Mullah's Eluded, Hijinks in the Hills." *The New York Times*. August 8, 1994.

Higgins, Patricia and Mehran Golnar. "Socialization of School-Children in the Islamic Republic of Iran." *National Women's Studies Association Journal*, Vol 3 no 2 (Spring 1991): 213–232.

Hijab, Nadia. *Women Power*. Cambridge: Cambridge University Press, 1988.

Jayawardena, Kumari. *Feminism and Nationalism in the Third World*. London: Zed Books, 1986.

Kandioyti, Deniz, ed. *Women, Islam and the State*. Bloomington: Indiana University Press, 1991.

Keddie, Nikki. *Roots of Revolution: An Interpretive History of Modern Iran*. New Haven: Yale University Press, 1981.

Keddie, Nikki and Beth Baron, eds. *Women in Middle Eastern History*. New Haven: Yale University Press, 1991.

Markaz-e Amari-ye Iran. Kholaseh-e Sarshomai-ye Sal-e Hezard Sisado Shasto Pans. (Summary of the Population Census for 1986). Tehran: Markaz-e Amari-ye Iran, [1365] 1986.

Massell, Gregory. *The Surrogate Proletariat*. Princeton: Princeton University Press, 1974.

Mernissi, Fatima. *The Veil and the Male Elite: A Feminist Interpretation of Women's Rights in Islam*. New York: Addison-Wesley, 1991.

Mernissi, Fatima. *Beyond the Veil: Male-Female Dynamics in Modern Muslim Society*. Bloomington: Indiana University Press, 1985.

Mies, Maria. *Patriarchy and Accumulation on a World Scale*. London: Zed Books, 1986.

Moghissi, Haideh. 1994. *Populism and Fundamentalism in Iran*. Boulder: Westview Press.

Moghadam, Fatemeh. "Commoditization of Sexuality and Female Labor Force Participation in Islam: Implications for Iran, 1960–1990." In Mahnaz Afkhami and Erika Friedl, eds. Pp. 80–97 and 200–203. *In the Eye of the Storm: Women in Post-Revolutionary Iran*. Syracuse, NY: Syracuse University Press, 1994.

Moghadam, Val. "Women, Work, and Ideology in the Islamic Republic." *International Journal of Middle East Studies* XX: pp. 221–243, 1988.

Molyneux, Maxine. "Mobilization Without Emancipation? Women's Interests, State and Revolution." In Fagen, Deere, and Coraggio, eds. *Transition to Democracy*. New York: Monthly Review Press, 1986.

Nashat, Guity. *Women and Revolution in Iran*. Boulder, CO: Westview Press, 1983.

Pahlavi, Princess Ashraf. "Notq-e vala Hazrat Shahdokht Ashraf Pahlavi" [Her Majesty Princess Ashraf Pahlavi's Speech]. In *Kongereh-e Bozorgdasht-e Cheomin Salrouz-e Azadi-ye Ejtemia-ye Zanan* [The Congress of Celebration of the Fortieth Day of Social Emancipation of Women]. Tehran: Women's Organization of Iran, [1353] 1974.

125

Parker, Andrew, Mary Russo, Doris Sommer, and Patricia Yeager, eds. *Nationalism and Sexualities.* New York: Routledge, 1992.

Petchesky, Rosalind. *Abortion and Women's Choice.* Boston: Northeastern University Press, 1984.

The Plan and Budget Organization. *Degarguniha-ye Ejtemai' va Eghtesai-ye Zanan-e Iran.* [Social and Economic Changes in the Position of Iranian Women]. Tehran: The Plan and Budget Organization and Statistical Center of Iran, 1974.

Ramazani, Nesta. "Women in Iran: The Revolutionary Ebb and Flow." *Middle East Journal,* XXXXVII: 409–428, 1993.

Salnameh-e Amari-ye Keshvar 1369. [Summary of National Census, 1990]. Tehran: Markaz-e Amer-e Iran, Statistical Center of Iran, [1370] 1971.

Sciolino, Elaine. "From the Back Seat in Iran, Murmurs of Unrest." *The New York Times.* April 23, 1992.

Sedghi, Hamideh. "Women in Iran." In L. Iglitzin and R. Ross, eds. *Women in the World: A Comparative Study.* ABC-Clio Press, 1976.

———. "An Assessment of Works in Farsi and English on Iran and Iranian Women: 1900–1977." *Review of Radical Political Economics,* XXIII: 37–41, 1980.

———. "The State and the Sexual Division of Labor in Iran." Paper presented at the Annual Meeting of Middle East Studies Association, New Orleans, Louisiana, 1986.

———. "Third World Feminist Perspectives or World Politics." In Peter Beckman and Francine D'Amico, eds. *Women, Gender, and World Politics.* Westport, CT: Bergin and Garvey, 1994.

———. *Veiling, Unveiling and Reveiling: Women and Politics in Contemporary Iran.*

Shahidian, Hammed. "The Iranian Left and the 'Woman Question," in the Revolution of 1978-79." *International Journal of Middle East Studies.* XXVI: 223–247, 1994.

Tabari, Azr and Nahid Yeganeh, eds. *In the Shadow of Islam: The Women's Movement in Iran.* London: Zed Books, 1982.

Tucker, Judith, ed. *Arab Women: Old Boundaries, New Frontiers.* Bloomington: Indiana University Press, 1993.

Urdang, Stephanie. *Fighting Two Colonialisms: Women in Guinea-Bissau.* New York: Monthly Review Press, 1979.

Yeganeh, Nahid and Nikki Keddie. "Sexuality and Shi'i Social Protest in Iran." In Juan Cole and Nikki Keddie, eds. *Shi'ism and Social Protest.* New Haven: Yale University Press, 1986.

Weiner, Myron and Ali Banuazizi, eds. *The Politics of Social Transformation in Afghanistan, Iran and Pakistan.* Syracuse, NY: Syracuse University Press, 1994.

Youssef, Nadia. *Women and Work in the Developing Societies.* Westport, CT: Greenwood Press, 1976.

THE DILEMMAS OF MODERN DEVELOPMENT:

Structural Adjustment and Women Microentrepreneurs in Nigeria and Zimbabwe

Mary J. Osirim

THE ECONOMIC crisis that affected sub-Saharan Africa in the 1980s followed by the adoption of Structural Adjustment Programs (SAPs) to remedy these problems have had their most devastating impact on Africa's most vulnerable populations—women and children. Recent socio-economic indicators reflect a declining quality of life on the continent including escalating unemployment/underemployment, growing malnutrition, and general deteriorating health conditions (UNECA, 1990; Wisner, 1992). Due to the high rates of unemployment and increasing male migration to cities in search of work among other conditions, more and more women are finding themselves the de facto heads of households and thus must assume even more financial and emotional responsibility for the rearing of children. At the same time, the legacy of colonialism and continued patriarchy reinforces the existence of a gender-segregated labor market, which limits the earnings potential of most African women. Under such conditions, many women have no choice but to enter the so-called informal sector as microentrepreneurs to provide them and their families with some cash income. However, current SAPs have circumscribed the abilities of these women to succeed as microentrepreneurs and have restricted their contributions to their families, their communities, and to national development.

Despite the claims of the Nigerian and the Zimbabwean governments that their SAPs are "home-grown," both of these policies were designed on the International Monetary Fund/World Bank model and adopted upon their strong recommendations. Thus, two dependent African states again find themselves limited in their actions by the demands of global capitalism. Such requirements for restructuring the economies in the Third World are resulting in undue hardship on the poor of these nations.

This study will explore the current dilemmas posed by SAPs on women microentrepreneurs in Nigeria and Zimbabwe, based on intensive interviews conducted among them in 1988 and 1991 respectively. Women self-employed as market traders, crocheters, seamstresses, and hairdressers were questioned about the impact of recent government policies on their lives, as well as about the operation of their firms, their responsibilities to their households and families, and their personal attributes.[1] The first of these areas will be examined against a backdrop briefly investigating the history of the economic crisis in these nations and the adoption of a SAP, the states' efforts to enhance the position of women in these societies, the role of the "second economy" and the reasons for women's participation in it as microentrepreneurs. Finally, some policy recommendations will be offered to improve the position of female microentrepreneurs and their contributions to these societies.

THEORETICAL FRAMEWORK

How can we understand the economic crisis that is engulfing sub-Saharan Africa, the response of states to this crisis, and its impact on women in these societies? What theoretical perspectives underlie and shape this work?

Within the sociology of development, world systems theory begins to explain these problems. Initially developed by Immanuel Wallerstein (1974) in his work *The Modern World System*, world systems analysis maintains that a basically exploitative relationship exists between core and peripheral nations, as also explained in the 1960s by the dependency theorists. Unlike scholars in the dependency school, however, world systems theorists argue that an identifiable system exists and extends beyond the boundaries of individual states or nations. This system is global capitalism, which emerged in its modern form in Western Europe in the 16th century. Diverging from earlier paradigms in the sociology of development, the world systems perspective is historical in its approach—it postulates that we can only understand the dynamics of social change and the contemporary problems of development if we explore the roots of these dilemmas in the emergence of the modern capitalist system.

According to Jan Kippers Black (1991), world systems theory does not focus on the interactions among governments, but calls attention to the transnational interactions of non-state actors, namely multinational corporations and banks. The economic organization of the world system consists of a single division of labor that unifies the multiple cultural systems of the world's peoples into a single, integrated system. Each area of the system has acquired a specialized role producing goods that it trades to others to obtain what it needs. The global economy is believed to be driven by international elites, particularly in the First World states, whose governments usually do their bidding. The control centers of the world economy are then the financial rather than the political capitals. The essential struggle for Wallerstein, then, is between rich and poor classes, rather than rich and poor states.

A more recently developed paradigm within the sociology of development, comparative political economy, better addresses the contemporary problems present in sub-Saharan Africa. This perspective aims to uncover, interpret, and explain distinctive patterns of development as they manifest themselves throughout various societies. Why do different countries exhibit distinct patterns of distribution and accumulation over the course of their development? (Evans, 1988) Thus, the global capitalist system remains a key variable in the analysis, but at the same time, the autonomy of the state and the strengths of dominant and subordinate classes are considered as critical factors in charting a society's development. Unlike the early dependency theorists, international political economists argue that the penetration of foreign capital does not necessarily result in the contraction of the economic role of a Third World state. The local bourgeoisies and workers in such a state, who are directly associated with transnational corporations might benefit from the latter's activities. Peter Evans, however, indicates that the expansion of the state's role, namely its involvement in the triple alliance with foreign capital and the indigenous bourgeoisie, does not necessarily advance other categories of development such as improving the living standards for the majority (Evans, 1979).

Comparative political economy further emphasizes the ability of subordinate classes to influence historical outcomes through class action (Evans, 1988). Therefore, the microenterprise sector is an important subject of analysis, since for many political economists, it is believed to contain the seeds of economic and political change. This is precisely the case because this segment of the economy often consists of some dynamic enterprises, associations and networks that offer the potential for strengthening civil society and transforming the state.

It is at this juncture, however, that feminist scholarship has broadened the parameters of comparative political economy. While these two frameworks acknowledge the existence of an international division of labor, feminist scholars have continued to draw our attention to the gendered nature of this

129

OSIRIM

segmentation. As many manufacturing and high-tech service activities are transferred from the high-wage core nations to the periphery, feminist theorists, such as June Nash (1983), Diane Elson (1992) and Kate Young (1984) draw our attention to not only how particular regions or nation-states are selected to become the producers of these goods and services, but to the differentiation in access to and returns from such activities based on gender. In addition to the effects of these relocations on the status of women in the labor market, these scholars are concerned more generally with the consequences of the international division of labor on culture and social structure.

With respect to the study of microenterprise development in Africa, feminist scholars have investigated the differentiation of activities in this sector by gender and the implications for social structure and development. In this regard, traditional culture, colonialism, continued patriarchy, the position of a nation in the global capitalist system, and the role of the state contribute to our understanding of not only the status of women in this sphere, but their current and potential contributions to local and national development. This discussion, situated within the discourse on comparative political economy, will focus on these latter two categories in its attempt to contribute to feminist scholarship in this area.

THE ECONOMIC CRISIS AND THE ADOPTION OF STRUCTURAL ADJUSTMENT PROGRAMS

Although both Nigeria and Zimbabwe have been victims of the economic crisis plaguing sub-Saharan Africa in the 1980s, Nigeria experienced the impact of the crisis earlier and more intensely than Zimbabwe. The decline in the oil market beginning in 1981 signaled the emergence of tough times for Nigeria and began to unmask the distortions in the economy. During the oil boom of the 1970s, Nigeria remained a monoproduct economy highly dependent on imports. With the exception of the government's attempts to begin a steel industry, which were unsuccessful, little to no diversification of the economy had occurred. Nigeria relied on oil for over 95 percent of its export earnings and virtually ignored the agricultural sector. As a result, the country moved from being self-sufficient in food production in the '70s to one heavily dependent on imports in the 1980s. By late 1981, Nigeria faced lower oil prices, mounting international debt, and declines in per capita income. Consequently, this country slipped from the middle-income to the low-income group in the World Bank's classification of Third World nations by the end of the decade (Bangura, 1989; The World Bank, 1990).

In an attempt to stem the tide of the crisis, President Shagari tried to gain a three-year extended facility loan from the IMF for 2.3 billion dollars in 1983 (Biersteker, 1986; Anyanwu, 1992). This began a series of negotiations between Nigeria and the IMF which extended over three regimes for more than two years. Debates between the government and the IMF raged over the

Fund's conditionality for the loan—over 17 conditions had been delineated for the government to meet, with the major disagreements surrounding three issues: trade liberalization; removal of the oil subsidy; and devaluation of the *naira*. Finally, after much public debate at the beginning of Babangida's administration in 1985, the Nigerian government rejected the loan (Biersteker, 1986; Anyanwu, 1992).

Although the IMF loan was formally rejected, Babangida introduced a SAP in July, 1986 which fit the standard IMF-World Bank model. Some of the major elements of this program included:

1. Efforts to correct for overvaluation of the *naira* by setting up a viable Second-Tier Foreign Exchange Market (SFEM).
2. Attempts to overcome the observed public sector inefficiencies through improved public expenditure control programs and the rationalization of parastatals.
3. Actions to relieve the debt burden and attract a net inflow of foreign capital, while keeping a lid on foreign loans (Anyanwu, 1992).

In effect, the government was embarking on a program to promote capital accumulation in a free market. Through the establishment of the SFEM, it was hoped that a rein would be placed on the previous corrupt system of obtaining import licenses and that importation would be minimized and rationalized. The government maintained that mismanagement and inefficiencies in production would be reduced by dismantling many of the parastatals. These measures would result in the retrenchment of workers, the removal of government subsidies from many products and services (including oil) and supposedly create an attractive climate for foreign investment, given the devalued currency. Such policies have had a particularly devastating impact on the poor, especially women, who are disproportionately plagued by escalating food, utility, health, education, and transportation costs.

Although one might expect that the initial socialist orientation of the Zimbabwean state might preclude it from embarking on a similar strategy to solve its economic problems, it nonetheless did adopt a SAP in 1990 based on the IMF-World Bank framework. How does the state come to enact a SAP in Zimbabwe? Unlike the situation in Nigeria, the Zimbabwean economy was more diversified— agriculture, mining, and industry contributed to national wealth. With the exception of South Africa, Zimbabwe was the most industrialized nation in Africa south of the Sahara (Stoneman, 1989b). To promote growth with equity, the government produced an economic program, The Transitional National Development Plan (TNDP), to delineate its major goals. This plan covered the period from 1982–1985 and set overambitious economic development targets of 8 percent growth per year with higher growth expected in goods production as opposed to services (Kadhani, 1986; Stoneman, 1989b). While Zimbabwe experienced significant growth exceed-

131

OSIRIM

ing 11 percent in the first two years after independence, this was not sustained throughout the decade. Growth was a negative 3 percent in 1983, and showed a modest improvement in 1984 of 1.3 percent, with growth in government-related services rising faster than goods (Kadhani, 1986). Several explanations were offered for the smaller growth period of 1982–1984, which included the drought from 1982–1984; continued fighting in Matabeleland; world recession; and continued destabilization in the region caused by South Africa (Stoneman, 1989b). Although growth for the 1988 and '89 period was 5 percent, formal sector employment growth had slowed considerably. Stoneman estimates that it is unlikely that formal employment has increased by more than 14,000 jobs per year since independence, and approximately 100,000 young persons enter the labor market every year. By the early 1990s, this figure was expected to reach 250,000 per year (Stoneman, 1989b). The recent drought has further exacerbated the Zimbabwean economy such that the government's earlier estimates of 2–4 percent growth in GDP in 1992 are far from correct. Actual figures are more likely to reflect a 9 percent decline in growth (Laishley, 1992). While the lack of significant growth in the economy by the beginning of 1990 heralded the economic crisis, the failure to create a sufficient number of jobs throughout the 1980s has arguably wielded an even more devastating blow to the current stability of the state.

Thus in an effort to improve the economy, the government enacted a SAP in 1990 which claims to be an indigenous plan, although it adheres to the major elements of the Nigerian plan and of past IMF-World Bank programs. Amid much discussion that neither the Congress nor the Central Committee had been consulted about the government's economic stabilization program, Mugabe launched a SAP with the following features, claiming that the relevant ZANU-PF members had been consulted (Training Aids Development Group, 1991; Moyo, 1992):

1. Trade Liberalization
2. Reducing Government Expenditures
3. Devaluation
4. Reducing Controls over Foreign Currency
5. Restricting Trade Unions

Although it is still too early to fully evaluate the effect of this SAP on the Zimbabwean populace, some early results already indicate that the poor, particularly women, have borne the brunt of the sacrifices. The removal of price controls coupled with the drought have thus far resulted in shortages and increased hunger among this population:

In March 1992—for the first time since independence—Zimbabweans not only queued for maize meal but also needed the protection of riot police. People in very dry rural areas have been forced to look for edible roots and leaves, and some residential facilities have had to close because of lack of water. Consumers were already experiencing severe shortages of sugar, cooking oil, margarine, matches and postage stamps, while the country was under the threat of blackout due to the shortage of electric power (Moyo 1992).

School, medical, and transportation fees have already increased and are having an especially negative effect upon the urban poor. The socioeconomic landscape is expected to worsen further under the SAP with retrenchment of 45,000–50,000 workers from the formal sector, disproportionately affecting the low-skilled, lowest-paid workers. It has been predicted that an additional 10 percent of the remaining formal sector workforce will see their incomes fall below the poverty line under this program (Gibbon, 1992).

One group that has been very adversely affected under the establishment of SAPs in Nigeria and Zimbabwe have been women microentrepreneurs. This population, who frequently begin very small firms as a result of structural blockage that impedes them from entering other fields, are considered members of the informal sector, an area where these governments expect to see employment generation under SAPs. The potential for growth among these businesspersons is restricted, however, by several factors. First, a gender-based division of labor persists even within this second economy, thereby restricting women's self-employment to service-oriented, low-return ventures, as opposed to manufacturing and advanced technology enterprises. Second, the persistence of patriarchy still limits women's access to capital, governmental and non-governmental sponsored support programs and business networks, thus restricting the possibilities for expansion and growth. Third, traditional gender-role socialization patterns still prevail in the household, within schools and society at large; thus, women's educational attainment levels and fields of study are circumscribed along strict gender lines further limiting them to low status occupations. Fourth, the retrenchment of government and other formal sector workers under SAPs means that for the most part, more men are unemployed, placing greater pressure on women to increase their earnings, often via the informal economy. Men are also encouraged to begin small firms and under these conditions, female microentrepreneurs often find themselves competing with men, who because of the privileges that their gender affords them are in a stronger position to outperform women in the informal economy. Finally, women self-employed at the margins of the second economy, who are facing greater responsibilities for the maintenance of their families, are even more disadvantaged by the removal of price controls, subsidies of vital social services and devaluation under SAPs than their male counterparts.

133

OSIRIM

FIELD METHODS

To explore the current status of female microentrepreneurs in urban Nigeria and Zimbabwe, two studies were undertaken in Lagos and Benin, Nigeria, in 1988 and in Harare and Bulawayo, Zimbabwe, in 1991. Intensive interviews were conducted with 54 women in Nigeria and 55 women in Zimbabwe self-employed as seamstresses, hairdressers, market traders, and crocheters (in Zimbabwe only). In Nigeria, the sample of traders included some who sold food and others who sold cloth, while only food vendors were included in the Zimbabwe study. The interview measures were divided into four major parts: 1) the personal attributes of the entrepreneurs; 2) the operation of their enterprises; 3) their roles and responsibilities in the family; and 4) their knowledge and use of governmental and non-governmental support services and the impact of government programs in the operation of their firms. The discussion here will focus on the responses contained in this fourth area, where the effects of recent adjustment measures upon the respondents were explored. The particular cases of Nigeria and Zimbabwe will first be placed in the more general context of the informal sector in Africa.

THE INFORMAL SECTOR AND WOMEN'S MICROENTREPRENEURSHIP IN AFRICA

In attempting to study the changing dimensions of global capitalism, socioeconomic development in the Third World and the international division of labor, scholars in the 1970s and 1980s increasingly directed their attention to the existence of a "second economy" or informal sector that was first defined as distinct from the formal economy. Early investigations of the informal sector often began with the definition developed in the International Labor Organization research on Kenya in 1972:

> This sector can be characterized by its ease of entry, reliance on indigenous resources, family ownership of enterprises, small scale of operations, labor-intensive and adapted technology, skill acquired outside of the formal school system, and unregulated and competitive markets (ILO, 1972).

Much of the early literature on the informal sector used the dual economy approach, which maintained that the formal and informal sectors were autonomous entities, operating within two different labor markets, with little to no relationship between the sectors (Mazumdar, 1976; Souza et al., 1976; Feldman, 1991).

Unlike these earlier studies, Portes recognizes the integral role that the informal sector can play in national economies (Portes et al., 1989). This sector often consists of small, unregulated activities that have grown as a result of worldwide economic restructuring. Large corporations in the West have increased their subcontracting arrangements with such firms in an effort to escape taxes, minimum wage and health and safety regulations, as well as the attempts of unions to improve wages and benefits. While acknowledging that the informal sphere does contain some illegal activities, Portes suggests that this sector should not be regarded as merely collections of survival strategies engaged in by the poor, since many of these enterprises are dynamic and yield incomes surpassing that of their formal sector counterparts (Portes et al., 1989).

OSIRIM

Feminist researchers have more recently advised that the term "microenterprises" replace the concept "informal sector" in describing women's very small, income-generating activities. This is an attempt on the part of women and development researchers to remove the negative, pejorative connotations, such as inefficient, often associated with the term "informal sector" (Otero, 1987; Downing, 1990; Horn, 1990). Further, such scholars have encouraged us to abandon the dual economy perspective that often accompanied "informal sector" and to consider women's ventures as more than simply survival activities. In this paper, the concept "microenterprises" is used within this feminist paradigm. The author maintains that although many of the businesses studied have encountered serious problems under the SAPs threatening their very survival, the women studied are indeed microentrepreneurs, who despite these dilemmas, are committed to their businesses and are making important contributions to their families and to their communities.

In recent analyses of microentrepreneurship in sub-Saharan Africa, several variables have been employed in attempts to define these activities, including: size of operations, legal status, the nature of production, and the role of the state (MacGaffey, 1986; Clark, 1988; Horn, 1988, 1990, 1991; Saito, 1991; Schoepf, 1992; Osirim, 1992). After agriculture, participation in the informal economy has been the major area of income-earning for women, due to the history of colonialism and the persistence of patriarchy previously discussed. Historically, West African women have been noted for their success in market trade, establishing a reputation for economic independence that enabled them to make substantial contributions to the maintenance of their families (Sanday, 1974; Robertson, 1984; Clark, 1988; Schoepf, 1992). In the contemporary period, some women throughout Africa south of the Sahara have achieved success through more long-distance trade, importing textiles, for example, from major urban centers in West and Central Africa (MacGaffey, 1986). Marriages to foreign men were also found to assist women in improving the profitability of their firms in some African states. In Zaire, for example, such husbands were beneficial in obtaining foreign exchange and inputs for production and sales that might be lacking or too expensive for an entrepreneur to obtain in her country (MacGaffey, 1986). In Zimbabwe's urban areas, food-related activities have been shown to be profitable ventures for women microentrepreneurs. Food-processing, such as the production of peanut butter and sunflower oil, as well as bakeries, "take-away" food shops, and catering have succeeded in meeting the growing demand for "ready-to-eat" foods by the growing urban population (Saito, 1991). Downing suggests that catering to the local urban and tourist markets are also potentially thriving areas for women's microentrepreneurship. Included among such activities are handicrafts, garment-making, rattan and hand-woven rugs (Downing, 1990). The persistence of traditional gender-role socialization patterns and the division of labor by gender has meant that for the most part, women are

OSIRIM

concentrated in such services, which are often an extension of their domestic duties. Because African women's entrepreneurial activities are centered in domestically-related services, these areas were chosen as the focus for this investigation.

WOMEN MICROENTREPRENEURS AND THE IMPACT OF ECONOMIC ADJUSTMENT PROGRAMS: TWO AFRICAN CASE STUDIES

As previously stated, microentrepreneurs were interviewed in two of the major cities in southwestern Nigeria and Zimbabwe to ascertain the effects of the government's recent economic policies on their performance and aspirations as businesspersons. The impact of these programs will be examined by sector; e.g., the responses of market traders will be discussed together across cities, as opposed to by ethnic group, given the very small samples of each population. The impact of the SAPs enacted in Nigeria and Zimbabwe will be considered by subsector.

Market Traders

When questioned about the effect of government policies on the operation of their businesses, both Nigerian and Zimbabwean market vendors reported that the removal of price controls, one of the major features of the adjustment programs, and the significant inflation that resulted are their major problems. Over half of the traders in the four cities studied noted that this was their most serious dilemma. Due to the national economy and increasing unemployment, consumers have less money to spend, even on the basic necessities such as food. Coupled with this is the fact that it now costs these vendors more to buy their commodities from the wholesalers, which in turn forced them to charge more for their goods. This action further reduced the demand for their products and resulted in fewer customers. These vendors expressed anger and lack of control in not knowing when such price increases would occur. One trader in Harare's Mbare Market notes this problem as:

> [In the market place] there is inflation of prices and relaxed demand. Fluctuation of prices of wholesale supply. Price increases affect everyone (Chera, 1991).

The rising prices of cloth have also meant fewer customers for cloth sellers in the market, since new clothing under such arduous economic conditions is of lesser demand than food.

Due to their meager incomes, market traders are extremely dependent on public transportation, and the higher prices for transport to bring their goods to the market is also making it extremely difficult for them to make a profit. In addition to increasing bus and taxi fares, transportation poses even greater problems for market vendors in Zimbabwe, because under structural adjustment, there are fewer operating buses, since the government lacks the necessary capital to repair them. Traders who were used to waking up at four A.M.

OSIRIM

to start their business day are now frequently beginning to join a bus queue at this time. These women often wait in lines for hours before obtaining transport to wholesalers and then to the market.

Among traders, increased competition (both from others working in the markets and from those owning stores) was viewed as another major problem affecting the profitability of their enterprises, especially for those in Zimbabwe. Vendors explained that the numbers of traders selling the same goods had increased markedly. As one Mbare trader remarked:

> The competition is stiffer, so the work was better in the past than now because there are too many sellers and we all sell the same things (personal interview, 1991).

Visits to markets in Zimbabwe not only revealed that many vendors were selling the same products, but that increasing numbers of men were selling fruits and vegetables in the marketplace. As discussed above, due to the reduction in the size of formal sector employment under structural adjustment, more retrenched workers are likely to be displaced to the informal sector. Female microentrepreneurs in both countries are particularly disadvantaged in this subsector, since they most often lack the connections, educations and skills to establish shops or diversify their activities into other areas. When compared to the other categories studied, Zimbabwean traders had the highest rates of divorce or widowhood, and thus the greatest responsibilities to provide for their children at a time when the state's policies were making it more difficult for them to accomplish this task.

137

The location of a market and harassment by the police were additional problems encountered by traders in Nigeria and Zimbabwe. Those working in Manwele Market in Bulawayo, for example, reported that they were experiencing declining sales in the recent period as more blacks were leaving the high density suburbs everyday for employment in the central city. In downtown Bulawayo, workers could shop at large markets, in grocery stores and supermarkets, as well as make their purchases from street vendors at the bus depot. Although hawking their wares in the latter case is illegal, some traders remarked that they and others have tried to sell goods very early in the morning at bus stations before the police arrive to fine them and confiscate their goods. This strategy engaged in as an attempt to stay in business involves yet greater daily physical sacrifices. They have to awaken even earlier to sell for a few hours at the depot in town, leave before the police come, and arrive back at their stall in Manwele Market between 7:30 and 8:00 in the morning. Women who succeed in taking on this extra shift can increase their profits, while for others, such women are only an additional source of competition. Although police harassment of market women is not a new phenomenon, it is particularly problematic under the current economic conditions with declining customers and sales.

OSIRIM

Although market traders face far fewer restrictions in Nigeria with respect to where they can sell, Lagos cloth vendors have experienced similar harassment by the police. Under the government's austerity measures, women selling banned imported cloth were not only harassed, but often had their stalls destroyed and their goods confiscated.

Crocheters

The crocheters, who were only in the Zimbabwe sample, also reported that with the removal of price controls, they were faced with higher prices for required inputs. Thirty-nine percent of the entrepreneurs in both cities discussed the rise in the price of cotton and their declining sales as a result of their need to pass these costs on to the consumers. Few crocheters were found to be making goods in colors other than white or beige due to the even higher prices charged for dyed cotton.

Declines in the number of customers were further cited by these businesspersons as a result of increased competition. As an observer at several of these streetside locations in Harare and Bulawayo, I witnessed that competition for buyers was indeed very keen. The most extreme example of this can be viewed at Enterprise Road in Harare, where potential buyers and passersby are often accosted by several crocheters at a time before they even get out of their cars. The dilemmas faced by these women because of increased prices for cotton and fewer customers are summed up in the comments of one Bulawayo crocheter:

> The problem is that there are not that many foreigners buying the goods and the cotton is too expensive. . . . [In the past] there was more success but now, you buy cotton today and it is one price; you buy cotton tomorrow and the price has gone up (personal interview, 1991).

While well over half the traders in Benin, Harare, and Bulawayo, and 100 percent of those in Lagos, reported that they had earned profits since they began their enterprises, only 44 percent of their counterparts in crocheting had earned profits. The participants in both sectors noted that much of the decline in profits occurred within a year after the passage of the SAPs in these nations. Under the present conditions, the profitability of trading and crocheting is likely to worsen.

Crocheters are also plagued by inadequate sites for their operations. These women would lose valuable workdays due to inclement weather, since they generally sat outdoors on the bare ground without the benefit of any protective covering. Although this situation predated the establishment of adjustment programs in Zimbabwe, promises made to these entrepreneurs by the City Councils of Harare and Bulawayo regarding the provision of sheds are less likely to be kept given the current restructuring demands. When coupled with the shortage of customers and the increasing costs of inputs, the problem of inadequate sites further reduces the economic viability of these activities.

Hairdressers and Seamstresses

Although the hairdressers and seamstresses were generally in a stronger financial position than the market traders and crocheters studied, the former had also experienced a decrease in the number of customers, difficulties in obtaining needed supplies, and increased competition in their fields since the adoption of SAPs. Among these entrepreneurs in Nigeria, the greatest dissatisfaction stemmed from the loss of customers, since many women decided that they could barely afford basic necessities and the services provided by these businesswomen were now considered luxuries. Further, the increasing costs of hair products and textiles has forced these respondents to raise their prices. These entrepreneurs clearly linked these problems to the maladies in the larger economy, directly caused by aspects of the adjustment policies:

> [Because of] removal of the oil subsidy, [we] can't get materials cheaply. Now only people with money are coming [to the business]. Not as many as should be (personal interview, 1988).

> Due to the changing of the money [devaluation] we couldn't make any sales. Even those who would come and give us part, couldn't pay the rest. [There are] problems: lack of sales, shortage of materials, wavering of prices, problems with customers (personal interview, 1988).

> Success is limited due to the depression. People need things cheaper than I can provide them with (personal interview, 1988).

> When women are coming, they bring their own supplies. They expect to pay you. I discovered some of our creams had gone moldy because [we were] unable to use them. Problem of getting the materials—scarce and very expensive (personal interview, 1988).

Further difficulties were noted by more than half of the Zimbabwean entrepreneurs in this area and many Nigerian businesspersons due to the inability to obtain needed inputs in the first place. In addition to the increasing costs of purchasing these products at home, these participants frequently lacked access to essential goods because of import bans, the costs of obtaining import licenses and/or paying customs duties, and the increase in prices of such imports due to the massive currency devaluations.

Finally, several entrepreneurs remarked that competition was escalating due to the increasing numbers of firms entering the market, especially as unemployment was soaring and more males were losing positions as a result of retrenchment in civil service positions. From my observations in Zimbabwe, it was noted that competition in opening beauty salons was not just among

139

OSIRIM

women, but men were also beginning many of these establishments. The difficulties faced by these businesswomen can be summed up in the words of a hairdresser in Zimbabwe:

> There is a lot of competition. No jobs in Zimbabwe. They [other businesses] grab customers off the street and grab your workers. Prices increase everyday. I go two-three days without customers but still have to pay bills as usual. If I increase prices, customers might stay away for a month (personal interview, 1991).

ASPIRATIONS FOR THE FUTURE AND
KNOWLEDGE OF SUPPORT SERVICES

Despite the many difficulties that microentrepreneurs in each of these sectors were facing under the SAPs, the majority of these women had aspirations for the future. Businesswomen in both Nigeria and Zimbabwe were first committed to securing their children's futures by providing them with further education. To succeed in this, the respondents believed it was necessary to achieve their occupational goals.

Most of the hairdressers and seamstresses studied hoped to expand their current activities by gaining more customers and expanding their work space. Many of them hoped to add related enterprises to their current operations, such as adding fitness centers to beauty salons, establishing factories to produce children's clothes alongside their current seamstress shops, and beginning factories to locally manufacture hair products. Several of the Nigerian entrepreneurs expressed their desire to expand the training of future seamstresses and hairdressers by beginning schools in fashion design, dressmaking, and cosmetology.[2]

Many of the traders and crocheters maintained that they would like to open shops in which to sell their products. Others had recognized the increasing demand for quickly prepared meals by the growing urban population and wanted to establish take-away food shops to meet these needs.

As demonstrated above, however, the problems engendered by the recent adoption of SAPs jeopardizes the potential for these entrepreneurs to make these contributions to their communities in the future. At the time of these interviews, even the government's programs to ease the strains of adjustment were not benefitting these women. In fact, knowledge about the existence of governmental and non-governmental support services for businesses generally, and those aimed at meeting the needs of those most devastated under SAPs, was quite low among the population sampled. Over 50 percent of the market traders in Nigeria and Zimbabwe and crocheters in Zimbabwe were unaware of such services and none of the participants had ever used any of them. Low levels of educational attainment and the failures of these agencies to fully advertise available services among these groups helps to explain the low knowledge base about institutions and programs such as vocational training programs and loan programs for microentrepreneurs. In addition to the lower levels of education that women have in these societies, female entrepreneurs know less about these services because of their blocked access to business networks. Male entrepreneurs, even those owning small-scale firms, are more likely to have formal sector contacts through employment and associations such as the Chamber of Commerce, that women even in comparable positions lack (Osirim, 1990).

The Zimbabwe government's efforts to improve the status of women are likely to have contributed to the fact that more traders there, when compared to their Nigerian counterparts, mentioned some government actions to improve their plight, such as providing markets and sanitation facilities. Traders in both nations did note that informal associations did exist, such as rotating credit schemes and market organizations based on the commodities one sold (e.g., Yam and Gari Associations) did assist them by providing loans and lumpsum payments to keep their businesses afloat. Nigerian vendors were more likely than those in Zimbabwe to mention such organizations. This can be explained by the longer history of market trade and the existence of such associations in West Africa (Sanday, 1974; Robertson, 1984; Seidman, 1984; Clark, 1988).

Among seamstresses and hairdressers, knowledge of and access to support services in general or the attempts of the government to ameliorate the strains of adjustment in particular were also limited. Only 24 percent of the Zimbabwean sample had ever obtained a bank loan for their businesses, compared to 12 percent in Nigeria. Zimbabwe's promotion of gender equality and the fact that the government is a major shareholder in ZIMBANK, one of the major sources of these loan funds, would probably explain the higher rate in Zimbabwe as opposed to Nigeria. The only other support services utilized by these samples included trade shows for advertising one's business (e.g., The Association of Cosmotologists in Nigeria) to obtain beauty products at reduced rates, and a government-sponsored training program in Zimbabwe.

Even under the current circumstances of economic adjustment, female microentrepreneurs could be assisted by the state's policies discussed above, which in the case of Zimbabwe would at least provide these women with some subsidized social services, and in the case of Nigeria could enable them to obtain business loans without the use of conventional lending criteria. However, without access to information about such programs, these women remain blocked in achieving the maximum benefits provided by the state for their firms and for their families, and thus, are further limited in the contributions they can make to their communities.

POLICY RECOMMENDATIONS

To improve the status and contributions of female microentrepreneurs to future development, several changes are needed in the present orientation and

141

OSIRIM

policies of these African states. At the micro level, both local and national governments need to provide information and access to support services and to programs addressing the social dimensions of adjustment. Women in this study and undoubtedly others lacked knowledge about the existence of the many training and loan programs that exist in these nations and had no information about these states' more recent aims to provide a "safety net" for those most victimized by their SAPs. Through the use of promotional campaigns advertising these programs and by employing urban outreach workers, microentrepreneurs could receive information about existing programs. The state could provide stipends for the businesswomen who attend classes and workshops as payment for the lost work hours and sales. Further, this author recommends that the model of The People's Bank developed in Nigeria be adopted in Zimbabwe. This bank provides microentrepreneurs with small loans as working capital for their businesses without the lending criteria, collateral requirements and interest rates of conventional commercial banks. Decisionmaking regarding loans and repayment is made by residents of the local community, with particular attention paid to the character, as opposed to the creditworthiness of the potential borrower.

With respect to providing a safety net, these states should also attempt to provide lower transportation costs for those working in the second economy. Some subsidy program for transportation to and from one's place of work needs to exist for those who earn very meager incomes but yet are completely dependent upon public transport.

For Zimbabwe's crocheters, local governments need to immediately address their need for facilities in which to work. The present situation where these women have to work outdoors on bare ground with no protective covering endangers not only the solvency of their enterprises but their health. The creation of new urban markets could house both these crocheters and also some market traders who lack stalls for their businesses. Given the economic problems of these states, the building of such stalls could be accomplished through self-help projects, where the state provides the materials and the entrepreneurs and their families provide the labor. Nominal rental charges could be collected by these local governments for the use of the land.

To promote more long-term change in the status of women microentrepreneurs and to advance the position of women at the bottom of the socioeconomic hierarchies in these nations more generally, both socialization practices and the division of labor based on gender need to be eliminated. Socialization practices that follow rigid gender prescriptions need to be replaced, such that the content of what young women receive in the classroom is empowering and provides them with expanding options for employment and lifestyle choices which are not restricted by gender. Classes in non-traditional areas, such as carpentry, welding, and high-technology fields, should be made available to women across the age spectrum. Such instruction will likely result

142

OSIRIM

in many women beginning more profitable microenterprises using the skills they have acquired and ultimately increasing their earnings.

It is not enough, however, for educators and students to change their thinking, but institutional practice is a critical component in the elimination of patriarchy. The state needs to more aggressively foster equality between women and men through promotional campaigns where it not only informs the public about its programs, but also advances a more egalitarian philosophy.

Such improvements in the lives of Nigerian and Zimbabwean women would require government expenditures which at this time, given the economic problems, would be very difficult. Thus more macro-level changes are required by these states. Regional cooperation in production and trade needs to be strengthened among the Economic Community of West African States and Southern African Development Community countries, so that member nations become more reliant on each other than on the international marketplace. Rather than just paying lip-service to promoting indigenous production, incentives, loan programs and training can be provided to truly encourage local manufacturing of required inputs and finished goods. Sub-Saharan African nations need to emphasize national and regional development goals, as opposed to the goals of multilateral agencies such as The World Bank and the International Monetary Fund and the international community which in the past have restricted their development and have increased their dependency. Rather than targeting Southern nations for adjustment and austerity programs, the aim of economic restructuring efforts needs to shift to the international level, where financial markets and transnational corporations, among other organizations, need to attempt at the very least to balance benefits between the Third World and the West. Only such macro-level changes in the global arena will ultimately improve the lives of poor women in the South for the long term.

CONCLUSION

The economic crises experienced by Nigeria and Zimbabwe in the 1980s resulted in their adoption of Structural Adjustment Programs upon the recommendations of the IMF and The World Bank. These policies have resulted in increased hardships for women microentrepreneurs among others in these nations. Although these states created additional programs to address the social dimensions of adjustment in these nations and to effectively combat the difficulties created by the SAPs, women microentrepreneurs were unaware of these policies and thus did not benefit from them. These women faced additional blockage with respect to credit, training, and other support services in these nations, since they lacked knowledge about the existence of these programs. Specific aspects of the SAPs, such as the retrenchment of formal sector workers, devaluation, and the removal of price controls and subsidies from vital social services have further disadvantaged these business-women. The effects of these policies can be readily seen in the escalating prices of commodities charged by wholesalers, increased competition from more firms entering a subsector as more workers are displaced from the formal sector, fewer customers, and the frequent inability of these women to gain import licenses for required inputs. To remedy this situation, these states need to implement new policies that involve fostering strong regional economic integration and domestic strategies to advance the position of women microentrepreneurs. Such efforts will further empower African women and increase their contributions to their families, their communities, and ultimately to national development.

NOTES

1. The respondents' anonymity was preserved in this study.

2. Many of the Nigerian entrepeneurs already provide apprenticeship training in sewing and hairdressing.

REFERENCES

Anyanwu, John. "President Babangida's Structural Adjustment Programme and Inflation in Nigeria." *Journal of Social Development in Africa,* 7 (1): pp. 5–24, 1992.

Bangura, Yusuf. "Crisis and Adjustment: The Experience of Nigerian Workers," In Bade Onimode, ed., *The IMF, The World Bank and The African Debt: The Social and Political Impact.* London: Zed Press, 1989.

Batezat, Elinor and Margaret Mwalo. *Women in Zimbabwe.* Harare: Southern Africa Political Economy Series (SAPES) Trust, 1989.

Biersteker, Thomas. *Reaching Agreement with the IMF: The Nigerian Negotiations.* Pittsburgh: University of Pittsburgh, Graduate School of Public and International Affairs, 1986.

Black, Jan Knippers. *Development in Theory and Practice.* Boulder, CO: Westview Press, 1991.

Clark, Gracia, ed. *Traders Versus the State.* Boulder, CO: Westview Press, 1988.

Downing, Jeanne. *GEMINI: Gender and the Growth and Dynamics of Microenterprises.* Prepared for the Growth and Equity Through Microenterprise, Investments and Institutions (GEMINI). Washington, D.C.: The Agency for International Development, 1990.

Downing, Jeanne. "The Growth and Dynamics of Women Entrepreneurs in Southern Africa." Paper presented at The Annual Meetings of the African Studies Association, St. Louis, Missouri, 1991.

Elson, Diane. "From Survival Strategies to Transformation Strategies: Women's Needs and Structural Adjustment." In Lourdes Beneria and Shelley Feldman, eds., *Unequal Burden: Economic Crises, Persistent Poverty and Women's Work.* Boulder: Westview Press, 1992.

Evans, Peter. *Dependent Development: The Alliance of Multinational, State and Local Capital in Brazil.* Princeton: Princeton University Press, 1979.

OSIRIM

Feldman, Shelley. "Still Invisible: Women in the Informal Sector." In Rita Gallin and Anne Ferguson, eds. *The Women and International Development Annual,* Vol. 2. Boulder, CO: Westview Press, 1991.

Gibbon, Peter. "The World Bank and African Poverty, 1973–91." *Journal of Modern African Studies* 30 (2): pp. 193–220, 1992.

Horn, Nancy. *The Culture, Urban Context and Economics of Women's Fresh Produce Marketing in Harare, Zimbabwe.* Unpublished Ph.D. Dissertation, Department of Anthropology, Michigan State University, 1988.

———. "Choice or Necessity? Women Selling Fresh Produce in Harare, Zimbabwe." Paper presented at the Annual Meetings of the African Studies Association, Baltimore, Maryland, 1990.

———. "Redefining Economic Productivity: Marketwomen and Food Provisioning in Harare, Zimbabwe." Paper Presented at the Annual Meetings of the African Studies Association, St. Louis, Missouri, 1991.

International Labor Office. *Employment, Incomes and Equality: A Strategy for Increasing Productive Employment in Kenya.* Geneva: International Labor Office, 1972.

Kadhani, Xavier. "The Economy: Issues, Problems and Prospects." In Mandaza, ed. *Zimbabwe: The Political Economy of Transition, 1980–1986.* Dakar, Senegal: Council for the Development of Economic and Social Research in Africa, 1986.

Kurian, George. *The Encyclopedia of the Third World.* New York: Facts on File, 1987.

Laishley, Roy. "Drought Dims Hope of Faster Recovery." *Africa Recovery* 6 (2) pp. 1, 6–7, 1992.

MacGaffey, Janet. "Women and Class Formation in a Dependent Economy: Kisangani Entrepreneurs." In Claire Robertson and Iris Berger, eds. *Women and Class in Africa.* New York: Africana Publishing Company, 1986.

Made, Patricia and Myorovai Whande. "Women in Southern Africa: A Note on the Zimbabwe Success Story." *Issues: A Journal of Opinion* XVII (2): pp. 26–28, 1989.

Mandaza, Ibbo, ed. *Zimbabwe: The Political Economy of Transition, 1980–1986.* Dakar, Senegal: Council for the Development of Social and Economic Research in Africa, 1986.

Mazumdar, Dipak. "The Urban Informal Sector." *World Development* 4, (8): pp. 655–679, 1976.

Moyo, Jonathan. "State Politics and Social Domination in Zimbabwe." *Journal of Modern African Studies* 30 (2): pp. 305–330, 1992.

Nash, June, and Maria Patricia Fernandez-Kelly, eds. *Women, Men and the International Division of Labor.* Albany: SUNY Press, 1983.

Osirim, Mary J. *Charactereistics of Entrepreneurship in Nigerian Industries That Started Small.* Unpublished Ph.D. Dissertation, Department of Sociology, Harvard University, 1990.

———. "Challenges in the Quest for Empowerment: Women in Small and Informal Sector Activities in Nigeria and Zimbabwe." Paper Presented at the First International Conference, "Women in Africa and the African Diaspora: Bridges Across Activism and the Academy," The University of Nigeria, Nsukka, 1992.

Otero, Maria. *Gender Issues in Small-Scale Enterprises.* Washington: The U.S. Agency for International Development, 1987.

145

OSIRIM

Portes, A. Alejandro, Manuel Castells and Lauren Benton, eds. *The Informal Economy: Studies in Advanced and Less Developed Societies.* Baltimore: Johns Hopkins University Press, 1989.

Robertson, Claire. *Sharing the Same Bowl: A Socioeconomic History of Women and Class in Accra, Ghana.* Bloomington: University of Indiana Press, 1984.

Saito, Katrine. "Women and Microenterprise Development in Zimbabwe: Constraints to Development." Paper presented at The Annual Meetings of the African Studies Association, St. Louis, Missouri, 1991.

Sanday, Peggy. "Female Status in the Public Domain." In Michelle Rosaldo and Louise Lamphere, eds. *Women, Culture and Society.* Stanford: Stanford University Press, 1974.

Schoepf, Brooke. "Gender Relations and Development: Political Economy and Culture." in Seidman, et. al., eds. *Twenty-First Century Africa: Towards a New Vision of Self-Sustainable Development.* Trenton: Africa World Press, 1992.

Seidman, Gay. "Women in Zimbabwe: Post-Independence Struggles." *Feminist Studies* 10 (3): 419–440, 1984.

Shannon, Thomas. *An Introduction to the World-System Perspective.* Boulder, CO: Westview Press, 1989.

Souza, Paulo, and Victor E. Tokman. "The Informal Sector in Latin America." *International Labour Review* 114 (3), 1976.

Stoneman, Colin. "The World Bank and the IMF in Zimbabwe." In Bonnie Campbell and John Loxley, eds., *Structural Adjustment in Africa.* London: Macmillan, 1989

———. and Lionel Cliffe. *Zimbabwe: Politics, Economics and Society.* London: Pinter Publishers, 1989.

Summers, Carol. *Native Policy, Education and Development: Social Ideologies and Social Control in Southern Rhodesia, 1890–1934.* Unpublished Ph.D. Dissertation, Department of History, Johns Hopkins Universitiy, 1991.

Sylvester, Christine. *Zimbabwe: The Terrain of Contradictory Development.* Boulder, CO: Westview Press, 1991.

The Training Aids Development Group. "Structural Adjustment: Changing the Face of Zimbabwe." *Read On* 3: 6–9, 1991.

United Nations Economic Commission on Africa (UNECA). *Economic Report on Africa 1990.* Addis Ababa: UNECA, 1990.

Wallerstein, Immanuel. *The Modern World System: Capitalist Agriculture and the Origins of the European World Economy in the Sixteenth Century.* New York: Academic Press, 1974.

Ware, Helen. "Polygyny: Women's Views in a Transitional Society, Nigeria, 1975." *Journal of Marriage and the Family,* 41 (1): 185–195, 1979.

Wisner, Ben. "Health of the Future/The Future of Health." In Ann Seidman and Frederick Anang, eds. *Twenty-First Century Africa: Towards a New Vision of Self-Sustainable Development.* Trenton, NJ: Africa World Press, 1992.

The World Bank. *World Development Report.* Washington, D.C.: The World Bank, 1990.

Young, Kate, Carol Wolkowitz and Roslyn McCullagh, eds. *Of Marriage and the Market: Women's Subordination Internationally and its Lessons.* London: Routledge and Kegan Paul, 1984.

GENDER AND THE GLOBAL HIV/AIDS PANDEMIC

Geeta Rao Gupta, Ellen Weiss, and Daniel Whelan

chapter 9

INTRODUCTION

THE GLOBAL pandemic of HIV/AIDS has emerged as a highly complex
and constantly evolving social as well as biological phenomenon that poses a
grave threat to societies and economies worldwide. Nowhere is this more
true than in developing nations, within which more than 91 percent of all
global HIV infections to date have occurred; heterosexual transmission of
HIV accounts for over 80 percent of those cases (Mann and Tarantola, 1994).
Of the estimated 20 million adults who have contracted HIV since the beginning of the pandemic, 8.7 million are women; in 1993 alone, more than
1.4 million women were newly infected, representing 40 percent of all new
infections that year (Mann and Tarantola, 1994). The male to female ratio of
HIV infection—which used to be about 3 to 1—continues to diminish
rapidly; many experts estimate that HIV infections among women have be-

gun to reach or even surpass infection among men in most areas of the world where the epidemic is well established.

Surveillance data reveal the degree to which HIV has penetrated vulnerable female populations—women with multiple partners and commercial sex workers. In the city of Bombay, for example, the seroprevalence rate for sex workers has increased from 5 percent in 1988 to over 30 percent in 1992 (Center for International Research, 1994). It was not until the late 1980s and early 1990s that public health experts began to pay more serious attention to HIV seroprevalence outside the so-called high-risk groups. Subsequently, data began to emerge in the early 1990s which showed startling increases of HIV infection among women who do not fit the generally accepted "high-risk" profile. The nomenclature of risk has changed: in some countries, especially in sub-Saharan Africa, the emerging incidence of HIV infection among low-risk women is so widespread that sex workers represent only a fraction of all women infected with HIV.

Seroprevalence data gathered at antenatal clinics since the mid-1980s demonstrate the pervasiveness of HIV infection among people considered to be at low biological or physiological risk for HIV infection. An antenatal clinic in Abidjan, Côte d'Ivoire, revealed an increase in HIV seroprevalence from 3 percent in 1986 to over 10 percent in 1990 (Center for International Research, 1994). In 1986, two percent of all women attending an antenatal clinic in Blantyre, Malawi, were HIV-positive—a figure that had risen to 31.6 percent by 1993 (Center for International Research, 1994). In São Paulo State, Brazil, HIV seroprevalence had risen from 0.2 percent in 1987 to 1.3 percent in 1990. Sentinal surveillance data from Bombay, India, reveals that in the three-year period from 1989 to 1992 seroprevalence among pregnant women rose from 0.1 percent to close to 1 percent (Center for International Research, 1994).

Although the specific costs posed by the rapid spread of HIV among women have not been analyzed, they are likely to be profound given the multifaceted roles women fulfill in every society. Insofar as they are mothers, food producers and processors, traders, and income earners, they make significant—albeit often overlooked and underrepresented—contributions to households and economies. Through their reproductive roles, for example, women's health is directly linked to child survival. This is particularly true in the context of HIV/AIDS, as women are becoming infected during their peak childbearing years, and it is estimated that there is a 25–40 percent chance that an infected mother will transmit the virus perinatally to her children in utero or during childbirth (Valleroy, Harris, and Way, 1990). As the pandemic among women of childbearing age progresses, it is inevitable that the advances that have been made over the past two decades in the area of child survival will be negated by increases in infant mortality due to HIV/AIDS.

Since the HIV/AIDS pandemic was first identified as a challenge to public health in the early 1980s, two basic questions have been central to research efforts designed to discover the reasons for the spread of the virus and possible solutions to prevent its spread: what are the biological, physiological, and behavioral factors that contribute to the epidemiology of HIV, and what prevention options can people adopt to protect themselves from becoming infected? Traditional health and medical research paradigms looked at the biological factors that figured into the spread of HIV, and more recently began to address the human dimension that plays such a significant role in fueling the pandemic—that "[p]eople, and specifically individual and collective human behavior, constitute the key dimension in the HIV equation" (Mann, Tarantola, and Netter, 1992).

The early focus on biological and physiological factors provided proof that women were more vulnerable to HIV infection than men. First, a woman's reproductive physiology makes her as much as five times more likely to contract HIV from an infected male partner than vice-versa (Panos Institute, 1990). Second, for younger women, the immaturity of the genital tract and the less proficient production of vaginal mucus provide less efficient barriers to HIV infection than is the case for older sexually active women (UNDP, 1993). Finally, women in developing countries are more likely to receive transfusions of blood or blood products as a result of anemia and blood loss during labor, miscarriage and induced abortion, and are therefore more likely to acquire HIV through transfusions of unsafe blood (Elias, 1991).

As for the behavioral side of the HIV equation, a paucity of data on women's sexual behavior revealed the gender bias inherent in the basic research questions that had driven HIV/AIDS social science research during the early years of the pandemic. Those efforts were (and, to a large degree, still are) targeted specifically to men, and the vast majority of women who were targeted were commercial sex workers. Nevertheless, it was becoming increasingly evident that women who could not be placed within a traditional "risk group," and had no known behavioral risk factors were contracting HIV, and that, therefore, the focus on individual behavior was not sufficient to explain women's risk.

Responding to the need for research into the behavioral, social, economic, and cultural correlates of women's risk for HIV infection, the International Center for Research on Women (ICRW), with support from the U.S. Agency for International Development, initiated the Women and AIDS Research Program in 1990.[1] The goal of the program was to provide a comprehensive understanding of women's HIV risk profiles. This goal was guided by the Center's belief that behavioral and social science research needed to look beyond biological factors to include not only an analysis of male and female sexual behavior, but more importantly, how sexual relationships are influenced by gender roles and relations.

149

GUPTA, WEISS, AND WHELAN

An examination of the HIV/AIDS prevention strategies upon which most behavior change interventions are based reveals the limitations of their usefulness for women. There are five basic recommendations that form the core of most HIV/AIDS control programs: (1) abstinence; (2) mutual monogamy; (3) reduction in the number of sexual partners; (4) consistent and correct condom use; and (5) accessing appropriate treatment for other sexually transmitted diseases (STDs). The success of these strategies in lowering an individual's risk of contracting HIV is predicated on two basic assumptions: (1) that any given sexual interaction is determined only by the intentions, emotions, and behaviors of the two individuals who participate in that interaction; and that, therefore, (2) reducing the risk of HIV infection is merely a matter of accepting and adopting HIV-preventive behaviors at the individual level. Research gathered through the Women and AIDS Research Program revealed another set of realities which, when taken into account, reveal the limitations of current prevention options. For one, there are powerful and broader contextual economic and sociocultural determinants of sexual behavior, and therefore of each sexual interaction. Second, and perhaps more obvious, is that women are put at risk not just by their *own* behavior, but by the behavior of their male partners, which in many instances is beyond women's control.

For many women around the world, sociocultural constructions of sexuality and male-female sexual interactions create formidable barriers to the adoption of risk-reducing behaviors. This matter is further complicated by the economic context of women's lives, in which the everyday assessment of what must be done to survive economically in the short run compromises the adoption of behaviors or practices which will reduce their risk of contracting HIV in the long run.

In examining a variety of contexts and populations within which women live, ICRW's Women and AIDS Research Program painted a vivid portrait of women's risk of HIV infection based on the realities of their lives. What is remarkable about the findings is how the stories that women tell about their sexual lives and experiences form common patterns and themes that transcend race, nationality, or culture. Arising from the synthesis of these findings are immediate and long-term recommendations to target the barriers women face in protecting themselves from HIV infection. Some of these findings have led to the development of interventions which currently are being developed and tested in the field as part of the second phase of the Women and AIDS Research program.

RECOMMENDATIONS TO REDUCE WOMEN'S RISK OF HIV INFECTION

The first set of recommendations presented below target the most immediate barriers of adopting risk-reduction behaviors—the knowledge and skills required to use a condom, to reduce the number of partners or ensure mutual monogamy, and to seek appropriate treatment for other sexually transmitted diseases.

Educate Women and Adolescent Girls About their Bodies and Sexuaity as Well as HIV and STDs

Studies carried out in India (George and Jaswal, 1994), Mauritius (Schensul et al., 1994), Guatemala (Bezmalinovic, DuFlon, and Hirschmann, 1994), Brazil (Goldstein, 1994), Thailand (Cash and Anasuchatkul, 1994), and South Africa (Abdool Karim and Morar, 1994) found that women and adolescent girls lack basic information about their reproductive anatomy and physiology, as well as STD/HIV prevention, and that this lack of information constrains their ability to adopt risk reduction behaviors. For example, some rural women from South Africa, and urban women from low income communities in India and Brazil, reported not liking condoms because they feared that if the condom fell off inside the vagina, it could get lost and perhaps travel to the throat and, if removed, might pull out the reproductive organs with it (Abdool Karim and Morar, 1994; George and Jaswal, 1994; Goldstein, 1994). For poor urban women in Bombay, India, lack of information limits their ability to identify abnormal gynecological symptoms that could signify a sexually transmitted infection (George and Jaswal, 1994). Even when women were aware of the symptoms of STDs, some took inappropriate measures for their treatment. For example, Jamaican women, working in the free trade zone of Kingston, generally were aware of the signs of STDs, but when they detected a symptom, some reported self-medicating themselves with antibiotics they shared with one another (Wyatt et al., 1994).

151

Educating women about their bodies also may help to limit the practice of certain high risk sexual behaviors. For example, some women from the South African study sample reported inserting drying agents into the vagina in the belief that the increased friction is sexually more satisfying for men (Abdool Karim and Morar, 1994). The agents used include herbs and roots, as well as scouring powders that can cause vaginal inflammation, lacerations, and abrasions, which significantly increase the efficiency of HIV transmission.

Accurate information on HIV transmission also will help women determine their level of risk. Data from the study conducted in Mauritius, for example, show that young unmarried women did not believe themselves to be at risk for pregnancy or STDs because they were engaging in "light sex," which they distinguished from sexual intercourse. In-depth questioning revealed, however, that "light sex" did in fact involve rubbing the penis against the vagina as well as some penetration, and therefore was a risky practice (Schensul et al., 1994). Young adolescent girls in Chiang Mai, Thailand, also believed that they were not risking infection because they were "good girls"

GUPTA, WEISS, AND WHELAN

and did not engage in sex unless they were in love with the man (Cash and Anasuchatkul, 1994). Clearly, women need to be better informed, because an accurate perception of risk is a critical first step in the process of behavior change.

Increase Women's Condom Literacy

Since condoms are the only HIV/AIDS prevention technology currently available, skills training workshops for girls and women on how to use a condom properly and on how to negotiate with a male partner to use one need to be designed and implemented. Existing condom promotion and education programs generally target sex workers and have not reached women who have to handle condom negotiation and use in more intimate or long-term relationships. Many women from the slums of Bombay, young women working in garment factories in Chiang Mai, Thailand, and secondary school girls in Khon Kaen, Thailand, had never before handled a condom and did not know how to use one (George and Jaswal, 1994; Thongkrajai et al., 1994; Cash and Anasuchatkul, 1994).

Innovative and creative methods must be developed to help desensitize women to the embarrassment of handling a condom and talking about sex. The research team in Chiang Mai, for example, developed a board game called anti-AIDS *siamsee* (which resembles the popular game *Monopoly*), in which players are rewarded with play money and free turns if they respond correctly to a set of questions on HIV/AIDS prevention. The team also developed a comic book about an invisible, flying condom who serves as a guardian angel for young women advising them on how to negotiate condom use. These materials, used as part of a peer education program for young female factory workers, have proven to be very popular in the factories and dorms where the girls work and live and have succeeded in helping them to overcome some of their reticence about talking about condoms and sex (Cash and Anasuchatkul, 1994).

Continue to Support Face-to-Face Education and Mass Media Campaigns that Destigmatize the Condom and Weaken its Association with Illicit Sex

Among women living in a rural area and a peri-urban squatter community of South Africa, nearly three-fourths of those interviewed indicated that a barrier to condom use was that it signified a lack of trust and intimacy (Abdool Karim and Morar, 1994). The studies in Brazil, Jamaica, and Guatemala reported similar findings: for those women, condoms are for having sex with "the other" and not with the stable partner. For women of Brazil and Guatemala the condom is for women "of the street, not the home"; in Jamaica, for "outside and not inside relationships"; and in South Africa, for "back pocket partners" (Goldstein, 1994; Bezmalinovic, DuFlon, and Hirschmann, 1994; Wyatt et al., 1994; Abdool Karim and Morar, 1994).

Provide Women with Opportunities for Individual Counseling and Group Interactions to Share Personal Experiences and Model New Behaviors.

Such opportunities enable women to discuss their sexual lives and the consequences of adopting or negotiating the risk reduction options, allow women to realize they are not alone with regard to their fears and worries, and permit them to adopt new behaviors in a non-threatening environment.

The young women factory workers in Mauritius, for example, reported feeling very alone with regard to their sexual lives. Because virginity among unmarried women is highly valued, these young women are afraid of asking peers or family members for information for fear that they will assume the girls are sexually active (Schensul et al., 1994). The researchers who conducted this study, as well as the researchers who conducted the studies with adolescent girls in Thailand, Brazil, and Zimbabwe, and with adult women in South Africa, Guatemala, and Brazil, reported that the process of data collection opened the floodgates—women were relieved they could finally talk to someone about their sexual concerns, and once they started talking, they demanded more information and additional opportunities to talk. They requested, for example, that focus group discussions or workshop sessions be continued past their scheduled hour or day of completion (Schensul et al., 1994; Cash and Anasuchatkul, 1994; Goldstein, 1994; Bassett and Sherman, 1994; Abdool Karim and Morar, 1994; Bezmalinovic, DuFlon, and Hirschmann, 1994; Vasconcelos et al., 1994). In the case of Chiang Mai, a research assistant on the team who was close in age to the girls being interviewed, began to get visits at home from young girls in the study sample who wanted to talk to her about their sexual experiences, fears, and worries (Cash and Anasuchatkul, 1994).

Providing opportunities for women to talk is a crucial step in overcoming the social norms that define a "good" woman as one who is ignorant about sex and passive in sexual interactions, and those that label interpartner communication on sex, particularly when initiated by the woman, as taboo. Such norms and beliefs make negotiating the use of a condom or raising the issue of monogamy a very difficult task. Women from Papua New Guinea, Jamaica, Guatemala, and India cited physical violence as a possible consequence of bringing up condoms or infidelity (Jenkins et al., 1994; Wyatt et al., 1994; Bezmalinovic, DuFlon, and Hirschmann, 1994; George and Jaswal, 1994). It is interesting that many women interviewed from Brazil and India reported choosing sterilization over other methods of contraception because they wanted to avoid discussing sex and contraception with their partners, often an unpleasant experience (Goldstein, 1994; George and Jaswal, 1994).

Make STD Services More Accessible and Available to Women by Integrating them with Family Planning and Maternal Health Services

Data from the program suggest that one of the reasons women do not seek treatment for STDs is that they are unaware of the signs and symptoms of

STDs (Bezmalinovic, DuFlon, and Hirschmann, 1994; George and Jaswal, 1994). Moreover, as reported by the study conducted with low-income women in Bombay, India, the vaginal discharge, itching, burning, and abdominal and back pain characteristic of STDs are accepted by many women as an inevitable part of their womanhood, or in the words of one woman, "it's a woman's lot" (George and Jaswal, 1994).

One way to overcome this reluctance to seek treatment is to integrate STD diagnosis and treatment services with family planning and maternal care services, which by all accounts are services women are more likely to regularly use. Regular screening procedures during a prenatal or a family planning visit could also help to identify asymptomatic STDs which increase women's risk of HIV infection.

Promote Sexual and Family Responsibility in Programs Targeted at Men and Adolescent Boys

The research results clearly indicate that women's ability to negotiate condom use or ensure fidelity in partnerships is largely dependent on men, because sociocultural norms give priority to male pleasure and control in sexual interactions. In São Paulo, Brazil, for example, some women factory workers reported engaging in anal sex not for their own pleasure but to satisfy their husbands. The women spoke of the pressure their partners exerted on them to engage in anal sex, and that their partners often threatened them with finding what they wanted on the street if the women did not consent (Goldstein, 1994).

The condoning of multiple partner relationships for men is another social norm that increases women's vulnerability to HIV. In many cultures both men and women believe that variety in sexual partners is essential to men's nature as men but is not appropriate for women. Adolescent boys in the Zimbabwean study recognize this double standard. As one young man said: "It feels O.K. about boys having more than one partner. But girls should be faithful to one boy" (Bassett and Sherman, 1994). Though many women expressed concern about the infidelities of their partners, they were resigned to their lack of control over the situation. Women from India, Jamaica, Papua New Guinea, Zimbabwe, and Brazil report that raising the issue of their partner's infidelity can jeopardize their physical safety and family stability (George and Jaswal, 1994; Wyatt et al., 1994; Jenkins et al., 1994; Bassett and Sherman, 1994; Goldstein, 1994).

Concern is rising in many communities with regard to the "sugar daddy" phenomenon, which involves young girls having sex with older men in exchange for money, gifts, or favors. When school girls in Zimbabwe were shown a picture of an apparently affluent man suggestively eyeing a young girl, the students acknowledged the existence of "sugar daddies" in their community, and one adolescent girl remarked: "These days there is ESAP (the

154

Zimbabwean structural adjustment program) so maybe this girl is not getting enough money from home, so she will be hoping to get a lot of money from a sugar daddy" (Bassett and Sherman, 1994).

There is a tremendous need, therefore, to design programs for men and boys that go beyond condom literacy by promoting partner communication and family responsibility. Some of the pregnant women sampled in the Guatemalan study felt that men would pay more attention to sexual responsibility if they were clearly told of the fatal consequences for their children. In addition, these women felt more empowered to discuss HIV/STD prevention with their husbands during pregnancy because they felt their partners would be more likely to listen and less likely to resort to physical violence because "I am carrying his child" (Bezmalinovic, DuFlon, and Hirschmann, 1994).

Support Biomedical Research Necessary to Develop a Female-Controlled Technology to Prevent HIV Transmission

The studies found that domestic violence and non-consensual sex is a reality in the lives of many of the women interviewed (Jenkins et al., 1994; Wyatt et al., 1994; Bezmalinovic, DuFlon, and Hirschmann, 1994; George and Jaswal, 1994). A repeated concern of women across the globe is the fact that the condom is ultimately a male-controlled device, and discussing its use raises the suspicion of infidelity—of both the woman and the man—which can result in violent interactions. Thus, these women fear bringing up condom use and monogamy for discussion with their partners. Moreover, women in Bombay, Guatemala City, and the highlands of Papua New Guinea pointed out that men often demand sex under the influence of alcohol, making condom-use negotiation an unrealistic option (George and Jaswal, 1994; Bezmalinovic, DuFlon, and Hirschmann, 1994; Jenkins et al., 1994). In addition, because the condom is a contraceptive, it interferes with many women's most cherished life goal—to be a mother.

One way to address these difficulties is to develop a technology that does not have contraceptive properties and that women can use without the knowledge or consent of their partners. The female condom, which is currently available, is unlikely to meet the needs of many women because it cannot be used surreptitiously nor does it permit conception. The diaphragm with nonoxynol-9, a female-controlled barrier method that can be used without partner consent, may be another alternative, although research on its effectiveness as a preventive technology for HIV remains inconclusive.[2] Moreover, the diaphragm, like the male and female condom, prevents pregnancy. The development of a microbicidal compound without spermicidal properties that can be used intravaginally without knowledge of the partner would be an ideal alternative for women who want to become pregnant and yet protect themselves from infection.[3] A microbicidal compound would also increase the range of available preventive technologies against HIV and other

155

GUPTA, WEISS, AND WHELAN

STDs for both men and women, and thereby be more likely to result in effective HIV prevention. It is important, however, that the development of a microbicide go hand in hand with efforts to change gender power dynamics and women's socioeconomic status, rather than be viewed as a technological fix in lieu of broader structural changes which affect women's lives.

ADDRESSING THE SOCIETAL CONTEXT OF VULNERABILITY TO HIV INFECTION

A second, broader set of recommendations target the economic and sociocultural determinants of women's risk for HIV infection, and highlight policies and programs to improve women's social and economic status in order to reduce their risk of HIV infection.

Provide Women with Economic Opportunities

Over the past few years, data from many studies have clearly shown that economic impoverishment is the root cause of women entering into multiple or temporary partnerships and for bartering sex for economic gain and survival (Schoepf et al., 1991; Bledsoe, 1990; Ngugi, 1991). For such women, "stick to your partner" or "love faithfully" messages are inappropriate to motivate behavior change. It is critical, therefore, that HIV prevention programs provide women for whom bartering sex is a matter of survival with alternative income-generating opportunities. Simultaneously, on a broader policy level, it is essential to improve women's economic status through appropriate measures, including access to credit, skills training, employment, and primary and secondary education.

Direct Resources Toward Strengthening Existing Community-Based Women's Organizations to Improve and Expand the Provision of Services

In addition to the provision of HIV/STD education, condom distribution, and STD diagnosis and treatment, the studies have highlighted the need for additional services which include support networks, income generation activities, and shelters for women who are victims of domestic violence, in order to facilitate individual behavior change in women. In many countries, community-based women's organizations already provide such services and address the micro- and macro-level socioeconomic determinants of women's risk through collective action by fighting legal, economic, and social discrimination. Typically, however, such groups struggle to survive with inadequate funds and technical resources. Findings from ICRW's Women and AIDS Research Program that highlight the extent to which women's health is compromised by lack of information, economic resources, support systems, and domestic violence underscore the urgent need to strengthen existing community-based women's groups to better meet women's needs.

GUPTA, WEISS, AND WHELAN

Design Programs Through Participatory Research that Mobilize
Communities to Question the Norms that Shape the Unequal Power
Balance in Relationships

HIV/AIDS, more than any other epidemic, has exposed the fatal consequences of women's powerlessness for all of society. The fatality of AIDS provides the undeniable moral and economic imperative to make the necessary
structural changes to empower women a reality.

Results from the Women and AIDS Research Program indicate that one
mechanism to begin a process of community mobilization around HIV/
AIDS issues is through the conduct of research. However, such a process of
questioning and change is more likely to occur if the research is of a particular kind: *action research,* in which the findings are translated into program intervention, and *participatory research,* which involves members of the community in the research process.

For example, while in the process of trying to ensure the participation of
adolescent girls in focus group discussions and educational sessions in an environment where young girls are very protected, the research team in Bombay held several consultations with male community leaders and elders and
with women who were held in high esteem within the community. The team
also organized a street play in the community which raised issues related to
women's low status and its implications for the health of families and communities. The play was interactive and required members of the community
to participate at several points as actors and discussants. As a result, not only
did the community elders permit their girls to attend the discussions and educational sessions, they encouraged them to attend; in the case of one particular father, who wanted to know why his daughter was not being included in
the sessions, even demanded that she attend. Moreover, the team reported that
the research process created an awareness about HIV/AIDS and a demand for
more information and services. More importantly, the research has set in mo-
tion a process of introspection on the link between women's status and the
health of communities (Bhende, 1994).

Participation of the community in the research process was achieved in
other ways as well. Research teams working in Brazil, Nigeria, and South
Africa involved members of the community in the design of the data collection instruments, discussion of the findings, and planning the interventions
(Vasconcelos et al., 1994; Uwakwe et al., 1994; Abdool Karim and Morar,
1994). In Papua New Guinea, South Africa, and Brazil, members of the study
populations participated as field investigators (Jenkins et al. 1994; Abdool
Karim and Morar, 1994; Vasconcelos et al., 1994).

As demonstrated through these experiences, participatory research leads to
community ownership of research findings and sustained participation in the
resulting actions. It is also an effective way to ensure the cooperation of the

GUPTA, WEISS, AND WHELAN

157

study population in responding to questions on sensitive and intimate topics such as gender relations and sexuality.

Promote the Collaboration of Researchers and Program Practitioners in the Conduct of Participatory Research

Experiences gained from ICRW's Women and AIDS Research Program indicate that linking researchers and program practitioners, such as those from non-governmental organizations, is an effective way to conduct participatory, action research that is useful and relevant for the community. Such partnerships help ensure the immediate utilization of findings for the design and implementation of interventions and maximize the skills and strengths of each partner, because each is responsible for what she or he does best. The researchers are responsible for the research design and methodology, and the program practitioners are responsible for ensuring that the goals of the research and the process of data collection meet the needs of the community and that the findings are translated into meaningful program interventions.

The program supported several collaborations of this kind. In Guatemala City, researchers from DataPro worked with the Asociación Guatemalteca para la Prevención y Control del SIDA (Guatemalan Association for the Prevention and Control of AIDS), a local non-governmental organization (NGO), to conduct an action research program targeting pregnant women. In Brazil, researchers affiliated with the University of Pernambuco worked with Casa de Passagem, an NGO in Recife to carry out a participatory research study with low-income adolescent girls.

In conclusion, ICRW's Women and AIDS Research Program has generated valuable, substantive data on women's lives and the factors that contribute to their risk of HIV and STDs. In addition, the program has elicited important lessons about the process of conducting applied research on sexuality and HIV/AIDS. But perhaps most importantly, by disseminating the findings of their research in-country, each of the research projects is serving as a catalyst for policy discussions at the national level on the critical importance of gender issues in HIV/AIDS prevention.

NOTES

1. The program supported 17 research projects in 13 countries worldwide: seven in Africa, five in Asia, and five in Latin America and the Caribbean. The studies collected data on topics related to women's and men's sexual behavior and women's vulnerability to HIV infection as well as opportunities for intervention. The study populations included men and women in community and workplace settings, adolescent girls and boys, community leaders, and members of traditional women's organizations.

2. Recent data show that the diaphragm used in conjunction with nonoxynol-9

does offer protection against cervical infection, including gonorrhea, trichomonoas and chlamydia (Rosenberg and Gollub, 1992; Cates and Stone, 1992).

3. The advantages of such a compound the possibilities to develop it are discussed in a recent paper by Dr. Christopher Elias and Lori Heise, entitled "The Development of Microbicides: A New Method of HIV Prevention for Women" (The Population Council, Programs Division, Working Papers, No. 6, 1993).

REFERENCES

Abdool Karim, Quarraisha and Neetha Morar. "Women and AIDS in Natal KwaZulu, South Africa: Determinants to the Adoption of HIV Protective Behaviour." *Women and AIDS Research Program Research Report Series.* Washington, D.C.: International Center for Research on Women, 1994.

Bassett, Mary T. and Judy Sherman. "Female Sexual Behavior and the Risk of HIV Infection: An Ethnographic Study in Harare, Zimbabwe." *Women and AIDS Research Program Research Report Series.* Washington, D.C.: International Center for Research on Women, 1994.

Bezmalinovic, Beatrice, Wende Skidmore DuFlon, and Annelise Hirschmann. "Guatemala City Women: Empowering a Vulnerable Group to Prevent HIV Transmission." *Women and AIDS Research Program Research Report Series.* Washington, D.C.: International Center for Research on Women, 1994.

Bhende, Asha. "Evolving a Model for AIDS Prevention Education among Underprivileged Adolescent Girls in Urban India." *Women and AIDS Research Program Research Report Series.* Washington, D.C.: International Center for Research on Women, 1994.

Bledsoe, Caroline. "The Politics of AIDS, Condoms, and Heterosexual Relations in Africa: Recent Evidence from the Local Print Media." In W. Penn Handwerker, ed. *Births and Power: Social Change and the Politics of Reproduction.* Boulder: Westview Press, 1990.

Cash, Kathleen and Bupa Anasuchatkul. "Experimental Educational Interventions for AIDS Prevention Among Northern Thai Single Female Migratory Adolescents." *Women and AIDS Research Program Research Report Series.* Washington, D.C.: International Center for Research on Women, 1994.

Cates, Jr., Willard and Katherine M. Stone. "Family Planning: The Responsibility to Prevent both Pregnancy and Reproductive Tract Infections." In A. Germain, K.K. Homes, P. Piot, and J.N. Wasserheit, eds. *Reproductive Tract Infections: Global Impact and Priorities for Women's Reproductive Health.* New York: Plenum Press, 1992.

Center for International Research. "HIV/AIDS Surveillance Database." Washington, D.C: U.S. Bureau of the Census, 1994.

Elias, Christopher J. "Sexually Transmitted Diseases and the Reproductive Health of Women in Developing Countries." *Programs Division Working Paper No. 5.* New York: The Population Council, 1991.

———— and Lori Heise. "The Development of Microbicides: A New Method of HIV Prevention for Women." *Programs Division Working Papers No. 6.* New York: The Population Council, 1993.

George, Annie and Surinder Jaswal. "Understanding Sexuality: Ethnographic Study of

Poor Women in Bombay." *Women and AIDS Research Program Research Report Series.* Washington, D.C.: International Center for Research on Women, 1994.

Goldstein, Donna. "The Culture, Class, and Gender Politics of a Modern Disease: Women and AIDS in Brazil." *Women and AIDS Research Program Research Report Series.* Washington, D.C.: International Center for Research on Women, 1994.

Jenkins, Carol and the National Sex and Reproductive Research Team. "Women and the Risk of AIDS: A Study of Sexual and Reproductive Knowledge and Behavior in Papua New Guinea." *Women and AIDS Research Program Research Report Series.* Washington, D.C.: International Center for Research on Women, 1994.

Mann, Jonathan and Daniel Tarantola. "AIDS in the World: Redefining the Pandemic." Paper presented at X International Conference on AIDS, August 5, Yokohama, Japan, 1994.

——— and Thomas Netter, eds. *AIDS in the World.* Cambridge: Harvard University Press, 1992.

Ngugi, Elizabeth. "Education and Counseling Interventions." Paper presented at the 18th Annual NCIH International Health Conference, Arlington, Virginia, 1991.

Panos Institute. *Triple Jeopardy: Women and AIDS.* London: Panos Institute, 1990.

Rosenberg, Michael J. and Erica L. Gollub. "Methods Women Can Use that May Prevent Sexually Transmitted Disease, Including HIV." *American Journal of Public Health* 82 (11): 1,473–78, 1992.

Runganga, A.M. Pitts and J. McMaster. "The Use of Herbal and Other Agents to Enhance Sexual Experience." *Social Science and Medicine* 35:1037–42, 1992.

Schensul, Stephen L., Geeta Oodit, Jean J. Schensul, Sadhna Seebuluck, Uma Bhowon, Jay Prakash Aukhojee, Satinder Rogobur, Bernadette Lee Koye Kwat, Shirley Affock. "Young Women, Work, and AIDS-Related Risk Behavior in Mauritius." *Women and AIDS Research Program Research Report Series.* Washington, D.C.: International Center for Research on Women, 1994.

Schoepf, Brooke Grundfest, Walu Engundu, Rukarangira Wa Nkera, Payanzo Ntsomo, and Claude Schoepf. "Gender, Power, and Risk of AIDS in Zaire." In M. Turshen, ed., *Women and Health in Africa.* Trenton, NJ: Africa World Press, 1991.

Thongkrajai, Earmporn, John Stoeckel, Monthira Kievying, Chintana Leelakraiwan, Soiy Anusornteerakul, Kanha Keitisut, Pramote Thongkrajai, Narong Winiyakul, Petchara Leelaphanmetha, Christopher Elias. "AIDS Prevention Among Adolescents: An Intervention Study in Northeast Thailand." *Women and AIDS Research Program Research Report Series.* Washington, D.C.: International Center for Research on Women, 1994.

United Nations Development Programme (UNDP). *Young Women: Silence, Susceptibility and the HIV Epidemic.* New York, 1993.

Uwakwe, C.B.U., A.A. Mansaray, and G.O.M. Ohwu. "A Psycho-Educational Program to Motivate and Foster AIDS Preventive Behaviours Among Female Nigerian University Students." *Women and AIDS Research Program Report-in-Brief.* Washington, D.C.: International Center for Research on Women, 1994.

Valleroy, Linda A., Jeffrey R. Harris, and Peter O. Way. "The Impact of HIV-1 Infection on Child Survival in the Developing World." *AIDS 1990* 4: 667–72, 1990.

Vasconcelos, Ana, A. Neto, A Valença, C. Braga, M. Pacheco, S. Dantas, V. Simonetti, and V. Garcia. "AIDS and Sexuality among Low-Income Adolescent Women in Recife,

Brazil." *Women and AIDS Research Program Research Report Series.* Washington, D.C.: International Center for Research on Women, 1994.

Wyatt, Gail E., M.B. Tucker, D. Eldemire, B. Bain, E. Le Franc, D. Simeon, and C. Chambers. "Female Low Income Workers and AIDS in Jamaica." *Women and AIDS Research Program Research Report Series.* Washington, D.C.: International Center for Research on Women, 1994.

161

AFRICAN WOMEN'S STRATEGIES TO ADVANCE HOUSEHOLD FOOD SECURITY

Ruth K. Oniang'o

chapter 10

INTRODUCTION

RURAL WOMEN'S contributions to agricultural productivity are now the talk of the day. Yet while women's contributions are significant, they have no say in making food policy. Produce from land is credited to the owner of the land, and while women in many African societies are not customarily recognized as land owners, men get the credit for women's efforts. Additionally, food policy focuses on cash crops—an area dominated by men and in which women are disadvantaged due to lack of capital and collateral investment—to the neglect of subsistence food production which is still a predominantly female occupation. In fact, the shift from subsistence to cash crop production is said to be linked with the heightening food crisis on the African continent. This assertion remains controversial.

Nevertheless, women continue to play a major role in ensuring food security at the household level. This has major implications for national food security, as over 70 percent of the population in many African countries is rural-based. For the urban woman, much of what is consumed within her household is actually produced by the rural woman. This study will thus focus on the efforts of the rural peasant women who not only grow and harvest the different foods, but also ensure that this food is made available to the household throughout the year.

Before we proceed with this discussion, let us define the two most important terms in this paper: *food security,* and *household.*

DEFINITIONS

Food security means that every individual has access to a sustainable food supply not only in quantity but also in quality, so that nutrient requirements are satisfied to maintain an active and healthy life. Even the Food and Agricultural Organization (FAO) has recently broadened its definition: "to ensure that all people at all times have both physical and economic access to the basic food they need" (FAO, 1983). In this context, food security is seen "to have three specific aims: ensuring production of adequate food supplies, maximizing stability in the flow of supplies, and securing access to available supplies on the part of those who need them" (FAO, 1983). Air, water, and food are people's most basic physical needs. Unfortunately, households do not always prioritize food. Access to food is a basic human right, and any democratic government would see to the fulfillment of this need not only to meet its constitutional responsibilities, but also to recognize people's rights and welfare.

The household in most societies is the smallest planning unit for production and consumption. Household sizes vary from community to community, and may also vary in terms of what is recognized as the functional unit. Basically, a household is a unit comprised of individuals who reside permanently together most of the time, have common resources, and share responsibilities. Rural and urban households are very different in seeking food security. Whereas most rural households produce food in ways which heavily tax women, urban households usually use men's income to purchase food.

Rural and urban survival strategies vary drastically. Rural households assess the food situation, make decisions about the amount and quality of land to be cultivated, the types of crops to be grown, when and how to plant, how to harvest and store, and how to utilize and dispose of the produce. Throughout this process, the focus is on ensuring household food self-sufficiency. Other considerations such as generating income from the produce or sharing with relatives who may be food-poor are important but secondary. A.O. Wagara (1988), writing on "household food security as a nutritional strategy," contends that households will not be able to achieve their goals except in the presence of agriculturally productive resources. Thus, we are concerned about the kind of environment and infrastructure that will guarantee continuous access to food that is adequate in both quality and quantity. For the rural community, such food must be produced, often on families' own land.

AFRICA'S FOOD CRISIS

The food crisis in Africa continues. Millions of people are dying, starving, and suffering from malnutrition. There seems to be no solution. Who will solve the problem? What role can the affected people themselves play? Food security must be addressed at the macro continental and national levels.

Since the early 1970s, the rate of growth in food production has lagged behind that of food demand in 32 of 41 sub-Saharan countries (Dey, 1984). High population growth (averaging 3 percent or more per annum), a high rate of urbanization at an increase of nearly 6 percent per annum, and increasing food demands due to rising real incomes have upset the food balance equation. During this time, food production has been far from steady. It has been adversely affected by protracted drought, precarious and unpredictable rainfall and other calamities including bush fires, desertification, attacks on crops and livestock by pests and diseases, civil strife and refugee problems, a shortage of production inputs, and short-sighted socioeconomic policies. A 1989 World Bank report paints an extremely grim picture. It states that to achieve food security for sub-Saharan Africa, 350 million new jobs must be created, and to register a modest improvement for the 1.1 billion inhabitants by the year 2020 the economies of the countries affected must grow by at least 4 percent annually. Is this possible?

In 1980, the Lagos Plan of Action called on "Governments to recognize women as vital instruments for solving the food crisis and make deliberate provisions to upgrade their skills and lessen their labors" (FAO, 1983). Similarly, at the global expert consultation on Women in Food Production held in Rome in December 1983, it was recommended that "greater attention and support be given to women's roles in food security at the household level; and to the policy and action implications this would require at the national level" (Dey, 1984). These recommendations have yet to be fully implemented.

If it is not possible to solve the food crisis globally, or even continentally, perhaps it can be attempted at the household/community level. After all, as was pointed out before, measures must begin at these levels before projecting globally. Food security is indeed a process that involves and affects households as single entities and as part of a community, nation, and world. The process that will eventually culminate in national level food self-sufficiency is, therefore, a complex one that affects families in a variety of ways.

WOMEN'S ROLES

Families and particularly women have employed a number of strategies to ensure household food security. Such strategies have included growing both primary and secondary staple foods, gathering wild fruits and vegetables,

165

ONIANG'O

planting drought-resistant crops, keeping small animals, and engaging in a wide variety of activities to generate income for household survival. The use of child labor is also an important food security strategy, not withstanding its negative implications for child development and survival.

Meeting household food needs has always been women's primary concern. Their roles as food caretakers have become even more critical since the introduction of the cash economy and subsequent relocation of men to areas where they earn a cash income. Such relocation has in many instances been geographical, thus leaving many female-maintained households with little capability to adequately produce and process family food. Worse still, women's time and energy get diverted to cash crop production and other activities intended to enhance the general well-being of the family.

In most traditional settings, the gendered division of labor allowed for complementary roles between men and women. Men prepared land for planting, while the women processed the food after harvesting. Some tasks were, shared, however. Marketing was done by both men and women, although they marketed different kinds of produce. Women, however, continued to shoulder the burden of extra "women's labor." This practice continues in some of the still-traditional communities. For example, 15 years of data from Kenya show that while women spend just as much or more time as men on cash crops such as coffee, tea, pyrethrum, and cotton, they spend at least 18 times more time on additional tasks such as water and firewood collection, food preparation, house cleaning and childcare (RKO, 1978, 1979). Women also spend more time tending to livestock and dairying than men. This is in part because men are leaving home to look for jobs or are just "idling" around; thus, most tasks get levied on women. For example, in some Southern African countries most men go to South Africa for work (U.N. Economic Commission for Africa 1988).

Women continue to hew wood for fuel and draw water. Women contribute to the family food base not only by producing the main family foods, but also by employing strategies that are meant to enhance food security at the most critical times.

Women and Natural Resources

Women have always taken advantage of the natural resources by collecting wild fruits and vegetables, and gardening vegetables along the river banks. Women also often gather wild foods and firewood on their way home from their farms.

These wild fruits and vegetables have unique nutritive attributes and are indeed survival foods for Africans, especially during droughts and pre-harvest seasons. With the environmental degradation, many rivers have become seasonal while forests have either receded or disappeared altogether, thus destroying all avenues for access to firewood, water, fruits, vegetables, and medicinal herbs. This trend has not only reduced women's capacity to meet family food needs, but also their capacity to address other aspects of survival.

Women and Supplementary Staples

In the agricultural sector, women are more likely than men to grow a greater diversity of crops which mature and become available as food at various times during the year. Women are also more conscious of the food crops to fall back on during periods of cereal deficits. Women will, for example, grow supplementary staples and snack-type foods for children, which include root and tuberous crops such as yams, sweet potatoes, cassava, and bananas. The "famine" crops include cassava and indigenous cereals like millet and sorghum—crops which thrive under harsh ecological conditions. The women also cultivate other essential foods like legumes and oil seeds, and also maintain gardens to regularly provide vegetables which are served as relish with the staple foods.

Secondary crops are usually grown in small fields near the major cash crops or planted at different seasons from the major food crops. In some cases, they are intercropped with the major crops. All this makes farming sense because it balances soil nutrients, provides ground cover water retention, controls erosion, helps reduce crop diseases and pests, economizes on energy and time, and provides well-balanced meals. Women often plant crops early so that they can mature ahead of the main crops and thus provide food before the main harvest season. Such practices have been documented in Gambia (Haswell, 1975), in the Ivory Coast (Capasso, 1981), and in Zimbabwe (Callear, 1983).

167

In rural Kenya, kitchen gardens have always been maintained to enhance food security at the household level since they provide vegetables throughout the year, even during the dry season. The gardens usually contain some drought-resistant plants. The other advantage of the kitchen garden is that it is small, near the house and can utilize waste water and garbage, therefore making it possible to get good yields. Extension workers have capitalized on the traditional practice of maintaining kitchen gardens and are working with women's groups not only to sustain this very noble practice, but also to enrich it. As well as providing a variety of foods on a continuous basis, kitchen gardens can easily serve an income-generating function.

In the Kakamega District of Kenya, surveys show that even during the dry season, about half of all households had kitchen gardens growing different kinds of vegetables (SIDA, 1987). Women also grow medicinal herbs in these gardens for treating a multiplicity of conditions including coughs, nasal and chest congestion, and diarrhea.

Women and Animal Production

Women's roles in animal production depend on the habitation patterns of the particular society. Nonetheless, in all types of animal production systems,

ONIANG'O

women play a major role in dairy processing. Women also keep small animals such as poultry, goats, and sheep. Women, too, are the main actors in marketing the fresh produce such as milk and eggs, as well as the processed products.

Increasingly, women own large farm animals. With the introduction of zero-grazing, more and more women own cattle, since this system does not require taking the animals from location; the animals are mainly sedentary and are fed and given water in the family compound. Whereas women often do inherit animals from family, they are beginning to independently purchase animals as a form of investment. The animals provide food and economic security as well as enhance the social standing of the women who purchase them. For example, among the Fulani of Nigeria, women process dairying products, sell the supplies, and purchase food for the family. In other words, women here have considerable control over the animals and the incomes that accrue from them. On the other hand, nomadic women in Kenya also process and sell milk products, but they generally give the proceeds to their husbands (Chavangi and Hansen, 1983).

Fish, available either naturally or from constructed ponds, is a major source of food security. Men do most marine fishing and inland fish production throughout the continent. Women may hire boats and pay fishermen to catch fish for them. Mostly, however, women play a significant (though not exclusive) role in smoking, drying, and marketing the fish. In some countries, such as the Ivory Coast, Togo, the United Republic of Cameroon, and Nigeria, males are completely absent from this process. In other countries like Madagascar and Kenya, both men and women market fresh and processed fish. In a few cases, women are involved in small-scale fish harvesting. For example, in the Central African Republic, Congo, Ivory Coast, Sierra Leone, Togo, the United Republic of Cameroon, and Zaire, women traditionally harvest fish in small streams, lakes, and swampy areas at the end of the dry season. In Kenya, women harvest fish in those areas which are routinely flooded. In situations such as these, sophisticated boats or even nets are not required (UN/ECA, 1974). Studies demonstrate that where women are involved in fish processing and marketing, there is little interference by husbands in women's financial affairs (UN/ECA, 1974).

Women and Post-Harvest Activities

Processing and storing produce is critical to achieving food security at both national and local levels. Sound practices in these areas ease price variations and assure more stable and sustained supplies. In most sub-Saharan African countries, storage facilities are inadequate and ineffective, while village-level food processing is completely undeveloped. It is estimated that one-fourth of all food produced is lost to spoilage, insects, and rodents. In Kenya, research has shown that most on-farm storage facilities are either lacking or inadequate (Maritim, 1985). Because of these constraints, the farmer hastens to sell

ONIANG'O

food at harvest time only to have to purchase it later in the season at much higher prices.

The processing of most food products, be they for sale or for home consumption, falls heavily on women. Women process the cereals and supplementary staples for storage and marketing; manage vegetables from planting through to processing; and process fish and dairy products. Usually, however, men must construct key storage facilities for staple foods. In the absence of such structures, the woman finds herself in a dilemma—she may have enough food to last until the next harvest season, but if she has nowhere to store it, the food may have to be marketed or disposed of (either by joint decision or by the man's decision). She will still be required to ensure the feeding of the family even in times of deficit. Sometimes women operate collectively to process and keep seed for next season's planting, and also keep some foodstuffs to market at a time when the exchange rates favor them.

Food processing procedures continue to be time and energy consuming. Little has been done to mechanize some of the tedious activities such as dehulling major grains such as sorghum, millet, and legumes (IDRC, n.d.). Nonmechanization of these procedures may create consumer demand for commercially processed non-indigenous cereals such as wheat, maize, and rice, which are comparatively less nutritious. Using these nonindigenous foods also negates efforts towards sustainability, as indigenous foodstuffs go to waste. Developing efficient and economical village-level milling systems would give products improved consumer appeal and thus increase the demand for locally available indigenous foodstuffs which the community produces.

169

Women and Personal Produce Plots

In many societies, both men and women cultivate personal fields from which they meet certain obligations to the household, clan, or community, and also finance personal expenses. Women reserve their personal produce to feed guests or workers recruited to work on their larger farms, for ceremonial obligations, and for seed, sale, or consumption at critical times. Such produce, therefore, significantly enhances the food and economic security of these women. The ability to operate a personal plot boosts a woman's morale as it improves her social standing and confidence.

Women and Food Preparation and Distribution

Women are the lifeline of society. Their roles as family caretakers hinge on providing food and childcare. A woman's traditional obligations as a wife and mother are to care for the infants and young children, rear her daughters, and provide the family's food and basic necessities (GOK/UNICEF, 1984). Fathers and other male elders are responsible for boys' upbringing beginning at age eight. Women are the "gatekeepers to child welfare," as they have primary responsibilities for the health and well-being of children. These responsibili-

ONIANG'O

ties include providing a clean and safe environment, fetching water, and accessing health services. The tasks associated with childcare have increased: more children survive and births are closely spaced, while modern-day childcare practices often require additional time, energy, and financial resources. Childcare is an awesome responsibility, since child health and nutritional status represent the well-being and general pace of development for any community. A healthy child population will unquestionably culminate in a healthy adult population. Traditional responsibilities of women thus remain largely the same, but the activities have increased in scope and complexity as a result of economic, social, and cultural dynamics. Women now face demands that exceed their available time, energy, and income.

In relation to food preparation and distribution, women are the principal actors; they decide how food should be distributed once it has been accessed. They make choices from among foods available in the market and in the home, and make the necessary allocations to individual family members. Their role enhances their knowledge about the quality and uses of different foods, enabling them to distinguish between varieties for characteristics such as taste, storage life, digestibility, and cooking time (Clark, 1985). With increased awareness, they can distinguish between essential and detrimental cultural beliefs and practices on child health.

Proper community education is essential. In Kenya, Home Economics extension workers have very close interactive links with grassroots women's groups all over the country. These professionals focus on nutrition and food utilization. Nutrition field workers in the Ministry of Health (MOH) teach nutrition education to mothers attending MOH clinics. Mothers are urged to participate actively in these programs rather than be passive listeners. New approaches get mothers and fathers involved in community weighing exercises where they learn about the development progress of their children by using a child health card. Extension workers and researchers are encouraged to put women at the forefront of their activities.

There is a large body of literature indicating that when women control household income, they are more likely to spend it on food. Women's control over food and economic issues at the household level results in better health and nutritional status of the children. Recent studies from southwestern Kenya comparing preschoolers among sugar and nonsugar producing households found that children in women-headed households had significantly better nutritional status than children from other households (Kennedy, 1988). Women should always be key players in development projects, as their participation and meaningful involvement affect the wider community.

IMPEDIMENTS TO WOMEN'S ROLES IN THE FOOD CHAIN

Women have played crucial survival roles to sustain society while their contributions have been quietly—though not publicly—recognized. Women themselves have had considerable and almost exclusive control over some spheres of operations; such operations have enhanced their self-confidence and status in society. Subordinate as they were, they felt fulfilled in their positions in a situation which appeared appropriate and functional at the time. Many of the impediments to women's development are new phenomena, brought about by inevitable sociocultural/economic changes and the failure by development proponents and activists to understand and build on traditional structures.

We shall now examine some of the constraints that have hampered women's progress and kept them out of mainstream development.

Monetization of the Economy

Monetization of the African economies hurt women. The cash earned from labor always found its way into the pockets of men, having devastating consequences for the family. Monetization was also the root cause of accelerated migration from rural to urban areas by able-bodied males in search of paid employment on the settler farms, which heavily depend on a cheap labor supply from the rural areas. This not only destabilized families, but also destabilized the complex mechanisms described earlier which ensured food security.

Rural-Urban Migration

Rural-urban migration and sometimes rural-rural migration may seem desirable—it relieves pressure on food supplies during periods of scarcity, reduces rural unemployment, and is likely to provide useful remittances. However, this migration increasingly creates more problems than it solves in both the rural and urban areas. With diminishing job opportunities and deteriorating living conditions, urban areas are no longer the "greener pastures" they used to be. The rural areas, on the other hand, continue to suffer from labor shortages as the most active and skilled men depart. The number of female-maintained households is increasing, while remittances to the rural areas can no longer be expected amidst increasing unemployment and rising costs of living in the urban areas. The result has been a drastic reduction in food yields in the rural areas, a phenomenon which is felt not only at the household/community level but also at the national level.

Cashcropping

While cash crops provide cash income for school fees and medical bills, essential nonfood items, transportation, and starting businesses, cash crops can also cause problems. For women, cashcropping competes for labor and land that would otherwise be used to produce food for household consumption.

Before the introduction of cocoa (which is now the leading cash crop in the Southern Volta region of Ghana), a complex food system existed in which

171

ONIANG'O

men were the main producers of the staple food, yam, while their wives assisted with weeding and harvesting. When cocoa was produced, it was planted on the best land while food crop production was moved to the less fertile lands, a move that posed a threat to household food security.

With men devoting more of their time and energy to cocoa production, women have become more responsible for food production, working on their own fields and also doing a great deal of planting, weeding and harvesting on their husbands' food-producing fields. The result has been a shift from yam production to the cultivation of the less labor-intensive but also less nutritious cassava, certainly a major detrimental shift in the people's dietary habits (Bukh, 1979). In a related case in Upper Volta, the tenure for land ownership for major cashcrop production was allocated to men only. Despite their tradition of growing household staple and secondary crops on their own plots, women were not given any personal plots (Dey, 1984).

Cash crops enjoy considerable inputs in terms of credit, fertilizer and marketing advice. Even where women contribute extensively to the labor requirements of cash crops, such services are usually channelled through men. In some cases, even women cashcrop farmers miss out on these services as they are directed to the male clientele. This leaves women unaware of possible improvements. For example, whereas technical advice was given to male rice farmers in the Ivory Coast when they received their fertilizer supply, their female counterparts were given no information regarding the use of fertilizers. As a result, they either threw the fertilizer away or had men use it on their cocoa crops (Dey, 1984).

Agricultural Intensification Programs

Technology transfers intended to increase agricultural yields have mixed results, because the intention and the practical outcome in implementing the schemes do not augur well. For example, attempts to transfer to Africa labor-saving equipment, new seeds, and agronomic practices developed in Asia have all met with disappointing results because of their inappropriateness to African conditions. In addition to technical problems, such as new crop species being unable to withstand Africa- specific diseases, the technologies failed to address sociocultural institutions and practices in food production and consumption.

Services have been channelled through men even where women are the main users. This displaced attention demonstrates a complete disregard for women's time allocation patterns. There are peak periods for certain agricultural activities which require long working hours for women.

A project in Nigeria aimed at improving yields in a variety of food crops appropriately illustrates the problem. The greatest demand in women's time fell during harvesting and post-harvest activities. Women do farm work for more than 25 days a month, three months of the year. The project's success

ONIANG'O

depended on women working 25 days a month for seven months, instead of the usual 25 days a month for 3 months; this was clearly unrealistic and un-workable. The men, on the other hand, never provided nor were they willing to provide in the future more than 15 days of work in any month of the year (Burfisher and Norestein, 1982). Women are by far the key actors in food production at great personal sacrifice.

Constraints in Getting Into Big Business and Policy

Women are invisible in big business, while the majority of vendors in small markets are women who usually founded the markets. Despite the fact that women can only engage in small business where the returns are low and competition stiff, they retain the spirit to keep going.

Both global and national business policies are beyond the comprehension of the small-scale and usually semi-literate rural market women. Yet it is these women whose involvement in the diversity of market activities contributes most to household and community-level food security. Their vulnerability is further accentuated by lack of any form of advocacy. Even those women in leadership positions may be unable to adequately represent the views of the rural market women, given the differences in their socioeconomic back-grounds.

The obstacles to women's effective participation in development lie in the complex mechanisms governing behavior patterns in African societies. In African indigenous societies, harmony was traditionally insured through "consensus," in which women were almost always subordinate to men. This aspect of tradition persists. Even in Lesotho, where women have better educa-tional opportunities than their male counterparts and participation in the job market is far better than in some African countries, the policymaking and managerial ranks are still male preserves.

Whatever their status, women are more sensitive to the needs of the fami-ly—particularly those that have to do with health and nutrition. Women spend their incomes on feeding and attending to the health of family mem-bers. Women have thus been identified as strategic actors for development, and agencies have begun to invest in women's income-generating projects.

CONCLUSIONS

Women have been described as "the life line of society," the "richest human resources," and the "backbone of society." Women are the very foundation of society while they prop up their male household heads. Women plan and manage a way into the future for their children and families, making careful decisions and avoiding jeopardizing their families' socioeconomic status. They are versatile and multipurpose actors and advisors in the home, roles which make them an extremely rich resource.

Women's lack of recognition and the failure to provide an environment for

ONIANG'O

the realization of their potential are tragic. In fact, most development programs initiated to help women have been counterproductive. Many community development advocates and donor agencies now recognize that programs must address the specific needs of women through participatory approaches.

The success of these programs depends on the involvement of consumers of goods and services, so that the beneficiaries, male and female, fully identify themselves with the intended programs. Leaving out men in the design and implementation of projects targeted to benefit women has created serious household conflict, disturbing traditional decisionmaking and production/consumption patterns.

Men are also a potentially rich resource and should be involved in ensuring household food security; women stand to benefit even if support from men is only moral. Development experts should build on traditional structures where these appear to be viable and functional, while they also work to change societal attitudes towards women. Only by giving due respect and support to women as equally useful members of society can we create sustainable development.

To be most effective, development programs should incorporate the following:

- Assisting women in their efforts to make money, since their money contributes more substantially to family survival. Examples of such support would include commercialization of women's produce such as indigenous fruits, vegetables, and supplementary staples; support of income-generating activities that do not threaten other crucial roles directly related to nurturing; and helping women to cope with these tasks by providing the necessary support at both the household and community levels.

- Efforts should be made to train women to venture into big business, while women in small trade should be encouraged to expand their activities to make them more profitable.

- Access to technology and information transfer and resources at all stages of the food systems chain. Such support would include designing of energy and time-saving implements for tedious tasks; providing timely extension information and inputs; facilitating access to credit and performance monitoring; providing child support arrangements; aggressively tackling the post-harvest processes to minimize food losses and improve on-farm storage; and providing a mutually workable arrangement that will ensure fair distribution of work loads and utilization of cashcrop income.

- Creating other opportunities for non-farm employment during the farming off-season, and to generate income for those without land.

- Advocating recognition of and support for women's crucial role in the survival of any nation, community, and household.

174

ONIANG'O

- Supporting women's education. Only when literate and aware can women create change in agricultural practices, health, and nutrition. Education is also fundamental to women's entry to decisionmaking bodies at the various leadership levels.

REFERENCES

Association of African Women in Research and Development. Occasional Paper Series No. 3. Dakar, Senegal: AAWORD, 1985.

Bukh, J. *The Village Woman in Ghana.* Uppsala, Sweden: Scandinavia Institute of African Studies, 1973.

Burfisher, M. and Norestein, N. *Sex Roles in the Nigerian TIV Farm Household and Differential Impact of Development Projects.* Washington, D.C.: International Economics Division, US Department of Agriculture, 1982.

Callear, D. *Women and Coarse Grain Production in Africa.* Rome: Food and Agricultural Organization Expert Consultation on Women in Food Production, 1983.

Capasso, F. *Rapport Sur Une experience de promotion feminine en milieu rural chez in Bete de Guiberoua* [Report on One Experience of Promoting Rural Women]. Prepared for the Animation Rural, Guiberoua, Ivory Coast, 1981.

Chavangi, N.A. and Hanssen, A. *Women in Livestock Production with Particular Reference to Dairying.* Rome: FAO Expert Consultation on Women in Food Production, 1983.

Clark, G. *Fighting the Food Crisis: Women Food Farmers and Food Workers.* UNIFEM Occasional Paper No. 1. New York: United Nations Development Fund for Women, 1985.

Cloud, K. *Sex Roles in Food Production and Food Distribution System in the Sahel.* Washington, D.C.: Office of Women Development, U.S.A.I.D., 1977.

Dey, J. *Women in Food Production and Food Security in Africa.* Rome: Food and Agricultural Organization, 1984.

———. *Women in Agriculture: Women in Rice Farming System.* Focus-Sub-Saharan Africa, Rome: Food and Agricultural Organization, 1984.

Food and Agricultural Organization. *Director-General's Report on World Food Security: A Re-Appraisal of the Concepts and Approaches.* Committee on World Food Security, April 13–20, 1983.

Government of Kenya/UNICEF. *Situation Analysis: The Well Being of Women and Children.* Nairobi, Kenya: GOK/UNICEF, Kenya Country Office, 1983.

Haswell, M. *The Nature of Poverty.* London: Macmillan, 1975.

International Development Research Centre. *Food Systems.* IDRC - 146 e, Ottawa, Canada, n.d..

Kennedy, E. *Effects of Sugarcane Production in Southern Kenya on Income and Nutrition.* Washington, D.C.: International Food Production Research Institute, 1988.

Maritim, H. "Maize Marketing in Kenya: An Appraisal of Storage Policies and Their Implications for Regular Food Supply." *Quarterly Journal of International Agriculture.* 25 (1): 12–19, 1985.

Nur, I.M. "Food Security for Africa." *Proceedings of the Third Africa Food and Nutrition Congress,* Vol. 1. Harare, Zimbabwe, September 5–8, 1988.

Republic of Kenya. *Integrated Rural Surveys, 1976–79 Basic Report, 74–77.* Based on the Division of Labour Module of IRS 4. Nairobi: Government Printer, 178–179.

ONIANG'O

Swedish International Development Association. *Towards Intensive Food Production in Kakamega and Kiambu Districts—Field Survey Results.* Report prepared for the Ministry of Agriculture, Home Economics and Rural Youth Branch, under the Intensive Food Production and Utilization Project. Nairobi, 1987.

United Nations Economic Commission for Africa. *The Changing and Contemporary Role of Women in African Development.* Addis Ababa: UN/ECA, 1974.

United Nations Economic Commission for Africa. *The Role of Women in Agro-Industries in Four Eastern and Southern African Countries: Botswana, Lesotho, Tanzania, Zimbabwe.* ECA/ATRCW/88/2, 1988.

Wagara, A.O. "Household Food Security as Nutritional Strategy." *Proceedings of the Third African Food and Nutrition Congress.* Harare, Zimbabwe, 1988.

The World Bank. *Sub-Saharan Africa—From Crisis to Sustainable Growth: A Long-Term Perspective Study.* Washington, D.C., 1989.

WOMEN'S HEALTH AND DEVELOPMENT

Kathleen M. Merchant

chapter 11

INTRODUCTION

THE HEALTH and nutritional status of women can be examined across several dimensions, revealing long standing inequities. There is a gender gap, resulting from a range of social & biological vulnerabilities; a maternal/child gap, creating a view of women limited to reproduction, valuing their importance solely in terms of ability to produce and maintain the health and nutrition of children; and an economic gap, demonstrated between affluent/less affluent countries and resulting in extreme differences in maternal mortality rates between nations.

The United Nations Decade of the Woman has played a large role in increasing the recognition of inequities and neglect in the areas of health and nutritional status. The series of conferences and papers commissioned through this forum launched a number of initiatives addressing problems women face in achieving health and obtaining adequate nutrition. An international dialogue has been stimulated and continues. Suddenly the health and nutritional needs of women are being considered and even prioritized by some international health agencies, research institutions and policy makers—not just to produce a larger baby or to deliver more and better breastmilk (although these goals still dominate the discussions and objectives), but to have healthier women who don't face high risk of death or debilitation from pregnancy or childbirth. And health issues of women beyond those related to their biological role in reproduction are receiving additional attention. For example, issues of genital mutilation, domestic violence, rape, depression, and sexually transmitted diseases such as AIDS—social/health issues that affect women to a greater extent than men in many settings, generally because of women's lower status in social relationships—are receiving recognition and calls for action from society and the health care community in particular.

Although this article emphasizes health problems faced by underprivileged women living in less affluent nations, there are many examples of inequities and gaps based on gender in the health care systems within affluent nations. In the United States and many industrialized nations, neglect of women's health needs exists in many forms, an example of which is health research priorities and study design. For example, within the research community nationally, attention has increasingly been drawn to the fact that very few major national studies of cardiovascular disease have included women in significant numbers, even though more women than men are affected in older age groups. Likewise, breast cancer research funding has been low relative to other diseases, particularly given the toll it takes on women's lives and the fact that it is the number one cancer in terms of prevalence among women in the United States. With the increased attention on these issues of gender inequity in health research, funding for such research is increasing. And yet, even research on the safety of medical procedures widely used on women has not been adequate at times. For example, scandalous gaps in knowledge regarding the safety of silicone breast implants have been revealed in recent years. Is this irresponsible neglect the result of political, economic, and health care systems being dominated by the priorities of men?

Returning to a global perspective, within the international health community, until very recently, the overwhelming emphasis has been on addressing and resolving the health problems facing *children*. Children have been correctly perceived as a vulnerable group. But increasingly, attention has been drawn to the fact that women are also a vulnerable group in terms of maintaining adequate nutrition and health status. The biological role of women in reproduction and their consistently lower social status throughout the world makes women vulnerable to lower health and nutritional status in settings of poverty, particularly within less affluent nations (Basta, 1989; McGuire and Popkin, 1989; Soysa, 1987; UNFPA, 1989).

To illustrate how overwhelming this influence of an emphasis on the child has been, a few years ago, an analysis of research on maternal child health revealed only 4 percent of the research articles dealt with at least one maternal health outcome, and the remaining 96 percent of the research articles addressed only child health outcomes (Howard, 1987). Clearly the mother was only significant in maternal child health as the producer of the child and the child's health (or lack thereof).

Economic power plays a large role in facilitating or preventing access to medical care for women. This is demonstrated in the poorer health status of women in lower socioeconomic groups relative to that of women in higher socioeconomic groups within nations, and in the poorer health status of women in less affluent nations relative to the women of affluent nations. The most dramatic illustration of this dynamic is the difference between the maternal mortality rates globally. Maternal mortality rates show the largest gap of *any* health indicator between affluent and less affluent nations.

The recognition of the multiple intervention points available when attempting to prevent a maternal death has been illustrated using the image of a "Road to Death," first introduced by Dr. Fathalla (WHO, 1986). In terms of that analogy, this study begins with an examination of the endpoint, maternal mortality, and travels back on the path to examine the immediate clinical causes of death. Next, reversing steps along this path, the contribution of high fertility rates to increased risk of mortality are highlighted, with consideration of the reduction in mortality that might be achieved if women had authority over their own fertility. And farther back up the path, the risks of malnutrition and their linkages to maternal mortality are examined, including a consideration of the impact of malnutrition from generation to generation. The social vulnerabilities of women with health consequences in each stage of the life cycle are briefly described. Also listed are some of the manifestations of these larger social problems affecting women's health disproportionately beyond their reproductive role, and throughout their life cycle. Finally, I identify a few of the difficulties with designing and implementing solutions that will improve the health and nutritional status of women.

179

MATERNAL MORTALITY

A maternal death is defined by the World Health Organization as "the death of a woman while pregnant or within 42 days (6 weeks) of termination of pregnancy, irrespective of duration of or the site of the pregnancy." Maternal mortality is thus being defined as a time of death measure analogous to infant mortality (note that this definition would include maternal deaths due to abortion and ectopic pregnancy). Deaths attributable to pregnancy and childbirth also occur outside of this time frame.

It is estimated that 500,000 maternal deaths occur each year. Six thousand of these death are in richer industrialized countries, which means that approximately 99 percent of these deaths occur in less affluent nations. This rep-

MERCHANT

resents the largest gap in *any* public health indicator. Women have the distinction of being the group that shows the sharpest contrast in health conditions between nations of differing economic levels. It is estimated that between 5 to 30 deaths per 100,000 live births occurs in the more affluent nations, and between 50 to 800 deaths per 100,000 live births occur in the less affluent nations. As an example of the magnitude, more maternal deaths occur in India in one day, than all of the affluent countries combined in one month. Another way of expressing the extreme gap is that women of reproductive age in Bangladesh have a 46 percent chance of dying from pregnancy-related causes relative to other causes, whereas women of reproductive age in the United States have less than a 1 percent chance of dying from pregnancy-related causes relative to other causes (Royston and Armstrong, 1989). And yet, these statistics represent only the tip of the iceberg; not only are the number of maternal deaths in less affluent countries generally underestimated[1], but they also do not capture much of the debilitation that results from obstetric complications that don't result in death.

Why Do So Many Die?

The alarming nature of the gap in health status and childbearing risk for women results in such dramatic differences in maternal mortality between nations that a desperate reaction has been triggered within sectors of the international health community. So far, it has been too tempting to policy and program planners to look for the "quick fix." These limited but well-intended efforts seek to quickly install "modern" obstetric practices and improve access and transport to such treatment facilities. Despite these efforts, it was recently reported that "the World Health Organization has found scant evidence of any progress in reducing maternal mortality in recent years" (WHO, 1992), whereas "infant mortality rates have fallen by one-half in the past thirty years, maternal mortality ratios have lagged behind, with little evidence of progress in the least developed countries" (World Bank, 1994: 2). Rushing to treat the symptoms without giving adequate consideration to the underlying causes of the tremendous gap in health status and childbearing risk will not lead to any sustainable and substantial reduction in poor health status among women.

In the rush to upgrade medical facilities and available technology, the primary health care approach or preventative approach should not be abandoned. In particular, the efforts to assure access to reproductive care and a range of contraceptive methods as well as adequate nutrition throughout the life cycle should be important components of improving women's healthcare and reducing maternal mortality. And yet the primary health care approach has been promoted for more than 25 years, so why is maternal mortality still so high?

The larger social context with the myriad of manifestations of discrimination against women continues to exert a strong influence on the health of women throughout the life cycle. Why are so many women dying and being debilitated from childbirth-related events? The answer to this question has many layers. Progressing from specific to more general, one can say that they are dying because:

There are no facilities, supplies, or personnel to cope with obstetric emergencies

They lack control over their own fertility

Nutritional and health needs are neglected

Social relations (gender relationships, family relationships, economic relationships) are unjust

UNAVAILABILITY OF OBSTETRICAL CARE

The major direct clinical causes of maternal death are hemorrhage (20–35% of maternal deaths), infection (5–15%), obstructed labor (5–10%), and eclampsia (15–25%). Induced abortion is also identified as a major cause of maternal mortality, estimated to lead to 40 percent of all maternal deaths (Coeytaux et al., 1993). Frequently hemorrhage and infection are the immediate causes of death from termination of unwanted pregnancies, which are often illegal and unsafely conducted. Women who die may have experienced several of these conditions. For example, obstructed labor can lead to the tearing of tissue, causing blood loss (hemorrhage), and ultimately an infection could set in and be recorded as the cause of death.

Depending on the health infrastructure of specific regions, the problems of unavailability of obstetrical care include: no money or fuel to transport a woman who is experiencing an obstetric emergency such as hemorrhaging; no blood or equipment available for transfusion of blood once she has arrived at the health center or hospital; no trained personnel to give such care; no antibiotics to treat a woman with a diagnosed postpartum infection; no knowledge to diagnose the infection and refer the woman to a health care giver; too long a delay before seeking additional help during a long and difficult labor; and no money available in the family to seek any care at all. The potential barriers to receiving necessary obstetrical care are unlimited.

FERTILITY

The actual risk of maternal mortality faced by any particular woman is also dependent on her fertility. The more times she is pregnant, the more opportunities for an obstetric complication to occur. In Africa, high maternal mortality rates are compounded by high fertility. The average number of live births per woman is 6.4. But in rural Africa, it is quite common for a woman to have given birth to eight live babies and to have been pregnant several more times. If, at each pregnancy, such a woman has a one in 140 change of dying (calculated for a maternal mortality rate of 700 per 100,000), she has a

181

MERCHANT

lifetime risk of dying from pregnancy-related causes of at least one in 15. Comparable figures for North America are 1 in more than 6,000, and 1 in 10,000 for Northern Europe (Royston and Armstrong, 1989).

"Too young, too old, too many and too close." This statement from the United Nations Population Fund (1989) summarizes the problem of high fertility rates and high mortality rates experienced in many settings of poverty. Maternal mortality rates are higher for adolescent women, for women over 40 years of age, for women with high parity, and for women with many pregnancies occurring in rapid succession. Women know of the burdens of frequent reproductive cycling through their life experience. They seek abortion—even though it may be illegal or unsafe—to avoid the additional burden of unwanted pregnancy and childbearing.

Adolescent pregnancy is a common occurrence in many regions. The percentage of women giving birth by age 18 is 28 percent in Africa, 21 percent in Latin America, and 18 percent in Asia (Royston and Armstrong, 1989). The percentage of first births to women aged 15–19 years is 44 percent in Costa Rica, 41 percent in Mexico, 29 percent in the United States, 24 percent in the Philippines, 19 percent in Malaysia, and 18 percent in Jordan (U.N. Population Division, 1986).

With the onset of puberty, early pregnancy poses an additional nutritional challenge to females, the first challenge being optimal growth. Although growth begins slowing for females by the age of approximately 14, gains in linear growth (particularly of the long bones), is not complete until the age of 18, and peak bone mass is not achieved until the age of 25 (FNB/NAS/NRC, 1989). Relevant to an early role in reproduction, "the development of the bony birth canal is slower than that of height during the early teenage period and the canal does not reach mature size until about 2–3 years after growth in height has ceased" (Harrison et al., 1985: 39). Therefore, increased nutrient needs for optimal bone growth are present throughout adolescence and into the early twenties.

The nutrient needs of pregnancy and lactation are in addition to the nutrient needs of growth. Although the impact of the competing nutrient needs of pregnancy on the young mother's linear growth may be minimal (unless the mother is 13 years of age or younger), there is little information on how bone formation and calcium deposition will be affected in a young mother. Fetal growth is likely to be affected. The incidence of low birthweight is higher among young mothers. Adolescent mothers have a higher risk of developing anemia (WHO/UNFPA/UNICEF, 1989). Increased food intake to cover needs of growth as well as pregnancy and lactation are crucial in adolescent pregnancies. Reduced growth or altered development through the stress of early pregnancy may have lifelong deleterious consequences for mother and child.

Data from the World Fertility Survey of the late 1970s, examining 40 coun-

MERCHANT

tries, suggests that if all those who said they wanted no more children were actually able to stop childbearing, the number of births would be reduced by about 35 percent in Latin America, 33 percent in Asia, and 17 percent in Africa. Many studies show that abortion-related deaths account for a very large proportion of maternal mortality: more than 50 percent in some Latin American cities, more than 25 percent in Addis Ababa, and more than 20 percent rural Bangladesh. The desire of women to limit their own fertility becomes a marker of increased risk for maternal mortality. It has been shown that women with an unwanted pregnancy are less likely to seek prenatal care or deliver with a trained attendant. Women who want no more children tend to be older and have a higher parity, and have a higher than average risk of maternal mortality. From available data, it has been estimated that one-fourth or 25 percent of current maternal mortality could be prevented if women had the ability to prevent unwanted pregnancies. This means that approximately 125,000 fewer women would die each year from causes related to childbirth.

NUTRITION

Infection, hemorrhage, and obstructed labor are some of the major complications related to childbirth that can be affected by the nutritional status of the woman. Significant blood loss through hemorrhaging is much more serious in an anemic woman (Alauddin, 1986; Mola and Aitken, 1984). Given the estimated prevalence of 47 percent iron deficiency anemia among women of developing countries, the severity of hemorrhaging—the top cause of maternal mortality—could be reduced through reduction of anemia. Approximately 50 percent of maternal deaths in Indonesia and Egypt and over 30 percent of deaths in India are due to postpartum hemorrhage (UNFPA, 1989). Maternal infection is probably exacerbated by malnutrition. Although severe deficiencies of micronutrients result in the most dramatic and easily assessed consequences, it is important to remember that milder forms of these deficiencies may also have consequences: "the severely deficient persons represent index cases, or the tip of the iceberg, in the spectrum of nutritional status within the population" (Buzina et al., 1989: 172). Even mild deficiencies of iron and vitamin A lead to reduced immunocompetence. Pregnant women are at increased risk for vitamin A deficiency. The potential hazards of micronutrient deficiencies to the immunocompetence of women should not be overlooked. A well-nourished mother with adequate iron status is much less likely to die from hemorrhage than a severely anemic mother, and a well-nourished mother will be better able to fight an infection than a malnourished mother.

Additionally, well-grown women face obstructed labor much less frequently than stunted women (Merchant and Villar, 1992). Most stunting in adults within deprived populations is directly attributable to poor childhood nutrition and health status; once again, adequate nutrition and health care in child-

MERCHANT

hood can prevent or reduce the likelihood of obstetric complications (in this case, obstructed labor). Stunting and malformed pelves are prevalent in populations that have suffered chronic malnutrition. (It is important to note that this is not a new finding; the malformed pelves of women in the United Kingdom were directly attributed to nutritional deficiencies and their consequentially increased risk of obstructed labor documented [Bernard, 1952; Thomson, 1959]).

Clearly the long-term nutritional solution for reduction of risk for difficult delivery is to optimize female growth through adequate nutrition from gestation to early adulthood, when growth of the bony pelvis is completed. Likewise, improved maternal nutritional status before pregnancy, particularly with respect to iron and vitamin A, will reduce the risk of death from hemorrhaging or infection.

The nutritional link with eclampsia is poorly developed, but there has been some indication that high calcium intake reduces the likelihood of developing eclampsia (Belizan et al., 1988; Lopez-Jaramillo et al., 1987). Maternal deaths resulting from unsafe abortions—generally as a result of infection or hemorrhage—can be linked to the greater ability of well-nourished women to withstand hemorrhage relative to anemic women, and the greater ability of well-nourished women to prevent and fight off infection relative to malnourished women. The ultimate primary health care solution to the complications of intentional termination of pregnancy, however, is adequate access to effective contraceptive and family planning methods.

Another linkage between nutrition and maternal mortality (via fertility) is lactation. It is well-known that breastfeeding, and particularly exclusive breastfeeding, depresses ovulation and therefore lengthens the interpregnancy interval. This means that the opportunity for nutritional recuperation of the mother is facilitated through breastfeeding[2] as well as the maximum health of the infant. The contraceptive effect of breastfeeding is well-documented, as are the advantages for adequate birthspacing. Therefore, the practice of exclusive breastfeeding during the first six months of life (and continued breastfeeding for the first two years, if possible) generally has a net health benefit for the mother, particularly where access to other methods of family planning is limited.

From these important relationships between conditions of extreme obstetrical emergencies and nutritional status, one can conclude that poor nutritional status is likely to be a hidden cause or contributing factor to the recognized clinical causes of maternal mortality. J. Leslie (1991) reports that conservative estimates suggest that among the 1.130 billion women 15 years and older living in developing countries in 1985, over 500 million were anemic due to iron deficiency, close to 500 million were stunted as a result of childhood protein energy malnutrition, about 250 million suffered effects of iodine deficiency, and almost 2 million were blind due to deficiency of Vitamin

184

MERCHANT

A[3] (DeMaeyer and Adiels-Tegman, 1985; Galloway, 1989; McGuire and Austin, 1987: Hetzel, 1988; Levin et al., 1991).

Intergenerational Effects of Undernutrition and Small Body Size

Health and nutritional problems are generally the consequence of earlier problems and the cause of later problems. They can rarely be assigned to a single stage of the life cycle, particularly as the consequences can be felt by later generations. For example, a cycle of suboptimal growth can be perpetuated across generations. Figure 1 (adapted from the UNFPA's Population Report

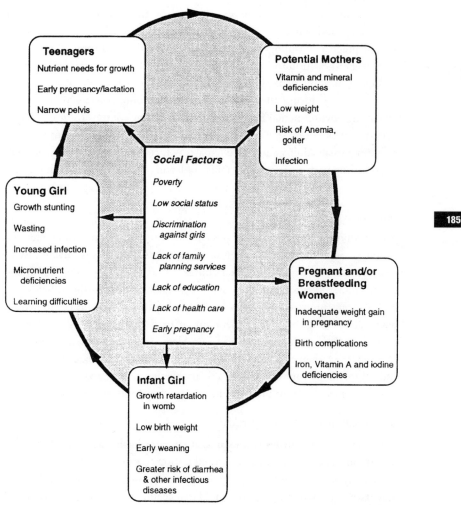

(Merchant and Kurz, 1993)

Figure 1: The Vicious Cycle of Malnutrition

of 1989) illustrates this intergenerational cycle. Many social factors contribute to the less-than-optimal growth from conception to puberty. Indirectly, factors such as poverty, low social status, and lack of health care play a role. More directly, factors such as infrequent feeding (small stomach capacity), low energy density of food, high exposure to infection, reduced immunocompetence, and anorexia due to illness (both during pregnancy and early childhood) contribute to growth retardation. It is also important to recognize that behaviors are passed on intergenerationally, and therefore behavioral patterns that contribute to growth retardation also will be passed on.

There is evidence that maternal size constrains fetal growth during the final stages of pregnancy. Small maternal size resulting from stunting during early childhood, and/or from very young maternal age, will constrain fetal growth beyond what it would have been had optimal childhood growth and/or pregnancy timing for the mother occurred. Compromised growth at early stages (gestation to 3 years) is particularly difficult to make up for at later stages (Martorell et al., 1990), in part because growth occurs at such an accelerated pace during this time period. In addition, because of the overwhelming environmental factors common in settings of poverty, it is unlikely that an initially poor start will be entirely overcome, which will most likely result in a small adult stature. The females will continue the cycle by producing offspring with a greater probability of having intrauterine growth retardation.

186

SOCIAL RELATIONS

It is beyond the scope of this chapter to address the influence of gender and economic injustice on maternal mortality in detail, but it is relatively easy to describe ways in which the social context contributes to poorer health and greater undernutrition among females. The conditions mentioned below are by no means universal and vary in their cultural patterns and combinations with each setting, but a consideration of their existence is essential in an analysis of the health and nutritional problems faced by women in any context where women face poverty and low social status. The social conditions and a broader picture of some health problems affecting women disproportionately at each of four phases of life are briefly characterized below.

Infancy/Childhood: Preference for Males

The preference for males can express itself from birth onwards through reduced food delivery, health care, and education to girls, particularly when resources are scarce. Additionally, children—and particularly female children—may have important roles in household management, including physically demanding tasks such as collection of fuel and water, often beginning at a very young age. A health risk of girls specific to the social situation, genital mutilation—sometimes referred to as female circumcision—is a cultural/religious tradition practiced in some regions that can have severe health consequences immediately and later when the child reaches the reproductive stages of life (Acsadi and Johnson-Acsadi, 1993). The form of mutilation varies, but it is estimated that 2 million girls are damaged in this manner (Toubia, 1993).

Adolescence: Early Reproductive Role

During adolescence a young girl can be rapidly shifted from childhood to marriage and pregnancy. She thereby misses opportunities for education and training as well as emotional maturation and physical growth required for reproduction and other productive responsibilities of female adult life. Contracting human immunodeficiency virus (HIV) is a growing health risk facing this age group. Women face a greater risk of contracting the HIV than men "when exposed to an infected partner, and young girls are the most vulnerable. Of all women infected, 70 percent are between the ages of 15 and 25" (World Bank, 1994).

Reproductive Years: Multiple Roles

In addition to reproduction, the responsibilities of adult life for women can be very physically demanding. These additional responsibilities generally include household management (cleaning, cooking, child care, family health care, collection of adequate water and fuel), in addition to agricultural food production, processing, and/or other production activities vital to survival. Health risks faced disproportionately by women that extend beyond the biological risks of reproduction include domestic violence, rape, and sexual abuse, often resulting in disability and sometimes leading to death. Again, these risks associated with gender originate in social and political relationships.

Later Years: Marginalization

In the final post-reproductive years, in some settings women are particularly vulnerable to undernutrition due to a loss of health through aging, coupled with a loss of valuable social roles. Women without secure financial or familial resources can easily be overlooked by the community and programs targeted to benefit those who are worst off. As the reproductive role tapers off, health risks associated with aging, such as heart disease and cancer, begin to become more prominent among women. "Cancer of the cervix, which peaks in women aged 40-50, accounts for more new cases of cancer each year in developing countries than any other type of cancer" (World Bank, 1994: xii). Regular screening and early detection are the best methods for reducing cancer and heart disease. Therefore, the social vulnerability of being "post-reproductive" and somewhat "invisible" in health programming and policy development increases the health risks of older women tremendously.

This overview illustrates how the social context can have a direct and spe-

MERCHANT

187

cific effect on the health and nutritional status of women. Additionally, it is useful to remember that the range of health problems affecting women disproportionately exists throughout the life cycle and extends beyond the biologically determined role in reproduction. These health problems are summarized in Figure 2.

Finally, it is important to recognize that the tremendous gap in an indicator of health such as maternal mortality is ultimately a result of the conditions of poverty and gender discrimination. Maternal mortality is a problem of such magnitude that it is crucial to recognize that there are many intermediary problems. It is not only the impaired access to adequate health care services and facilities essential for medical emergencies of labor, delivery, and recovery from childbirth that leads to death; poor health status before pregnancy also increases a woman's vulnerability to developing conditions of a medical

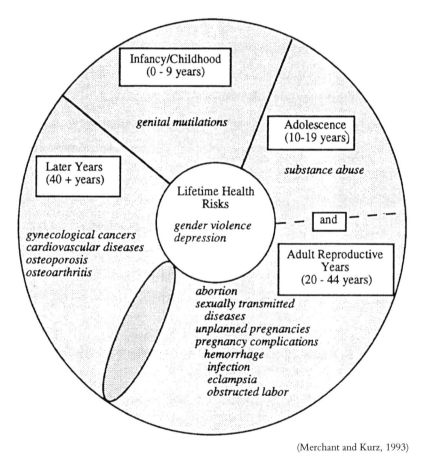

(Merchant and Kurz, 1993)

Figure 2: Some Health Problems Affecting Women Exclusively or Disproportionately during the Life Cycle

emergency. And a woman's health and nutritional status is affected by the presence or absence of manifestations of gender discrimination throughout her life.

BARRIERS TO SUSTAINABLE IMPROVEMENT IN WOMEN'S HEALTH STATUS

The elusive quality that all development projects hope to capture but rarely are able to is "sustainability." There are some major barriers within the system of development that frequently prevent the quality of sustainability from being achieved. Rather than listing a menu of policy, research, and community action recommendations, I would like to provoke and challenge us to acknowledge and consider some commonly encountered dynamics that stand in the way of positive change. First, I will choose a specific situation and touch upon problems encountered when attempting to reduce maternal mortality through "alarm and transport" strategies, and second, I will examine a few general problems encountered when attempting to design and implement programs using a top-down approach.

REDUCING MATERNAL MORTALITY QUICKLY

Programs attempting to improve early recognition of emergencies and transport to better facilities for women with severe obstetric complications are not experiencing success in regions with weak to nonexistent "western" medical health care infrastructure, such as is the case in the remote rural and highland Andean regions of Bolivia. One cannot begin to respond to high maternal mortality by instituting a system of emergency transport when the more basic needs of nutrition and health care in that community are not being met.

Understandably, one obstacle to use of such a system is the lack of trust, knowledge, or experience on the part of these remote communities regarding the efficacy of using such emergency transport and the health system at the other end of the journey. Why should they partake of such services? It is more appropriate to create the trust in and demand for such services within a community through demonstration of the ability to meet health needs by incorporating health services into existing health care networks. These services must address broad and basic health needs and thereby avert some obstetric emergencies, a task that is much more long-term, comprehensive, and therefore difficult to sustain. When health care resources perceived to be useful are available, they will be utilized.

At times, responding to the less dramatic chronic health and nutrition problems of women and a community may appear to be tedious and less dramatic in terms of the immediate number of maternal lives saved that are directly attributable to a new program, but it is also likely to have a greater constructive impact on women's health and the local health care system. Reducing the number of obstetric emergencies through prevention will ultimately

189

MERCHANT

increase the resources available to develop the appropriate responses to complex emergencies.

Additionally, without a solid local health care system of support for referrals, and widespread acceptance of the "external" medical system, the risk approach which relies on early recognition of an emergency and provision of immediate transport cannot be maintained. Current screening methods are not exact enough to provide much warning for most obstetric emergencies, such as hemorrhaging or obstructed labor prior to the onset of labor. Accurate screening is an important limitation because resources in remote areas cannot support the effort of transporting a high number of false positives, (women exhibiting characteristics of risk that don't result in emergencies).

Therefore, supporting development of pre- and post-natal care consistent with the needs which can be met by the materials and services available, and using local knowledge and belief systems enriched by additional education and training, should be one of the major goals to improve the safety of childbirth in underserved and remote areas.

Short-Term Focus

Problems with complex causes cannot be solved by a limited and short-term focus. Unfortunately, because programs that lack quick and measurable indicators of improvement are not fundable and are therefore without "seed" money, it is difficult to organize even for a minimal exchange of information to define problems and propose solutions. Money is available for large-scale policy pieces and research efforts, but very little is available for the long, arduous road to community-level implementation and sustainability. So much of the information and experience available remains segregated between those defined as "experts" operating on an international and national policy level, and those struggling day-to-day at the community level—whether from non-governmental organizations, local health posts, or local community members themselves.

Inability of Those in Power to Share or Release Decisionmaking Power

Inherent in the lower social status of women and those in poverty throughout the world is their almost complete absence in policy sessions from discussions of problem definition and problem solving. The system that supports the low status of certain members perpetuates that hierarchy and resists raising the status of those members. A top-down relationship is built into the situation. Although most policy papers have a section addressing the importance of "listening to women", too few are able to carry through and actually let go of authority or their self-image of possessing greater knowledge. Decisionmaking power is almost never delegated. The mistrust of local understanding of their own struggles and problem solving ability, or the impatience inherent in the unrealistic timeframe for demonstrating results, prevents funders, concerned government officials (national and local), and NGOs from allowing groups without authority—frequently local women and other minor community members—from taking charge of community projects to improve health and/or the status of women.

To overcome these natural barriers, these issues must be recognized and acknowledged. Only then can true innovations be made in approaches to development. Efforts must continually be made to work in partnerships and exchange information between those with regional, national, and international information and those with local knowledge and experience. The desire to segregate, disrespect, and mistrust the other party's intentions and/or abilities is strong.

NOTES

1. For example, most deaths occur outside of hospitals in remote regions often because the women are unable to get to health care facilities. A thorough discussion of the challenges to estimating maternal mortality accurately is contained in *Preventing Maternal Deaths* (Royston and Armstrong, 1989).

2. This is provided that the mother is consuming enough to cover the additional nutritional needs of lactation.

3. Information specifically addressing prevalences among women is difficult to find for Vitamin A and iodine deficiencies. Therefore, the estimates are based on population preferences, most likely leading to an underestimation of the deficiency among women.

REFERENCES

Acsadi, G. T. F. and G. Johnson-Acsadi. "Socio-economic, Cultural, and Legal Factors Affecting Girls' and Women's Health." *Women Health and Nutrition Work Program Working Paper Series.* Washington, D.C.: The World Bank, Population, Health and Nutrition Department, 1993.

Alauddin, M. "Maternal Mortality in Rural Bangladesh: The Tangail District." *Studies in Family Planning,* 17 (1):13–21, 1986.

Basta, S. S. "Some Trends and Issues in International Nutrition." *Food and Nutrition Bulletin* 11 (1): 29–31, 1989.

Belizan, J. M., J. Villar, and J. Repke. "The Relationship Between Calcium Intake and Pregnancy-Induced Hypertension: Up-to-Date Evidence." *American Journal of Obstetrics and Gynecology,* 158: 898–902, 1988.

Bernard, R. M. "The Shape and Size of the Female Pelvis." *Edinburgh Medical Journal* 59: 1–15, 1952.

Buzina, R., Bates, C. J., van der Beek, J., Brubacher, G., Chandra, R. K., Hallberg, L., Pollitt, E., Pradilla, A., Suboticanec, K., Sandstead, H. H., Schalch, W., Spurr, G. B. and J. Westenhofer. "Workshop on Functional Significance of Mild-to- Moderate Malnutrition." *American Journal of Clinical Nutrition* 50: 172–76, 1989.

Coeytaux, F. M., A. H. Leonard, and C. M. Bloomer. "Abortion." In *The Health of Women: A Global Perspective* M. A. Koblinsky, J. Timyan, J. Gay, eds. Boulder, CO: Westview Press, 1993.

191

MERCHANT

DeMaeyer, E. and M. Adiels-Tegman. "The Prevalence of Anaemia in the World." *World Health Statistics Quarterly* 38: 302–316, 1985.

Food and Nutrition Board/National Academy of Sciences/National Research Council. "Osteoporosis." In *Diet and Health: Implications for Reducing Chronic Disease Risk.* Washington, D.C.: National Academy Press, 1989.

Galloway, R. "The Prevalence of Malnutrition and Parasites in School-Age Children: An Annotated Bibliography." Washington, D.C.: The World Bank, Education and Employment Division, 1989.

Harrison, K. A., C. E., Rossiter and H. Chong. "Relations Between Maternal Height, Fetal Birthweight and Cephalopelvic Disproportion Suggest that Young Nigerian Primigravidae Grow During Pregnancy." *British Journal of Obstetrics and Gynaecology* supplement 5: 40–8, 1985.

Hetzel, B. S. "The Prevention and Control of Iodine Deficiency Disorders." ACC/SCN State-of-the-Art Series Nutrition Policy Discussion Paper No. 3. Rome, Italy: Food and Agriculture Organization, 1988.

Leslie, J. "Women's Nutrition: The Key to Improving Family Health in Developing Countries?" *Health Policy and Planning* 6: 1–19, 1991.

Levin, H. M., E. Pollitt, Rae Galloway, and J. S. McGuire. "Micronutrient Deficiency Disorders." In Dean T. Jamison and W. Henry Mosley, eds. *Disease Control Priorities in Developing Countries.* New York: Oxford University Press (for the World Bank), 1991

Lopez-Jaramillo P., M. Narvaez, and R. Yepez. "Effect of Calcium Supplementation on the Vascular Sensitivity to Angiotensin II in Pregnant Women." *American Journal of Obstetrics and Gynecology* 156: 261–62, 1987.

Martorell, R., J. Rivera, and H. K. Kaplowitz. "Consequences of Stunting in Early Childhood for Adult Body Size in Rural Guatemala." *Annales Nestle* 48: 85–92, 1990.

McGuire, J. S. and J. E. Austin "Beyond Survival: Children's Growth for National Development." New York: UNICEF, 1987.

——— and B. M. Popkin. "Beating the Zero-Sum Game: Women and Nutrition in the Third World, Part I." *Food and Nutrition Bulletin* 11: 38–63, 1989.

Merchant, K. M. and J. Villar. "Effect of Maternal Supplementation on Risk of Perinatal Distress and Intrapartum Cesarean Delivery." Abstract. *Experimental Biology '93. The FASEB Journal* 7 (3): A282, 1992.

Moerman, M. L. "Growth of the Birth Canal in Adolescent Girls." *American Journal of Obstetrics and Gynecology* 143 (5): 528–32, 1982.

Mola, G. and I. Aitken. "Maternal Mortality in Papua New Guinea, 1976–1983." *Papua New Guinea Medical Journal* 27 (2): 65–71, 1984.

Royston, E. and S. Armstrong. *Preventing Maternal Deaths.* Geneva: World Health Organization, 1989.

Soysa, P. "Women and Nutrition." *World Review of Nutrition and Diet* 52: 1–70, 1987.

Thomson, A. M. "Maternal Stature and Reproductive Effciency." *Eugenics Review* 51 (3): 157–62, 1959.

Toubia, N. *Female Genital Mutilation: A Call for Global Action.* New York: Women, Ink, 1993.

United Nations Population Division. "Contraceptive Practice: Selected Findings from the World Fertility Survey Data." New York: United Nations, 1986.

United Nations Population Fund. "State of World Population 1989. Investing in women: The Focus of the Nineties." New York: UNFPA, 1989.

World Health Organization. "Maternal Mortality: Helping Women Off the Road to Death." *WHO Chronicle* 40 (5): 175–83, 1986.

World Health Organization/United Nations Population Fund/United Nations Childrens Fund. "The Reproductive Health of Adolescents: A Strategy for Action." A joint WHO/UNFPA/UNICEF statement. Geneva: World Health Organization, 1989.

World Health Organization. "Women's Health: Across Age and Frontier." Geneva: WHO, 1992.

The World Bank. "Development in Practice: A New Agenda for Women's Health and Nutrition." Washington, D.C.: The World Bank, 1994.

193

MERCHANT

WAR AND VIOLENCE AGAINST WOMEN

Vesna Nikolić-Ristanović

chapter 12

INTRODUCTION

ALTHOUGH MANY people experience violence in peacetime, wartime violence affects people more drastically: war involves whole communities and results not only in individual deaths and injuries, but in widespread destruction of property, homes, families, and economies. War affects women's lives differently than men's whether women remain in targeted areas, reside in areas which are out of the "combat zones," or flee in refuge. Women are non-combatant victims of violence in all forms of warfare—international and internal, religious, ethnic or nationalist, and from both enemy and "friendly" forces. Women comprise the majority of civilian casualties of modern forms of warfare (Chinkin, 1993) and suffer from a large range of violent acts—the majority of which remain invisible. Most public attention is focused on rape, so that it is often thought to be synonymous with violence against women in war. However, women also suffer from other kinds of sexual abuse, as well as from torture, killing, malnutrition, psychological violence, fear, domestic violence from men who return from war, loss or forced separation from their children, husbands and other relatives, and from different kinds of discrimination and violence in refuge. Including emotional, psychological, and physical consequences of war in lives of women broadens our definition of wartime violence. Women who experience wartime violence teach us to take all these forms of violence seriously.

This study uses the war in the former Yugoslavia to examine two forms of violence against women: 1) sexual violence related to torture and killing of women; and 2) domestic violence in wartime. The analysis of the first is based on interviews of 69 women refugees temporarily settled in Serbia who spoke about their own and other women's experiences of violence in wartime.[1] The examination of domestic violence is based on the statistical data and qualitative analyses of cases reported to the Belgrade SOS hotline, as well as on the above-mentioned interviews with refugee women.

The majority of interviewed women were Serbs (59), while 7 were Moslems, 2 Croats, and 2 Slovenians. The ethnic structure of the women interviewed does not represent the overall ethnic structure of the women victims of war in former Yugoslavia, but it is fairly consistent with the ethnic structure of refugees in Serbia, who are mainly Serbs. According to the official statistics of the *Commissariat for Refugees of the Republic of Serbia*, at the beginning of 1994 77.1 percent of refugees were Serbs, 8.9 percent were Moslems, 2.5 percent were Croats, and 11.5 percent belonged to other nationalities. Although we can assume that, given the balance of power in this war, Moslem women suffered most, we want to demonstrate the common features of victimization of women in war regardless of their nationality. Also, we want to draw attention to the victimization of Serb women, which was largely ignored because of Serbia's politics and military role in the war. While the majority of interviewed women were Serbs, they did not only speak about the experiences of Serb women. On the contrary, a significant number of Serb women were from mixed marriages and families or have friends of other nationalities—thus they spoke about the violence against Moslem and Croat women as well.

SEXUAL ABUSE, TORTURE, AND MURDER

Men have been raping and otherwise sexually abusing women throughout history, in times of peace as well as in war. In wars men only continue to do what they did before but in a more mindless and indiscriminate way (Vickers, 1993) and with more "comprehension" and "excuses" for their behavior. Rape has accompanied all wars: religious wars, revolutionary wars, both world wars, and civil wars. Rape is not bound by definitions of "just" or "unjust" wars (Brownmiller, 1975). Unfortunately, rape is equally a reality of the current war in former Yugoslavia. However, since, as McGeough points out

(Vickers, 1993), the military rarely details what they euphemistically call "collateral damage," reliable statistics on rape and other kinds of sexual abuse in this war (as well as in other wars), are not available. Furthermore, the unreliability of statistics on rape in war is also connected to their use as a means of political manipulation. During the war, as Brownmiller wrote, emphasizing rape as the atrocity of soldiers of only one side or nation is used to promote hate and provide the emotional groundwork that leads the other side into the war. All sides in conflicts usually do not admit that their soldiers rape, but rather point out the rapes of their enemies. When the war is over, predictably, the crime that is "the easiest to charge and the hardest to prove" has traditionally been the easiest to disprove as well. "The rational experts found it laughably easy to debunk accounts of rape and laughably was the way they did it" (Brownmiller, 1975: 31). Thus, the details on the suffering of civilians in war are left to refugees. What they experience, see, and hear may also be the best source of our knowledge about sexual violence against women in war.

The women we spoke with indicated that even though the public focused on rape as the most violent form of sexual abuse, it is only one form in a broad spectrum of wartime sexual victimization of women. The sexual abuse of women in war includes also rape threats (i.e., intimidation by rape), different kinds of sexual harassment, sexual slavery in the form of forced, regular favors via the mistress system, and forced prostitution (military prostitution and prostitution as a survival strategy). Women were abused sexually in the militarized areas (during operations and occupation), as well as in the areas which were free of combat but in which different ethnic groups still live together. Women were abused during the procedures of interrogation and search, as well as in detention, when seeking welfare assistance and in refuge.

As Susan Brownmiller points out, rape is seen as an

Unfortunate but inevitable by-product of the necessary game called war. Women, by this reasoning, are simply regrettable victims— incidental, unavoidable casualties . . . Rape is more than a symptom of war or evidence of its violent excess. Rape in war is a familiar act with a familiar excuse (Brownmiller, 1975: 43).

However, as in peacetime, rape in wartime results from power imbalances rather than from sexual motives. The sexual meaning of rape in war is marginal and is used as a means for achieving aims which have nothing in common with sexuality. The wartime rape includes three "sides:" the man-rapist, the woman-victim, and the man-war adversary of the rapist. The victim and the rapist depend on the balance of power in a particular time period.

Patriarchy means that women are regarded as men's property, a pure addition to the territory and other things that men possess. Rape is to male-female relations what conquering troops are to occupied territories, and imperial authority is to colonialism (Chinkin, 1993). Sexual conquest becomes an

acceptable way of validating masculinity, of demonstrating dominance and superiority over women. "If sexuality were not bound with power and aggression, rape would not have been possible. When these attributes of masculinity
are accentuated, as in war, rape reaches epidemic proportions" (Jackson, 1978:
25). The male nature of war accentuates the power gap between men and
women. Rape in war is not merely a matter of chance or of women victims
being in the wrong place at the wrong time (Chinkin, 1993). The power of
men is intensified by the weapons in their hands so that "ordinary Joes are
made unordinary by entry into the most exclusive male-only club in the
world" (Brownmiller, 1975: 32). On the other side, women—deprived of
both weapons and male protection, with their class and ethnicity and with
their educational or professional background—are exposed in different ways
to male sexual violence.

The cruelty of wartime rape is furthered in that in the eyes of the offender,
the victim symbolizes the enemy. According to patriarchal principles, women
are the male enemy's property, and they should be used as an instrument to
defeat the enemy. As Brownmiller writes, "a simple rule of thumb in war is
that the winning side is the side that does the raping. . . . First, a victorious
army marches through the defeated people's territory, and thus it is obvious
that if there is any raping to be done, it will be done on the bodies of the defeated enemy's women" (Brownmiller, 1975: 35). Men from the losing side
also rape but as a means to retaliate and get revenge. Thus rape becomes a
manifestation of the heroic fighting man engaged in a good fight (Brownmiller, 1975). When roles are changed and the former losers become winners,
they equally tend to demonstrate their power and finally defeat the enemy.
This was the case of the Russian soldiers who raped German women at the
end of World War II. This is also the case in the Bosnian war, where the nationality of rapists depends on the balance of power in geographic areas.

During attacks, men rush into homes, kill the men, rape and kill the
women, rob and destroy property, and burn houses. Sometimes, men are first
forced to helplessly watch the rapes, torture, and killing of their wives. Sometimes they are the first killed or wounded and, after the women are deprived
of potential protectors, they are raped, tortured, and killed. A Serb woman
spoke about her woman neighbor, a compatriot, who was raped and tortured
by four Moslem soldiers in Bratunac, Bosnia. Soldiers first rushed into her
apartment and shot at her husband. He was wounded and still conscious but
he pretended he was dead. Thinking that the man was dead, soldiers raped the
woman. After raping, they tortured her, extinguished cigarettes on her body,
cut her breast, and left her in the bathtub. When they left, the husband asked
for help. After four days the woman died in the hospital.

Very often brothers, fathers, or fathers-in-law have also been forced to
watch acts of rape. As one raped woman said, it is not rare that fathers are
forced to have sexual intercourse with their daughters. For the rapist, rape of a

NIKOLIĆ-RISTANOVIĆ

woman in war may be as much an act against her husband, father, or brother as an act against a woman's body (Brownmiller, 1975).

In some cases men prove their power and humiliate the enemy by raping old women who live alone, so that their helplessness is increased by their immobility and absence of any protector. As a Moslem woman said, in the Bosnian town Foča, Serbs raped and killed a 90-year-old woman who lived alone. Another Moslem woman, 78-years-old, who also lived alone and was ill, was raped and tortured by Serbs in her house in Brčko; she died from the violence.

In the territories occupied by the enemy's army or in the areas under siege, women are also raped, tortured, and sought out and killed. Soldiers often effectuate searches under the pretext that they are looking for weapons. Sometimes they rape and torture women in their own homes, but more often they take them away to prisons, camps, bordellos, or other locations. Sometimes women are abducted from the shelter or when walking around. Soldiers take them away supposedly to witness searches of other people's apartments. Sometimes women are arrested because of their alleged membership in some political party or participation in some other political activity against the enemy. Their imprisonment is occasionally due to the political or military activities of their husbands, sons, and fathers, although it is likely that they are imprisoned simply because they belong to the enemy's nationality. A striking example of the latter is the statement of a Serbian woman who, when arrested by Croats, was told that she was apprehended because she had danced *kolo* (a traditional Serbian folk dance) at her wedding. A Moslem woman spoke about two young Moslem girls, about 14 years old, who were taken away from their homes and kept in prison. She met them in the hospital where they had abortions, performed late in their pregnancies. They were psychologically devastated; their parents were completely ignorant of their whereabouts and utterly unable to help them. Sometimes men do manage to protect female members of their families, but often their efforts simply fail. As a Serbian woman pointed out, in urban areas the fact that a woman has a male protector can sometimes prevent her from being taken away and raped, but in more primitive, rural areas, this is not the case. She spoke about Moslem soldiers who attempted to take away her 14-year-old relative under the pretext that she should witness the search of her house. The girl's grandfather managed to prevent them from taking her by saying that she was only a child who looks like a girl.

The interviews indicated that sometimes the residents of whole villages were taken away and at times put in different prisons, while others were imprisoned in the same dungeon. In some cases women were put in bordellos while men were imprisoned. In prisons, men are tortured while women in both prisons and bordellos are raped and tortured. One woman said: "In the center of Sarajevo a Moslem, known as a criminal, ran the bordello for young girls. When I passed near this house (a former restaurant) I heard them screaming. . . ." A Serbian woman, who was in a Moslem prison for both women and men, spoke about a special kind of torture used against Serbs: all prisoners, women and men equally, were tied with wire and forced to stay out during Serbian shell attacks. Once, a 76-year-old woman was untied and raped in front of all the prisoners, so cruelly that she died.

In the camps, prisons, or bordellos women are systematically raped with even more violence and humiliation than peacetime rapes. As the research suggests, cruelty toward the victim increases with an increase in the number of offenders. While peacetime rapes are most frequently committed by one offender against one victim, wartime rapes usually involve a number of offenders who consecutively rape each victim, causing horrible suffering by the victim.

Apart from being raped, women who experienced the war in former Yugoslavia were beaten and threatened with knives against their throats. In prisoner-of-war camps women were forced to watch other prisoners being beaten or slaughtered. As a Serbian woman raped by Moslems said, "We were raped by three men; they put their knives on our throats, and wanted to cut our throats. Having beaten our prisoners, they cut them in pieces or drowned them in pools, while forcing us to witness these scenes. There were about 200 of us prisoners, and even now I do not know how many of us have been killed."

In areas which are not directly affected by war, women were also raped because of their nationality. Rapes often followed abduction of women by fraud, committed by their neighbors or other men whom they had known for years and who suddenly turned on them. A 21-year-old Serbian girl living in a village where Serbs were the majority spoke about the way she was abducted and raped: "My house was at the beginning of the street, but young people from the village usually met each other for entertainment at the end of the street. It was quite usual for us to invite each other and go out together. He was a Croat, 22 years old, and we were friends. Once when we were walking, as usual, on our street and came to its dark part, he suddenly put his hands on my mouth and called two other men who seized me and put me in the car. They also tied my eyes and mouth and hit me on the head so that I lost consciousness. When I woke up I realized that they left me at a meadow near my village. Every part of my body was hurting. I felt nauseated and I realized that I had been raped . . ."

In civil wars the vulnerability of women, apart from belonging to the side of the enemy, is often influenced by the history of relationships between a particular woman and particular man who knew each other for years. Thus, women had to pay for their previous behavior toward a particular man, or, as a woman said, "It was usual that if one had some conflict in the peace time he tended to retaliate in the war. When it is the matter of women it is always

NIKOLIĆ-RISTANOVIĆ

something related to sex." Especially vulnerable are pretty young girls who had previously refused some men's proposals for love. As revenge, these men raped them. Sometimes this means that the earlier imbalance of power, mirrored in an important social position of the woman and a low social position of the man, are reversed and brought into the traditionally expected order, which implies an imbalance of power favoring males. In Dretelj, a Croat prison for Serbs and Moslems, almost half of the women detained were raped. As a woman said, the majority were young girls, with two of them being a physician and a teacher. The latter were raped in an especially cruel manner. They were tortured and told that they had to give birth to an Ustaša (Croat). Their lives were threatened. The woman physician was taken to wash houses and raped again. The rapists were people whom she had helped several times as a physician. Also, the teacher was raped by her students. As Brownmiller wrote," . . . the gun in the hand is power. The sickness of warfare feeds on itself. A certain number of soldiers must prove their newly won superiority—prove it to women, to themselves, to other men" (Brownmiller, 1975: 38).

More often, women had to pay for the attitudes and behaviors of their husbands, sons, brothers, or fathers; thus rape is used as indirect punishment. A Serbian woman, who was detained in a Moslem camp because her husband and son had refused to surrender, was raped by many men she had known previously. Some of them were regular customers of the shop where she worked, and some were people punished by her husband, who worked as a policeman before the war. During her stay in the camp, details about her rape and torture were broadcast on a local radio station. Her husband was killed, her son lost his eyes as a consequence of torture, and her house was burned down.

Women who were married to men of other nationalities were vulnerable to victimization by men from both ethnic groups. A Moslem woman from the city of Mostar—which was divided between Croats and Moslems—witnessed her sister's fate: "She was mistreated by Croats because her husband, who is a Serb, stayed in the Croat section of the city while she, as a Moslem, came to stay with her mother in the Moslem section. Croats from the Moslem part of town assumed that her husband fought against the Croats. The woman's Croat neighbors kidnapped the woman and her mother. They verbally abused them, threatening to massacre and rape them. It is likely that my sister was raped too, because she was in such terrible psychological condition that she could hardly speak about the details." A Croat woman, married to a Moslem, was raped by Croats while her daughter witnessed the rape. Rape was obviously intended as a message for her husband. Men whose wives belonged to the other nationality could not protect their wives from the men of their own ethnic group. A Serb woman, married to a Croat, and whose mother is Moslem, wrote to her sister, a refugee settled in Belgrade:

NIKOLIĆ-RISTANOVIĆ

"My husband is not able to protect me and my mother. It was suggested to the men who are married to Serbs and Moslems to leave or drive away their women. Otherwise, both of them would be in danger. I am so afraid."

While men are obliged to go into combat, women and young girls are forced to clean houses, and these tasks are often followed by rape. Rape is used as an instrument of war and a method of ethnic cleansing. Intimidation by rape is used as "an instrument of forced exile, to make you leave your home and never want to come back" (MacKinnon, 1993: 88). A woman spoke about how she decided to send her two daughters to refuge: "We lived in Sarajevo. There was shelling, and murders; girls were raped. One day my 15-year-old daughter came home completely terrified and said that she would prefer to be killed rather than raped. I exploded and said to my husband that our daughters are young and pretty and, therefore, in danger of rape. I said that I would have survived if I were raped but they could not, because in such a case their life would be destroyed. Later on, we made efforts and managed to send them to Serbia."

In Bosnia wartime rape is used as a method to produce children of the rapist's nationality. According to patriarchal patterns, women symbolize the family, and the family is seen as the basis of society. Humiliation and rape of women, in order to give birth to the children of the enemy's nation, represent an effort to destroy the very base of the enemy community. Wartime rapes also serve as a means for destruction of a nation. The idea of rape as a method of ethnic cleansing is based on a very deep patriarchal construction: women are seen as objects, as "dishes" which passively accept men's seed and do not add anything original to it. Thus the identity of the child, the identity of a human being, depends only on men; consequently, women impregnated by their enemies give birth to children who belong to the enemy's ethnic group. It is time to deconstruct the notion of ethnic cleansing and accept that it is a war crime—forced impregnation—which the international community and International War Crime Tribunal still do not designate as such. We agree with Chinkin that rape as a means of ethnic cleansing should be separately investigated and prosecuted. This would underscore both the gravity of rape and the violent sexual abuse of women in armed conflict, irrespective of their association with other tactics such as "ethnic cleansing" (Chinkin, 1993). From our point of view, it is ethnic mixture rather than ethnic cleansing—although males from all sides do not define it as such, resulting in horrible suffering of women. Rapists want to be sure that raped women will give birth to children of *their* nationality—children who will also remind women of their terrible experiences. Feeling the child of the rapist in her womb and being convinced that everybody will know that it is the child of the enemy, but knowing at the same time that it is also her child, is the most cruel form of torture. Rapists also want to send a message to husbands and other males from the enemy side that their women are worthless once they give birth to

202

the children of the enemy. The husbands of raped women and other men detest and reject these women because they were raped and bore children to the enemy. A husband gave a pistol to his wife (a Bosnian Serb) and suggested that she shoot herself. Sometimes husbands do not believe that their wives were raped and accuse them of adultery.

In some areas girls, often as young as 14 years old, were systematically raped and abducted. The women who spoke about this practice in West Lika, a part of Croatia, said that all the raped girls were Serbs abducted by Croat soldiers. There is some indication that the girls were put in bordellos or made sexual slaves through the mistress system. A Serb woman who survived World War II spoke about similar practices in that war, with actors who belonged to the same nationalities as the current war. She spoke about Serb girls who were raped in a grain elevator. After being raped, some of them were killed and taken to live with rapists to be their mistresses and run their households. When the war ended they were released. It is interesting that the men of their own nationality did not label them as raped women or as prostitutes; all of these women, save one, were later married to Serbs. Perhaps this made some women choose to become mistresses of men from other ethnic groups in order to survive. This survival strategy sought to preserve some of their dignity. As one woman said, "Nobody can criticize me that I was a whore during the war." However, some women could not cope with their survival problem in this way. Women who lived in combat zones, as well as refugee women, were sometimes forced to sell their bodies for 10 eggs or a can of food in order to feed their children. In the sieged town of Sarajevo, women sometimes became mistresses of men who could issue them permission to leave the city and join their children.

Men's abuse of female sexuality and reproductive rights is unlimited and depends on men's immediate political and military needs. For example, in comparison to Serbs and males of other ethnic groups involved in the conflicts in former Yugoslavia, Germans had different needs in World War II. They were forbidden to rape Jews under the stern prohibition against "race defilement," which is similar to the prohibition against "the mixture of the races" that was the legal code in the American South before and after slavery (Brownmiller, 1975). Thus we see variation in the form of wartime violence against women in relation to the social and political context of the war in question.

DOMESTIC VIOLENCE: THE IMPACT OF WAR

As in all patriarchal societies, domestic violence is an everyday reality for many women living in the former Yugoslavia. Although there is no reliable statistical data about women's victimization, the research as well as the practice of SOS hotlines reveal that battering is widespread, often having serious consequences.

203

Recent research (Nikolić-Ristanović, 1994) demonstrates that more than half of women (112 or 58.3 percent) from a sample of 192 women[2] reported that they had been victims of some kind of spouse abuse. Ninety-four (or 49 percent) of the women reported psychological violence, while 36 (or 18.7 percent) revealed that they were victims of wife battering. 18.7 percent of the women reported that they had been raped by their husbands. Wife battering was usually followed by other kinds of violence. Women who were beaten by their husbands were at the same time victims of psychological abuse (38.9 percent), sexual violence (25 percent), or of both (52.8 percent).

Records from the Belgrade SOS hotline, which was founded in March of 1990, show that the number of women who call the SOS telephone increased from 499 in 1990 to 701 in 1991; the numbers continued to rise, to 1096 in 1992 and 978 in 1993.[3] In 1994 some 1,300 calls were recorded up to the month of December. Although the increase of the number of women who reported their victimization to the SOS hotline might be related to different factors, including women's increasing awareness of the existence of the SOS line, these data obviously confirm our assumption that domestic violence is widespread in our society. The invisible war was present in the private lives of women before it broke out publicly (Fischer, 1994) or, as a woman victim of her husband's violence said, "The war is nothing new for me, I have been living in war for years." But "traditional" male violence against women has intensified under the influence of the publicly recognized war (Fischer, 1994). Like domestic violence in peacetime, which is seen as a private matter between women and men rather than a crime, domestic violence in war is not treated seriously. As Chinkin points out, these "effects of conflict that are suffered by women as harms or loss are not categorized as such by legal norms. . . . These situations are simply accepted as unfortunate side effects of conflict and are unrecorded in the catalogues of war crimes" (Chinkin, 1993: 204).

Since the beginning of the war, the number of violent crimes and the degree of violence used has increased. Violence against women is influenced (apart from other factors) by the concentration of weapons in the hands of ordinary men—former soldiers from the war in Croatia and Bosnia who are usually frustrated, nervous, intolerant, and very aggressive. The aggression of these former soldiers, as well as of other people who are permitted to have weapons, has been also reinforced by media campaigns against people belonging to other ethnic groups as well as against opposition parties (Lukovi, 1993). The patterns of violence are widespread in media and state agencies as well as on the streets and within families. The news and other political broadcasts present violence as an acceptable form of conflict resolution. Violence related to political intolerance is widespread in all human contacts, and is a consequence of differences in either political opinions or ethnic groups. The large number of refugees living in poor conditions and without any clear future also contributes to conflict and violence both among refugees and between them and other Yugoslavian people who live in poverty, fear, and insecurity. These factors all coalesce to make violence against women, especially domestic violence, more dramatic. At the same time, cooperation with the police becomes more difficult because "given the general surge of violence, they are less inclined than ever to intervene in cases of violence against women" (Fischer, 1994: 165).

According to Belgrade SOS statistics, in 12 percent of all calls recorded in 1993, women reported that molesters were men who spent some time fighting in the war. The findings of the analyses of the Belgrade SOS hotline in 1991, 1992, and 1993 (Mršević 1994) suggest that offenders are most often actual husbands and partners (65 percent), or former husbands and partners (13.3 percent). From the beginning of the war the number of violent acts committed by sons has increased from 6.4 percent in 1991 to 7.6 percent in 1992, and 11.4 percent in 1993. Women reported psychological violence (77.4 percent) and physical violence (70.7 percent) by sons, as well as sexual violence (15.5 percent) and economic abuse (6 percent). Women reported death threats twice as often in 1993 than in the previous years. Also, the use of weapons in domestic violence has been increasing since the war began, after which some 40 percent of women who called SOS telephones reported that their partners were threatening them by the use of pistols, grenades, and similar weapons. According to the Zagreb SOS hotline, a similar situation regarding the impact of war on domestic violence exists in Croatia (Fischer, 1994).

To analyze the influence of war and economic crises on domestic violence against women, we used 33 cases reported to the Belgrade SOS hotline and the shelter for battered women, as well as four cases reported by refugee women. In all cases, the violence was related to warriors returning home; nationalism; the aggravation of social and financial position as a result of refugee status; or economic dependence of either husband or wife as a consequence of economic crises/refugee status caused by the war.

Twenty-four molesters were husbands; 11 were sons. One boyfriend molested his girlfriend and one refugee molested his landlady. The majority of the women were Serbs, while there was one Moslem and two Croats. Seven women lived with husbands of different nationalities: two women lived with Moslems, one lived with a Croat, one with an Albanian, and the rest of the women lived with Serbs.

All of the sons who molested their mothers and 12 husbands who molested their wives were those who returned from warfare, bringing weapons with them. Some of the men also molested their sisters, children, and other relatives living with them. All of these men regularly used weapons (pistols, grenades) to threaten their victims. Some of them became more violent after their war experience; some started to consume alcohol and beat their mothers and wives for the first time after they returned home from warfare.

Some started to rape their wives. One woman said that her husband slept with his machine gun under the bed, woke up at three a.m. and forced her at gunpoint to have sex with him. One other woman said that she did not want to sleep with her husband since, after he returned home from warfare, he had became violent when they had sex: "It is like he rapes me. I am completely blue . . . He has nightmares . . . I am afraid of him, I am afraid that he had raped in warfare." Some women described their husbands as "persons who had became crazy after their war experience." Even women who were not beaten called the SOS telephone for help. A striking example comes from a woman who lives in a little town in Serbia, who said of her husband: "He was mobilized by the Yugoslav army one day after our wedding. He did not want to go to fight but he finally decided not to refuse. He was afraid that we may have problems because, in our circles, those who desert are seen as betrayers and cowards. When he left I was pregnant. In his absence I gave birth to twin sons. Before our wedding we dated for four years and loved each other very much. He came back from warfare as a gray-haired alcoholic who was unable to communicate with anyone except his friends from warfare. He regularly goes out, stays in bars and drinks with them. When he is at home, he is nervous, molests me and our children and destroys the furniture. When he calms down he feels pangs of guilt and asks forgiveness. He says that he experienced horrible things in war but he does not want to speak about the details."

At the very beginning of the war some women reported so-called "post TV violence syndrome" (Fischer, 1994: 164). This means that their husbands became very aggressive after watching TV News, since the main war propaganda was conveyed through this broadcasting. Some men made decisions to go to war after watching this broadcast, and when women told their husbands about their worries and fears for them, they became violent. The men became nervous because they felt they should go to fight but feared doing so, causing them to take out their anxieties on their wives. Or as Mladjenović points out: "In the 'hinterland,' men cannot simply kill people in the street, so their wives at home become a suitable replacement for the enemy" (quoted in Fischer, 1994). Women related stories such as: "My husband watched the TV news and then he beat me for the first time. We have been living together for twelve years and he has never done such a thing." Another woman said: "He simply got up and went to look for the pistol which his father has been keeping in the closet since World War II." Some of these women were beaten for the first time in their lives by their husbands, and sometimes violence was unexpected and more drastic than previously.

Spouses belonging to different ethnic groups or having differences in political opinions also created conflicts and violence. In some cases violence became more drastic because the wife belonged to a different ethnic group than her husband, while in other cases nationalism provoked violent behavior. Nationalism did not dominate only in politics and the media, but rather in all—including personal—relationships. As Smith points out, "everything that happens in global society is reflected in the family" (Smith, 1989: 25). The abstract hatred of other nationalities was transformed into the concrete hatred of very close persons such as wives, children, and other relatives. These close persons symbolized the enemy. But wives were also seen as their husbands' property, and thus a source of shame.

A Croat woman reported that in the last two years she "has been suffering from awful violence committed by her husband because of her nationality." He also molested her before the war, but with the beginning of the war, he became completely uncontrollable. Another Croat woman was divorced, but because of a bad financial situation had to continue to live in the same apartment with her Serb husband. Her husband's family blamed her for the war, and with the emergence of nationalism, her former husband became violent, beating her several times so severely that she was hospitalized.

One Moslem woman, whose husband was Serb, was beaten regularly since the beginning of war. She used to be happy with her husband, but when the war broke out friends began to berate her husband saying: "Why did you choose to marry one Moslem among so many Serbian women?" They blamed her for everything that was done by Moslems against Serbs. Her husband started to beat her every night after drinking with his friends. She had serious injuries and tried to flee with their child. However, he did not allow her to bring the child with her, saying: "This is a Serbian child and must stay here."

Domestic violence against women is also related to the frustrations produced by refugee status. Conflicts in refugee families sometimes result from the drastic change in social status, lack of financial security, or a new situation in which husband or wife or both of them are dependent on others. In some cases husbands spent time in warfare and still have weapons with them, making the violence more dangerous and the victim more helpless. One woman refugee from Bosnia living with her husband and child in a rented apartment suffered when the husband came back from warfare. He began to consume alcohol, to rape, beat, and threaten his wife at knifepoint. She would like to leave him, but since she is unemployed she has nowhere to go.

A special problem exists in families which have accepted refugees. Women who have both refugees and violent husbands in their homes report that their husbands become more violent. The imbalance in the family created by newcomers is used by men as a rationale for violence against women. This violence occurs regardless of the nationality of the wives. Some male refugees molest the women who give them refuge.

The majority of women called the police for help. However, the police either did not intervene or their intervention was ineffective. Police did not take weapons away from the offenders, and sometimes police even supported

207

molesters who, as volunteer soldiers, had participated in the war in Bosnia and Croatia. Police tended to justify the violent behavior of former soldiers as a consequence of war trauma, and even mocked the battered women. They made comments such as "what do you expect me to do, I was not the witness at your wedding," "he is obviously in love with you," "wife battering is a Serbian custom," and so on.

It would be unfair not to mention the positive effects of the war in some cases of domestic violence. It is known from other conflicts that crises can empower women and sometimes encourage them to rely less on marriage as a means of support (Bushra and Lopez, 1993). A war can help women leave violent husbands under the pretext of fleeing in refuge to protect themselves and their children. Some women we spoke with failed to leave violent husbands earlier because they were afraid of being unable to support themselves and their children. Now as survivors of war, who learned to cope alone with the difficulties of life in refuge, they felt empowered to realize alternatives to their earlier life.

CONCLUSION

War magnifies the gendered structure of violence, as it increases the power gap between men and women. Not only are women deprived of weapons as opposed to men who become more "masculine" having them, but they are deprived of the protection which they normally have as citizens and subordinates to men. The complete mechanism of protection embedded in patriarchal societies is paralyzed so that women do not have protection from either the state or the men in their lives. Their husbands, sons, and fathers are often absent from the home as they have gone to fight the war, or have been arrested, tortured, and killed. Women, who have no voice in deciding to go to war, are those who pay for men's decision to fight. Women from all sides are used, more or less, depending on the balance of power, as a means to achieve men's political and military ends. Not only are they left alone to cope with violence, destruction, and fear, but they are molested even more cruelly by those who, in patriarchal societies, are traditionally expected to protect them. Women are those who have to pay the price for their men's participation in war, either as victims of their aggression—justified as psychological trauma resulting from war—or as "possessions" of the enemy. Women are left to cope alone, not only with violence, but also with supporting their families and running households in the impossible conditions of war. They are often forced into disguised prostitution, and as refugees, also suffer from sexual harassment and abuse.

Although there have been important advances in recognizing rape as a war crime through international law, many of the effects of conflict suffered by women are not categorized as such by legal norms (Chinkin, 1993). Forced

NIKOLIĆ-RISTANOVIĆ

impregnation, violence from partners returning from warfare, and malnutrition caused by U.N. sanctions, for example, are not prohibited by international law. International law must recognize that women from all sides in conflicts suffer from violence, and offenders from all sides should be prosecuted (Chinkin, 1993).

NOTES

1. This is part of the material collected through interviews conducted by a group of researchers who are now analyzing the impact of war on women, based on analyses of women's personal experiences and definitions of violence. The interviewers and authors of the book are Vesna Nikolić-Ristanović, Slobodanka Konstantinovic-Vilić, Nataša Mrvić-Petrović, and Ivana Stevanović.

2. The research on spouse abuse, which we carried out at the Institute for Criminological Sociological Research in Belgrade, is the first research of this kind in the Federal Republic of Yugoslavia. The research was originally planned for a large sample, in order to estimate the number of crimes (a victimization survey). However, unfavorable economic conditions forced us to change course and study a smaller sample of 192 women. The women were asked whether they had experienced violence in their marriages (psychological, physical, or sexual). Those who replied affirmatively were then asked about the characteristics of their experiences, about their own reaction to these events, and about the subsequent social reaction that might take place.

3. The decrease in the number of phone calls in 1993 occurred because the Belgrade SOS hotline telephone number was changed in July of 1993, thus only 10 calls were recorded for the whole month of July 1993.

REFERENCES

El Bushra, J. and Piza E. Lopez. *Development in Conflict: The Gender Dimension*. Report of an Oxfam AGRA East Workshop held in Pattaya, Thailand, February 1–4, 1993.

Brownmiller, S. *Against Our Will*. New York: Simon and Schuster, 1975.

Chinkin, C. M. "Peace and Force in International Law." In *Reconceiving Reality: Women and International Law*, D.G. Dallmeyer, ed. New York: Asil, 1993.

Commissariat for Refugees of the Republic of Serbia. *Refugees in Serbia*. Belgrade: Commissariat for Refugees of the Republic of Serbia, 1994.

Fischer, E. "War, Women and Democracy." In *Test the West: Gender Democracy and Violence*. Vienna: Austrian Federal Ministry of Women's Affairs, 1994.

Jackson, S. "The Social Context of Rape: Sexual Scripts and Motivation," *Women's Studies International Quarterly* 1: 33–47, 1978.

Luković, P. "Media and War: Yugoslavia, the Mirror of Hatred." In *Yugoslavia Collapse War Crimes,* S. Biserko, ed. Belgrade: Center for Anti-War Action, 1993.

MacKinnon, C. A. "Comment: Theory is not a Luxury." In *Reconceiving Reality: Women and International Law*. D.G. Dallmeyer, ed. New York: Asil, 1993.

Mršević, Z. "Ženska prava su ljudska prava" (Women's Rights are Human Rights), SOS telefon za zene i decu zrtve nasilja, Beograd. (SOS Hotline for Women and Children Victims of Violence, Belgrade: Serbia.)

Nikolić-Ristanović, V. "Domestic Violence against Women in Conditions of War and

Economical Crises." Paper presented at the 8th International Symposium on Victimology, Adelaide, Australia, August 21–26, 1994, 1994.

Smith, L. *Domestic Violence: An Overview of the Literature.* London: Home Office Research and Planning Unit Report, 1989.

Vickers, J. *Women and War.* London: Zed Books, 1993.

NIKOLIĆ-RISTANOVIĆ

WOMEN'S VISIONS OF PEACE:

Images of Global Security

Betty Reardon

The need for women's perspectives on human development is critical since it is in the interest of human enrichment and progress to introduce and
weave into the social fabric women's concept of
equality, their choices between alternative development strategies and their approach to peace, in ac-
cordance with their aspirations, interests and talents
(Forward Looking Strategies, 6).

chapter 13

TOWARD A NONVIOLENT WORLD: WOMEN'S WAYS OF KNOWING

THE IMPORTANCE of introducing women's thinking into public affairs,
recognized in The Nairobi Forward Looking Strategies, reflects a recent trend
in feminist scholarship. Over the past several years, research into women's
ways of knowing, reasoning, and decisionmaking has demonstrated that, at
least in Western countries,[1] women's thinking is different from that of men;
and it has been argued, as noted above, that this difference can shed new light
on, and often produce unprecedented solutions to, some of the world's major
problems. With regard to issues of security and peace, as has been recounted,
women's thinking has already contributed significantly constructive direc-
tions. These "feminine" modes of thinking and problem solving can be
learned and applied by both women and men; thus, as indicated earlier, they
are an important influence in peace education.

Women's thinking and learning develops best when women's identities, values, and perspectives are affirmed in the learning process. They tend to learn most as "connected knowers" whose learning takes place in, and is related to, community. The significance of affirming identities and confirming learners as bearers of knowledge of value to the community has, I would argue, great significance to learning for global community building. Women's ways of knowing may well be applicable to others such as traditional peoples who, like women, have had little voice in global policy making.

> In the masculine myth, confirmation comes not at the beginning of education but at the end. Confirmation as a thinker and membership in a community of thinkers come as the climax of Perry's story of intellectual development in the college years. The student learns, according to Perry, that "we must all stand judgment" and must earn "the privilege of having [our] ideas respected." Having proved beyond reasonable doubt that he has learned to think in complex, contextual ways, the young man is admitted to the fraternity of powerful knowers. Certified as a thinker, he becomes one of Them (now dethroned to lower-case them). This scenario may capture the "natural" course of men's development in traditional, hierarchical institutions, but it does not work for women. For women, confirmation and community are prerequisites, rather than consequences of development. . .
>
> . . . It is clear from our data that women's sense of self and voice flourish when they become what we call connected and passionate knowers. We argue that educators can help women develop their minds and authentic voices if they emphasize connection over separation, understanding and acceptance over assessment, collaboration over competition, and discussion over debate, and if they accord respect to and allow time for the knowledge that emerges from first-hand experience. We have learned these things by listening to the woman's voice (Belenky et al. 1986: 25–26)

The mode of learning outlined above as women's ways of knowing may well be what is needed to engage the disparate and conflictual members of world society in a process of common learning for authentic global security. The adversarial proving of merit Belenky et al. allude to as the masculine confirmation process has been a style of politics as well as academics that has produced the very kind of thinking, described by Stephen Kull (1986) and Carol Cohn (1987), that women peace activists have begun to challenge.

Other feminist research, such as that of Carol Gilligan (1984), has shown that women tend to see reality as a set of interconnected experiences and interrelationships. They measure the desirability of an action in terms of its human consequences, a characteristic often sorely lacking in policy making. Because of their concern with relationships, women tend toward holistic views of the world that focus on problems in their general context over a longer time period, including past as well as future. For example, women in the peace movement tend not to focus on specific weapons in isolation from the overall arms development dynamic, not to see the arms trade as separate from

and enhancement of life and maintaining vital, mutually enhancing relation-ships. Thus nonviolence is a crucial element in feminist peace strategies.

While nonviolence as a philosophy or strategy is not feminist per se, it is consistent with women's modes of thinking and feminist approaches to con-flict resolution. Many feminist peace activists are practitioners and advocates of nonviolent change. Women struggling for peace and justice know the world can be very different, and they can and do envision alternative futures in which the peoples of the world can live together so as to enhance the quality of life for all. Feminine visions of the future involve the achievement of authentic, comprehensive global security. Through such exercises as "imag-ing a world without weapons," both women and men have envisioned a non-violent global society. Some have formed networks to refine and work for the achievement of such visions. One example of such a network is the Feminist Utopian Network that grew out of an international conference on Women and the Military System held in Finland in January 1987.

Yet it is not only feminist scholars and peace researchers who have the op-portunity to engage in international networks who are working for a nonvi-olent global society. The movement involves a great variety of women the world over.

From all walks of life, applying feminine values and perspectives to direct non-violent actions for peace have demonstrated ingenuity, creativity, tenaci-ty, and courage. Women have disrupted the patterns of their own lives and risked their careers and well-being in a series of actions throughout the world intended to raise public consciousness about the serious threats to survival and the human costs of the arms race, to demonstrate to their governments their knowledge and concern about these issues, to bear witness to their per-sonal and corporate commitments to reverse the arms race, and to achieve a just international economic order and to ultimately abolish war. As their abo-litionist and suffragist grandmothers before them, who helped abolish slavery and enfranchise women, they consistently and insistently declare and work for a more humane and equitable society. And they have achieved much.

Many women in their own homes and communities are making every ef-fort to overcome the violence that pervades society. In their personal relations and families, they practice constructive conflict resolution. They bring up their children in the knowledge that conflict can be conducted constructive-ly, humanely, nonviolently. They encourage cooperation among their children and advocate its emphasis in the schools. They monitor their children's read-ing, play, and, where TV sets are common in average households, their televi-sion viewing—not only to prevent the children's being inundated with mes-sages and images of violence, but also so that they can discuss these images and messages to encourage critical reflection and consideration of alterna-tives.

In their workplaces outside the home, many women are encouraging more communicative and cooperative, and less competitive, atmospheres. As they demand freedom from sexual harassment for themselves, they also demand that all workers be treated with dignity. They try to raise issues related to peace, conflict, and disarmament to raise consciousness about the problems and the possibilities for resolution. Many of them who are educators of young children try to convey attitudes of respect for others and knowledge of techniques for nonviolent conflict resolution. Some who are teachers of older children and in universities are active in the development of peace education and peace studies.

In their places of worship and in their community organizations, many women are initiating study-action programs. Many are leaders in peace organizations, and women make up the majority of the volunteer workers who administer and support the programs and demonstrations of the peace organizations that comprise the major part of the worldwide peace movement. They are as well the backbone of the disarmament movement and provide the major source of energy for the non-governmental organizations (NGOs) that spearhead that movement and the related campaigns for human rights, development, and the environment.

Women can do and are doing much to bring about a nonviolent world. But perhaps the most effective thing women can do is to become significant voices in policy making, to bring feminist perspectives, feminine values, and feminine modes of thought into equal consideration with masculine perspectives, values, and modes in confronting the major questions of peace and security. Certainly women should make every effort toward the implementation of the Nairobi Forward Looking Strategies for the Advancement of Women. These measures call for women's input into all aspects of peacemaking, from the highest levels of policy making and international negotiation through the educational process in all spheres and at all levels, including the local, grassroots level where the full impact of war and militarism are felt and where the basic constituency for peace must be built. At all of these levels of policymaking and implementation, and in all these spheres of action, there is need of both the energies and the concrete contributions of women, but also, and most especially, of women's views and experience and feminine values and perspectives.

The Nairobi Forward Looking Strategies lay stress on women's participation in decision making in regard to public policy and technology, especially at the regional and international levels, and set a specific goal for the United Nations: "All bodies and organizations of the United Nations system should therefore take all possible measures to achieve the participation of women on equal terms with men at all levels by the year 2000" (FLS, para. 356). Similar goals for all public policymaking bodies are being actively pursued by women throughout the world in their local communities, in provincial and national politics, and in international organizations. Such goals can be enhanced by the implementation of the strategies. The U.N. Secretary General himself has called for more women's participation.

> The world-wide contribution of women to the promotion of peace, to social equity, and to global development is increasingly evident. So, too, is the degree to which women suffer from the persistence of conflict, from hunger and malnutrition, and from an unending arms race. More than ever, women are becoming active in seeking to overcome these negative phenomena. In this they have demonstrated commitment and determination, standing in the forefront in pursuit of the requirements of a peaceful global society. Women have brought energy and inspiration to the struggle for social justice and economic progress to the common benefit of all humanity, regardless of sex, race, or belief.

> Unfortunately, women remain inadequately represented at national and international decision-making levels. Where women's views and experience are absent, the political process remains incomplete.

> . . . It must be the mutual goal of governments, intergovernmental and non-governmental organizations, and of individuals to act for the preservation of peace, for sustained economic development and for social justice. The full and equal participation of women in these endeavors is essential. While there is ground for encouragement in the progress achieved during the United Nations Decade for Women, work must continue towards full implementation of the Nairobi Forward Looking Strategies for equality between women and men in all spheres of life (Perez de Cuellar, 1987).

Thus, one of the primary things women can do for a nonviolent world is to work to assure that the implementation of the strategies is monitored and that national policies and programs are derived consistent with the goals and purposes of the International Women's Decade. Continued cooperation between intergovernmental agencies and non-governmental organizations is essential to this end, as is the continued infusion of feminine thinking and its capacities for imaging peace. Women's ways of knowing, rooted in connectedness, cooperation, and discussion, have enabled women to envision a transformed world characterized by real human security.

IMAGING AN ALTERNATIVE FUTURE

Because women carry most of the social responsibilities for nurturing and preparing the young for their adult lives, anticipating the needs of aging relatives, and struggling for community improvements to assure a better quality of life, they are practical futurists. Many have developed the capacity to live in two realities. On the one hand, they have mastered the arts of survival and nurturance within the context of the present reality of conflict, human suffering, and inadequate resources. On the other hand, they also exercise capacities to envision a better world and to struggle for its achievement as they see to

REARDON

217

the daily needs of those in their care. Women's lives, women's movements, and women's peace organizations are animated by clear and positive visions of a world at peace. While there may be no common definition of peace with which all women throughout the world would agree, there are emerging notions of what constitutes peace and how it can be achieved. Some are even envisioning, in systematic, intentional programs, what peace would be like, how it would affect our daily lives and the social structures in which we live them.[2] Such visions provide images of a transformed world that inform and energize women's efforts for peace. Four such visions reflect the major issues of peace and security, reviewed in major U.N. reports,[3] and reflected in U.N. conventions and standards on human rights. Each vision reflects women's concepts of authentic global security.

The four visions: "The birthright vision" images a world in which the basic human needs of the Earth's peoples are met; "the vision of women as equal partners" centers on the full equality of women and men in the public and the private spheres; "the transcendence of violence vision" projects a world free of war and the physical abuse of women; and "the vision of an ecological community" perceives a world built on common interests and sharing, and respect and care for the planet Earth. All four are distinct dimesions of the comprehensive image women hold of a total system of authentic global security. Each vision reflects possibilities for meeting a fundamental human need or expectation of well-being, and offers a goal against which to measure progress toward overcoming the various forms of violence and peacelessness.

218

The Birthright Vision: Vision of an Equitable World Order

Because women's visions of global security are comprehensive and universal, the alternatives they seek offer authentic security to the whole human family. The first and most fundamental vision is one in which the essential security requisite of the fulfillment of basic human needs would be not only the aspiration of security policy planners but the primary criteria by which policy choices are made. If such were the case, women believe, the minimal security expectations of every child born into the world would assure them fulfillment of these basic needs:

- Food in adequate amounts, and of appropriate types and quality, to assure normal growth and physical development
- A home in a clean, sturdy structure appropriate to the climate and adequate to the size of the family
- Parents or caring guardians whose own basic needs are sufficiently met so that they can in fact fulfill their parenting responsibilities
- A community provided with clean water, basic sanitation facilities, health care services, and education at least at the primary level
- An environment that offers the possibility for sustainable development

based on respect for the ecology of the planet, provision of clean air, and preservation of the fundamental natural beauty of the Earth, all essential ingredients in fulfilling the aesthetic needs manifested by all people

- A world community actively committed to the pursuit of peace, justice, and sustainable, ecologically responsible development

Women, particularly mothers and teachers, see such conditions as the basic requirements to be fulfilled for all children if they are to develop, learn, and mature into persons capable of pursuing their unique capacities and becoming responsible, constructive members of society. Indeed, the world community recognized this to be so in 1959 with the Declaration of the Rights of the Child and the Convention on the Rights of the Child adopted by the U.N. General Assembly in 1989. The convention, in fact, sets forth in detail a set of standards as entitlements of every child, entitlements that provide physical, social, psychological, and cultural security. A world moving toward peace would be a world where the interests of the children and the vulnerable formed major policy criteria. Seeing these possibilities, women's groups such as the Women's International League for Peace and Freedom joined child advocacy groups such as Defense for Children International to work for the adoption of the convention by the General Assembly, and in a campaign for its ratification by the United States and other nations. All cooperate with UNICEF toward its implementation.

Women as Equal Partners: A Vision of a World of Equality

The nature of women's lives and of the inequalities between men and women is such that throughout most of the world, women, as we have seen, bear a double social and economic burden. Economically, they form a major part of the productive work force in both agriculture and industry, and they produce the entire work force in bearing and raising children. Socially they are responsible for providing the major share of fundamental health care, education, remedial, and compensatory services to those in all kinds of need, usually with resources they must produce themselves. In times of economic stress or social crises, they are called upon to absorb the stresses through the means of household management with little, often no, public assistance. Women provide their societies with fundamental and essential unrecompensed services but have little or no say in deciding the purposes to which these services will be put.

Most of the world's women put in a double work day, rising and retiring hours before and after the rest of the family to perform household chores and provide meals before and after full days in fields, factories, and offices.[4] Women are, and are expected to be, at the service of their families at all hours, under all circumstances. In few societies, and in not too many more individual instances, do men share fully in the tasks and responsibilities of running households and

REARDON

caring for families. Yet they have the almost exclusive right to decide upon the social and economic policies that determine the conditions in which households exist and to dispose of all the resources available to the family. Women, who provide the fundamental bases of the society and the economy, have only a minor share in the benefits of both. Owning less than 1 percent of the world's wealth, they have virtually no power to decide how that wealth will be used, or how the products of their own labors, including their children, will be used by the society, and little or no control over their own time and their own bodies. And, as we have seen, they have been, and are, subject to every possible form of violence, including some particular to their sex.

For centuries many women and men have been aware of these inequities, but comparatively few have sought to remedy them. With the United Nation's International Women's Decade, however, the attention of the whole world was called undeniably to the injustice of the imbalance in the contributions made by, and the benefits accorded to, women. While the fundamental unjust conditions have not been redressed, the struggle for equity has been universalized and accelerated and is now pursued in light of a vision of equality that would assure an equitable distribution of time, wealth, and power between men and women. Women envision a transformation in the relations between women and men that would bring to the sphere of social and economic management and policy making the perspectives of women and feminine values, on an equal footing with masculine values and perspectives, affording us a more fully human view of social reality and a more holistic approach to public issues, global problems, and world security. Such a transformation would first and foremost renounce violence against women and the vulnerable. The vision of human equality arises from the principles articulated by the Universal Declaration of Human Rights and spelled out in the international legal standards created to implement them.

The Women's Decade and the Forward Looking Strategies represent a major challenge to the world community to implement these standards on behalf of women. The Convention on the Elimination of All Forms of Discrimination against Women provides the international legal standards that support and uphold the policy changes called for by the strategies, including a blueprint for change and the concretization of this vision of equality. The survival needs of the human family and their planet home require that the skills, energies, perspectives, and insights of women not be undervalued and repressed by discriminatory laws and customs. Further, if men are to have a greater stake in the continuation of human life and the improvement of its quality, they must take more responsibility for and participate more fully in the activities that provide care and the fulfillment of human needs. A more equal balance between women and men in all spheres of social and family life is essential to the achievement of global security.

So it is that women envision a world in which they share equally with men in guiding and governing the social order and carrying the responsibilities for maintaining and improving the quality of human life. This new vision of the world would be managed by equal numbers of women and men in the policymaking councils, in the legislative halls, in the administrative offices, as well as in all diplomatic delegations and all bodies of the United Nations. In carrying out their responsibilities, these governing and guidance agencies would call equally on the experience and capacities of both women and men. In the formulation of public policy, feminine as well as masculine insights and criteria would be brought to bear. Equal attention would be given to the need for care as to the need to control. Many feminists argue that such equal representation of women and men, of feminine and masculine values, could so change the climate of policy making that the possibilities to transcend war, significantly reduce structural violence, and achieve authentic peace would be greatly enhanced. We could make strides toward a global society in which the rights enumerated in the universal declaration are actual norms not just aspirations.

The vision of women as equal partners also foresees women playing a significant role in the planning and management of the economy. No longer serving merely as cheap and disposable labor, or as food producers whose production needs are ignored, women would contribute as much with their minds as with their eyes, hands, and backs to the production of economic goods. Such goods when produced by feminine criteria would be more directed to fulfilling human needs, providing authentic economic security rather than the continued technical advancement of war preparations. Public expenditures would be of an entirely different balance between social and military than now reported in *World Military and Social Expenditures*. Serving in such capacities will require equal educational and employment opportunities for women, a condition far different from present circumstances. The 1995 World Conference to assess the Forward Looking Strategies should call for more than the 30 percent goal suggested by Boulding and the Economic and Social Council for women's participation in the United Nations and other policymaking and implementing bodies. The goal should be expanded to 50 percent.

Such a public world cannot be achieved without comparable changes toward equality in the private sphere, which exerts the main influence over the relations between women and men. If women are to take up equal responsibility for the public order, then they can no longer be expected to carry the major burden of the household and family. In a world of equality, women and men would share these tasks as they would the tasks of running the economy and the polity. Each would contribute equally to the common good of the society and to providing a nurturing environment in the family and the household and strive toward personal relations of equality, complementarity and mutuality. Equality also would pervade educational practice with

221

REARDON

changes, advocated by feminist peace educators, such as the development of caring and nurturing capacities in boys and men and the enhancement of political and technical capacities in women toward the achievement of a true partnership society (Eisler and Loye, 1990).

The vision of women as equal partners is extremely significant in strengthening the possibilities for peace. Enjoying the rich satisfactions of participating in the growth and development of young children enhances the quality of men's lives and provides nurturing male role models as strong as that of the warrior for little boys and adolescent males. Men so invested in the development of the young, in the maintenance of daily life, may well experience greater inhibitions on placing human life at risk through waging or planning wars. They would come in touch with those feminine and nurturant aspects of all human beings that have long inspired the struggle for peace.

Such a world would offer healthier communities and a stronger social order with all members equally considered, concerned, and invested in the success of public policy. This vision is far from the reality in which we now live. However, it is a vision of a practical possibility, a possibility that informs the international human rights standards and inspires women's movements and peace and human rights movements throughout the world.

The Transcendence of Violence: Vision of a Demilitarized and Disarmed World

Women suffer the violence of the world on three levels. As has been described, they are themselves the victims of the generalized violence of war and oppression and of special forms of violence inflicted specifically on women. They suffer the pain of often being helpless to save their loved ones and those in their care from the violence of armed conflict and economic structures that impose cruel deprivations. They are the victims of the violation of the integrity of their persons by sexual abuse and rape, by lack of control over their own bodies. And they suffer, as well, from caring deeply about the plight of all who fall victim to the disasters resulting from militarism and militarization.

Women the world over yearn for a world in which order is maintained by consensus, goals are pursued by constructive rather than destructive means, conflict is resolved without violence, and women are free of the constant fear of sexual harassment and rape. These yearnings lead women to envision a disarmed, demilitarized world in which violence has become a tragic aberration rather than the social norm. The vision of the transcendence of violence brings forth an image of a world constructed on the basis of some of the fundamental values of global feminism. First, the sanctity of the Earth, underlying traditional peoples' reverence for nature, is now essential to preserving our planet. Another value focuses on the oneness of humanity, recognizing the universality of human needs and aspirations, and calls us to understand that the human species will survive or perish together. And last, an emphasis on the integrity of persons demands that the inequities of the global economy and political system be reformed by such measures as a New International Economic Order and a respect for the human rights of all persons. These life-affirming values, when applied to present world conditions, clarify the extent and nature of the violence of the world and the severe and insidious consequences of world militarization.

Militarization, as Ruth Sivard and other peace researchers have demonstrated, has increased apace with the spiraling arms race. With the arms race came an erosion of the fragile trends toward human liberation and the fulfillment of fundamental rights and freedoms that seemed so vigorous at the end of World War II.[5] Indeed, the tragic truth is that within a few short years of the promulgation of the Universal Declaration of Human Rights, the trend toward its realization was reversed, and an alarming increase in its violation has been documented annually by intergovernmental and non-governmental organizations. During the 1970s and 1980s especially, gross violations were on the increase. Often committed in the name of national security, repression of civil liberties, disappearances, and torture still infected politics and almost invariably accompanied the exertion of the power of the military and the imposition of military rule and militarist values. The militarization of the world also strengthened institutionalized commercial prostitution and other forms of sexual slavery. However, while armed conflict has been on the increase, it has been only one of the direct causes of higher levels of violence against women. Industrialization and corporate enterprises have also spawned new forms of exploitation and prostitution, and although the number of military governments has been reduced in recent years, the legacy of repression and human rights violations continues to be a source of much human suffering. Women, therefore, see the need to devise policies and strategies to reverse all trends toward militarization and to root out the militarist thinking and value system that is the cause of most of the violence pervading our contemporary human experience.

Such policies might be derived from images of a demilitarized world that portray new social institutions, and processes incorporating the values and techniques of nonviolence. Women envision a world in which negotiation, arbitration, mediation, and the rule of law have replaced the role of force and armed conflict to resolve disputes and impose the resolution on the losing party. They envision vast numbers of persons trained in nonviolent conflict management operating at every level of social organization, from the rural village or urban neighborhood to the international level, using skills and techniques now available to all and applying feminist modes of compromise and reconciliation, as a means of achieving win–win solutions where no one need be a loser.

Women envision a process of transarmament and demilitarization in which national armed forces are gradually replaced by nonviolent civilian defense forces trained in passive resistance and nonthreatening defense postures. They

223

REARDON

see this reduction of national armed forces as occurring simultaneously with the building of mediation forces and a United Nations standing peacekeeping force that relieves nations of the burden of each being the sole defender of its own interests and borders. They understand that the establishment of such a force would signify the existence of sufficient communal interest to substitute peacekeeping policing mechanisms in the place of preparation for war. The world would have acknowledged that order and cooperation are more in the interest of every nation than the anarchy of an unpredictable and dangerous system of "self-defense." Moving toward a system of "common security" is seen as a way of increasing authentic world security.[6]

Women see the nurturing of international understanding and the building of consensus as developing through cooperative efforts at the resolution of world problems, through more open and regular communication among potential adversaries, through mutual trust building and independent and collaborative initiatives in the reduction of armed forces and the ending of the arms trade. They see the possibilities of major cultural exchanges involving local communities as well as national agencies. They see the savings of resources and reduction of tensions to be gained through economic cooperation and economic conversion.

A demilitarized world would be one in which sexual slavery and sexist repression would be guarded against by world agencies and institutions established to protect and enhance human rights and fundamental freedoms. Rape, enforced prostitution, involuntary pregnancy and the gross exploitation of women's bodies would not be tolerated in a world committed to the development of nonviolent institutions and systems.

What is most essential in this process of transcending violence is the demilitarization of the mind. As we have been instructed by the UNESCO charter, and reminded in quotations from Nancy Shelley, Charlene Spretnak, and Carol Cohn, "wars begin in the minds of men," especially in the minds of men who believe force and violence to be the necessary or appropriate means of achieving human purposes. The willingness to use violence for public purposes stems from a form of thinking that sanctions violence and sees human beings as inherently unequal. As I have argued elsewhere (Reardon, 1985), the inequality between women and men has been a fundamental cause of the social toleration of many forms of violence against women, and of the perpetuation of war.

Many women believe that only through a carefully orchestrated, sincerely and zealously pursued process of demilitarization can the violence of the world be reduced—all violence, the direct violence of armed conflict arising from political and ideological struggles, and the indirect structural violence of economic exploitation from greed and competition. Understanding the links between military violence and particular forms of violence against women, highlighted by the statement of the IPRA Consultation on Women, Mili-

224

REARDON

tarism, and Disarmament, leads many to see disarmament and demilitarization as important as the reduction of the abuse of women through laws regarding rape, family violence, and economic equity. Both routes must be pursued, but the primary path to the envisioned transcendence of violence is
through comprehensive demilitarization of economic and political structures,
social custom, and ways of thinking.

Those now working for a demilitarized world are formulating and lobbying for nonmilitary solutions to contemporary international crises, as they
strive to educate policy makers about the possibilities for alternative security
systems. They have gone directly to the leadership of hostile nations. As did
their foremothers before World War I, Women for Mutual Security sent a delegation of women to Baghdad in an attempt to avoid the Gulf War. One day
before the hostilities were initiated by the United States, they issued the following message to President Bush.

We are a delegation of women representing women's organizations from all over
the world, and have just returned from a trip to Baghdad. We spent four days
there and had full and lengthy discussions with the following people:

(1) Mr. Latif Nusaif Jasim, Minister of Culture and Information
(2) Mr. Saadi Mahdi Salif, President of the National Council
(3) Mr. Taha Yasim Ramadan, First Deputy to the Prime Minister
(4) Glanes Aziz, Vice President of the National Council
(5) Adel Abdel Karim, Foreign Affairs Head, National Council
(6) The Executive Board of the Federation of Iraqi Women

225

In all of our discussions with ministers and other officials there was, of course, a
common line on the situation and a genuine conviction that Iraq was right in its
analysis and evaluation and right in its stand.

Reading between the lines, however, but sometimes from comments made more
overtly, we understood that there was flexibility, and a willingness to consider
other options along the lines of their proposed peace plan of August 12, 1990.
There were no changes in substance, but changes in the tone of the presentation.
Clearly they want to sit down and truly discuss the issues.

In more specific terms, we believe the withdrawal from Kuwait is negotiable:

This is why we ask you, have all efforts at peace been made? We believe they
have not. Although there have been some sketchy overtures on both sides, the
possibilities were allowed to disappear in the shifting sand. One "last effort" is
not enough. The last efforts must continue. It is never too late to stop a war.

Our women's plea, and in the name of justice, and for the sake of humanity, we
ask you to reject the rivers of blood that will flow in the Gulf region and find a
political solution. This is the only solution in harmony with human intelligence
and civilized behavior.

Margarita Papandreou, Co-ordinator, Women for Mutual Security

REARDON

Nawal El Saadawi, Arab Women's Solidarity Federation (Egypt)

Flora Abdrakhmanova, Women's Int'l League for Peace and Freedom, Soviet Women's Committee

Joan Drake, Institute of Policy Studies, Madres (Lat. America), WILPF

Maude Barlow, Voice of Women, Canada, Women World Parliamentarians for Peace

Kay Camp, Women's Int'l League for Peace and Freedom

Fathieh Saudi, Arab Women's Solidarity Association (Jordan)

On behalf of the International Women's Gulf Peace Initiative (Women for Mutual Security, 1991b).

Earlier, on January 10, 1991, they had explained the nature of their concerns in a statement at a press conference in Baghdad.

We are a delegation of women here in Baghdad representing women's organizations from all over the world which came to get a more comprehensive view of the situation, and to see if there was any way we could play a role in an authentic peace process.

As women, there are many elements in this brinkmanship strategy that create deep anxieties for us . . . we have the problem of the double standards in international law. We have fought the double standard in male-female relationships for decades now, so we are particularly sensitive to the hypocrisy of such standards. . .

And last, but not least, we are against the use of force in settling conflict situations. When people develop the attitude that differences can be settled through violent means, then we perpetuate a mentality that brings violence into all human relations, and right into the home, where women and children are the primary victims. War cannot be diplomacy by other means. War must become obsolete . . .

Women have always been the true advocates of peace. We believe in living for a cause, not dying for it. If we had the power in our hands, we would sit at the negotiating table, and we would search for as long as it takes for a peaceful solution. Disputes cannot be settled without discussion (Women for Mutual Security, 1991a).

In calling for discussion, these women were calling for not only an alternative approach to conflict, but an alternate way of thinking. The same mode of thinking that sees people as inherently unequal also makes possible the use of violence against others who are perceived as less important, evil, or in opposition to authority. Violence against women, cultural and political repression, as well as war, all begin in the minds of men, and all are interrelated. The way we think, and the way we teach the young to think, about the world and others will be the main determinant of the future security of the world. The processes of demilitarization and moral inclusion required to lead us to human equality, a just peace, and authentic global security must begin with the demilitarization of the mind, and that step can be initiated by first becoming fully aware of the nature and extent of violence against women as the main indicator of the general level of violence in the society. Awareness of a problem is the beginning of learning that can change the way we think about the world. Feminist peace researchers argue that there is a need to change our way of thinking so as to see all people as persons equally endowed with dignity, fundamental human rights, and integrity, within one moral community, the universal human community (Opotow, 1990). Moral inclusion will lead us to reject the belief in the inferiority of women and the concept that adversaries are not entitled to their human rights; indeed, to transcend the very concept of "enemy" that is fundamental to the war system (Reardon, 1985).

An Ecological Community: Vision of Comprehensive Authentic Global Security

When the various visions of global security women have projected merge into one comprehensive vision of global security, we see a world in which all the feminist criteria for security are used to establish social goals and guide policy formation. Such a world would be striving for ecological balance and the health of the biosphere through the application of a comprehensive, exigently observed set of planetary environmental standards. All peoples of the Earth would be adherents to the Earth Covenant, a document drafted by an international group of men and women under the initiative of the feminist peace researcher, cofounder of Global Education Associates, Patricia Mische. The document reflects the belief in the efficacy of observing agreements and standards such as those set forth by the United Nations. Its substance also embodies ecofeminist principles of the organic interrelatedness of living systems and the imperative to survival of nurturing relationships.

> We and all living beings depend upon the Earth and upon one another for our common existence, well-being, and development. Our common future depends upon a reexamination of our most basic assumptions about humankind's relationship to the Earth. We must develop common principles and systems to shape this future in harmony with the Earth.

Principles and Commitments

In covenant with each other and on behalf of the whole Earth community, we commit ourselves to the following principles and actions:

- *Relationship with the Earth*. All Life forms are sacred. Each human being is a unique and integral part of the Earth's community of life and has a special responsibility to care for life in all its diverse forms.

Therefore, we will act and live in a way that preserves the natural life processes of the Earth and respects all species and their habitats. We will work to prevent ecological degradation.

227

REARDON

- *Relationship with Each Other.* Each human being has the right to a healthful environment and to access to the fruits of the Earth. Each also has a continual duty to work for the realization of these rights for present and future generations.

Therefore—concerned that every person have food, shelter, pure air, potable water, education, employment, and all that is necessary to enjoy the full measure of human rights—we will work for more equitable access to the Earth's resources.

- *Relationship Between Economic and Ecological Security.* Since human life is rooted in the natural processes of the Earth, economic development, to be sustainable, must preserve the life-support systems of the Earth.

Therefore, we will use environmentally protective technologies and promote their availability to people in all parts of the Earth. When doubtful about the consequences of economic goals and technologies on the environment, we will allow an extra margin of protection for nature.

- *Governance and Ecological Security.* The protection and enhancement of life on Earth demand adequate legislative, administrative and judicial systems at appropriate local, national, regional, and international levels. In order to be effective, these systems must be empowering, participatory, and based on openness of information.

Therefore, we will work for the enactment of laws that protect the environment and promote their observance through educational, political and legal action. We shall advance policies of prevention rather than only reacting to ecological harm.

Declaring our partnership with one another and with our Earth, we give our word of honor to be faithful to the above commitments (Mische, 1989: 33)

Standards of well-being much like those listed in the International Covenant on Economic, Social, and Cultural Rights (1966) would be used to steer the human family toward policies designed to meet human needs, in a framework respectful of the limits of the Earth. The statistics that now appear annually in *World Military and Social Expenditures* would be drastically altered as all societies put a higher priority on serving the social needs of their people than on keeping up with a costly and destructive arms race. Relations among nations would be strengthened by a variety of cooperative and confidence-building programs, and peace and security would be maintained by the non-violent institutions of an alternative security system.

Central to this vision is the process of economic conversion, with a shift in resources from military to civilian production along with a concomitant process of disarmament and the building of peacekeeping capacities so that the world could ultimately achieve general and complete disarmament. The twin tasks of economic conversion for development and disarmament as a process of peacemaking are the main foundations for a planetary human community. Development pursued with a respect for the health of the planet would demonstrate the ecofeminist perspective in global economic policy.

228

REARDON

When women's visions take the form of intentional imaging, actual steps, events, and policies are articulated that could bring the vision into being. These histories of the future are sometimes called "transition scenarios." Here is one such feminist transition scenario on how peace might come to the world, devised on the eve of the second special session on disarmament of the General Assembly. It follows actual history until 1992 and then imagines possibilities for the next century. Some details have been added since the first writing.

Disarmament is the major transformational task for our historical period and the key to this transition scenario, which envisions general and complete disarmament as only a first step toward exorcising coercive force from the world political system. When we consider a total peace system as the overall goal, disarmament does not seem so remote or unattainable. It is but one part of the total system. If, as in Elise Boulding's frame of reference, we see an historical period as 200 years, we can look forward and backward at the peace-building process at work and perceive disarmament not as an end but as the turning point. Elise uses the 200-year period primarily to stretch the visioning process in somewhat the same way the World Order people talk about relevant utopias. It places the immediate present's problems in a different dimension and makes them less overwhelming . . .

I find it helpful to think of disarmament as a turning point in the transition scenario. Disarmament would be the structural manifestation of a commitment to peace, to the reduction of violence and coercive force. If we look at the historical process in a 200-year framework with our era as a turning point, it might look something like the following in terms of historical landmarks:

1899	The International Court of Justice at the Hague—an attempted institutional alternative to war through the adjudication of international disputes
1915-17	Founding of major international women's peace movement—forerunner of Women's International League for Peace and Freedom
1928	The Kellogg-Briand Pact—a treaty to which more than 50 nations ultimately adhered that renounced war as an instrument of national policy
1945	The United Nations Charter that declared its purpose as ending war
1962	McCloy-Zorin Agreement on General and Complete Disarmament stating that total disarmament was the ultimate goal of the negotiating process
1975	Mexico City International Women's Year Conference beginning of U.N. Decade for Women
1978	The UN Special Session on Disarmament (SSD I) which declared disarmament as a basic requirement for peace and development; provided an outline of needed steps toward disarmament

1979   Convention on the Elimination of All Forms of Discrimination Against Women; more women come into politics

1980   Copenhagen mid-women's decade conference asserts essential link between women's emancipation and peace

1982   The Second Special Session on Disarmament (SSD II) launched the World Disarmament Campaign to inform and educate about the needs and possibilities for disarmament

1985   Nairobi Conference formulates Forward Looking Strategies for the Advancement of Women; links women's rights and peace
Beginning of changes in world political and power relationships

1991   General Assembly establishes registry to record and control arms trade

1992   U.N. Summit on Environment and Development adopts principles for ecologically sound development based on criteria for healthy societies and a healthy planet; Secretary General issues Agenda for Peace; Chemical Weapons prohibition adopted

1995   International prohibition of the use, production, deployment or development of weapons of mass destruction called for by World Women's Conference, Beijing

2000   International prohibition of the arms trade results from NGO efforts

2020   General and Complete Disarmament Agreement (GCDA)—member nations of the United Nations acknowledge their adherence to a worldwide agreement; total disarmament process begun; Agreement negotiated by an assembly of equal numbers of women and men

2050   Nonviolence Accord (NVA)—the nations of the world renounce the use of violence as a means to social, economic, and political ends by signing the NVA; delegates cite the Seville Statement

2100   Confederation of Human Communities on Planet Earth—formal acknowledgment of an institutionalized system of global peace, based on the Universal Declaration of Human Rights and the Earth Covenant

In working toward a peace system, by about 2050 we should achieve a Nonviolence Accord. Institutionally and technologically, the accord (NVA) would be preceded by three-quarters of a century of a nation-state system that attempted arms control while continuing to build stockpiles and distribute arms. Those states chose military values and security at the cost of human values and human security. Finally, the deterioration of the quality and potential for continuation of human life becomes so apparent that a major value shift occurs, away from militarism and toward humanism. This shift was largely the result of the women's peace movement struggling to replace military values with human values.

Movement toward NVA begins in the last quarter of the 20th century with various nonviolent strategies applied to actual conflicts, staged disarmament, and global institution building that would bring about general and complete disarmament under global institutional control, with compulsory, peaceful conflict-resolution machinery for the settlement of international disputes. A global security force would maintain world security and gradually obtain the exclusive right to use force internationally. National forces trained in nonviolent intervention methods would be reduced to the minimum necessary to preserve domestic order . . .

The disarmament movement, merging with environmental and human rights and women's movements, outlines economic and political conversion based on principles of ecological balance and social justice.

By the end of the 21st century the nonviolent social order could be institutionalized into a functioning peace system. The system would be officially inaugurated with a charter for the Confederation of Human Communities on Planet Earth. Such a charter would officially recognize as global regulatory agencies those institutions that the global community had devised over the last century and a half to assure equitable enjoyment of peace and justice by all the peoples of the world, and the health and viability of the planet.

Through the humane application of technology, as envisioned by Boulding and such feminist science fiction authors as Ursula LeGuin, the forces of community and consensus could build so that coercion of any kind, even nonviolent, would simply fade away from the repertoire of socially acceptable human behavior. The former consequence—mutual empowerment of formerly competitive human groups and nation states, even women and men—would enhance the development of the synergic types of power that futurists and feminists envision now. Thus the human capacity to achieve goals would be increased enormously, even to the point of creating such a true peace system by the beginning of the 22nd century (Adapted and expanded from Reardon, 1980).

231

To envision such possibilities is the first step in bringing them about. Without such visions we cannot move into an uncertain and unknown future, a future that conforms more explicitly to our feminist values. It is from these values of care, inclusion, fairness, nonviolence, and mutuality that we determine policies and implementation plans. And it is from today's policies that tomorrow will be born.

FEMINIST QUESTIONS FOR ASSESSING SECURITY POLICY

I have tried to make two things sharply evident in this review of the relationship between women and peace: the need to change the modes of thinking we bring to issues of national and world security, and the need to change the structures that exclude women's full and vitally needed contribution to the peacemaking process. To bring about structural change we need policy change. In other words, just as women are now asserting a new and unprecedented effort to gain a voice and articulate their perspectives to the public, they must also find ways to be heard by policy makers. Feminists in seeking ways to bring women's experience into politics are raising new policy questions based on criteria derived from women's ways of thinking.

From such questions, steps toward the evolution of a transition scenario may arise.

As I have tried to demonstrate, women's ways of thinking lead to a distinctly feminine approach to security issues that is quite different from the current approaches to national security applied by the dominantly male political leadership. Throughout, I have tried to demonstrate the need to bring the feminine approach into policymaking, and to bring more women into the policymaking process, to introduce feminine perspectives and criteria, and to provide the benefits of women's ways of thinking. The feminine approach suggested here produces a particular set of criteria that women bring to the assessment of security policy. These criteria, like women's visions of a world at peace, derive directly from the four essential security expectations outlined in the introduction that comprise the feminist concept of authentic global security. They can be designated as sustainability, vulnerability, equity, and protection.

Sustainability

Sustainability derives from the expectation that the Earth will sustain life and demands that unnecessary damage to the environment and the natural order and basic resources be avoided. Sustainability is a criterion that requires raising questions about the ecological dimensions and consequences of every policy decision. Any action taken for public purposes may have ecological consequences. Much media attention has been given to personal action and behaviors in regard to "cleaning up" the environment. Equal attention needs to be given to public policy in regard to sustaining and restoring it. Questions about long-term as well as short-run effects on the environment need to be raised in consideration of every public issue. Local as well as potential global impacts must be anticipated. The fundamental question to be asked is whether the policy in question will harm or enhance any of the fragile ecological systems of the Earth. The principles of the Earth Covenant should be applied to every policy in the exercise of the criteria of sustainability. If the Earth is to sustain humanity, then humanity must sustain the Earth.

Vulnerability

Vulnerability derives from the expectation of the meeting of basic human needs and requires that policies not result in further deprivation of the weak and the poor. Vulnerability recognizes the fragility of most life forms, of social systems as well as ecosystems. It recognizes, too, that harm to one part of any system affects the whole system. Deprivation in one sector of society ultimately weakens the whole of society. The structural violence of ignoring the human-needs implications of any policy decision makes the nations and communities experiencing poverty less secure and ultimately the world less secure. Respecting and accounting for vulnerability determine the level of

justice in a society. If justice is to be achieved, every policy should be examined in the light of its actual or potential effect on the vulnerable. As every
public policy is considered, questions should be raised as to how it will affect
the poor and the environment, and whether it will increase or decrease the
total deprivation suffered by the human family and the environmental health
of the planet. The Convention on the Rights of the Child, the Forward
Looking Strategies, the Convention on All Forms of Discrimination against
Women and Agenda 21 issued by the Rio Earth Summit on environment and
development provide particular indicators for assessing social and ecological
vulnerability.

Equity

Equity derives from the expectation that humans will be nurtured by their
own societies and necessitates a process of policymaking that is based upon
full and fair representation of all, and thus requires that the policymaking
process involve equal numbers of women and men. Equity ultimately rests on
the full and universal recognition of human rights and dignity. Equity in such
universal terms can best be assessed by taking account of the effects a policy
will have on the human rights of women. Limits on, or denial of, the rights of
women affect the rights of others, those who depend on them, and the communities in which they live. A policy should be assessed in light of whether it
will protect or violate the fundamental rights of any and all groups affected,
and the rights of women are the best indicator of the wider effects. In every
decisionmaking process, we should ask what results might accrue to ethnic
minorities, indigenous peoples, oppressed persons, as well as women. The
Universal Declaration of Human Rights and the conventions derived from it,
particularly those related to discrimination against women, racism, and
apartheid, provide readily applicable standards of equity.

233

Protection

Protection derives from the expectation of defense against harm, be it from
other persons or groups or from natural and sometimes unexpected sources.
It calls for serious efforts both at creating positive, constructive relationships
with others and at avoiding putting society at risk of harm of any type—two
skills women have perfected over the centuries. It requires more efforts at establishing positive interdependence, and the avoidance of national policies
that weaken or damage relationships, create hostilities, or threaten the health
and well-being of any sectors of society. It demands the end to the development of ever more "sophisticated" arms and a cessation of the arms trade as
the greatest security risks we face. New and creative efforts in international
cooperation, confidence building, and conflict resolution must be devised and
pursued. Protection from harm, the criterion now most influential in security
policy, can best be assured by prevention and anticipation, or avoidance. Pro-

REARDON

tection of peace and security lies in causing no threat to others, preventing harm by not courting it, and certainly not by preparing to harm others, the purpose of arms development. Nonthreatening security systems and measures must be designed and pursued. Communication and negotiation, as well as constant monitoring of issues of controversy and conflict, need to become a normal part of all social systems. For every policy, we must ask: Will it threaten or cause harm to others? Will it strengthen or weaken positive, constructive relationships? Will it detract or add to the total security of all? The Final Document of the first special session on disarmament (*Final Document 1978*) provides an excellent set of guidelines for protection through demilitarization and disarmament. It contains many possibilities to consider in the search for alternative security systems.

In every case, a primary barometer of positive or negative security policy is measured by the effects on women. In light of their visions of security, women are the ones who are, and have been, raising these questions in the interest of all. If women's questions, women's visions, and women's voices can be brought fully into the planning of our future, the problems of peace will be approached from perspectives that will open new and hopeful possibilities. Feminist visions of global security are inspired by hope and informed by possibilities. Women dream of peace and craft the future from their dreams.

> Let me explain. The dream, the utopia, is a world without weapons. This must be the highest peak a civilization can reach. When our quarrels, our conflicts—which will always exist as long as we are varied and different human beings—are resolved without resort to violence. Our policy will be to prevent the use of arms until they can be eliminated. When we see life between human beings as a partnership and life among nations as a larger partnership, we have the possibility of redirecting this world away from war and violence to one of peace (Papandreou 1991).

234

NOTES

1. Mary Belenky, B. M. Clinchy, N. R. Goldberger, J. M. Tarule, (sociologists), Carol Gilligan and Nancy Chodorow (psychologists), and Jean Baker Miller (psychiatrist), have revealed a good deal about women's thinking. Their research bases, however, are not global.

2. "Imagining a World Without Weapons" workshops have been developed by Elise Boulding and Warren Zeigler. These workshops are offered by the Futures Invention Laboratory. Work of a similar nature has been done for decades by the World Order Models Project.

3. The reports appear in volumes known by the names of the chairs of the independent commissions that produced them—Brandt, Palme, and Brundtland.

4. Two excellent films depicting these circumstances are *Portrait of Teresa* from Cuba and *Raji and Kamala* from India.

5. See especially *World Military and Social Expenditures,* 1984 and 1986.

6. For a consideration of alternative security systems and a proposal for common security, see Harry Hollins et al., *The Conquest of War* (Boulder, CO: Westview Press, 1989).

REFERENCES

Belenky, M., B. Clincly, N. Goldberger, and J. Tarule. "Implications for Human Development." *Breakthrough,* Summer, 7 (4): 25–26, 1986.

Burns, R. "Development, disarmament, and women: Some new connections," *Social Alternatives* 3(1): 159–164, 1982.

Cohn, C. "Nuclear Language and How We Learned to Pat the Bomb." *Bulletin of the Atomic Scientists,* June: 17–24, 1987.

Eisler, R. and D. Loye, eds. *The Partnership Way.* San Francisco: HarperCollins, 1990.

Gilligan, C. *In a Different Voice.* Cambridge: Harvard University Press, 1984.

Kull, S. "Winning the Unwinnable: An Interview Study of the Beliefs About Winning a Superpower War." Research paper, 1986.

Mische, P. "The Earth Covenant: The Evolution of a Citizen's Treaty for Common Ecological Security." *Breakthrough* 10 (4): 31–33, 1989.

Opotow, S. "Moral Exclusion and Injustice: An Introduction." *Journal of Social Issues* 46 (1): 1–20, 1990.

Papandreou, M. "A Feminist Foreign Policy: Will it Work?" CSWS Review presented at a Feminist Conference, Montreal, June 1991 and published in Annual Magazine of the Center for the Study of Women in Society. Eugene: University of Oregon, 6–9.

Perez de Cuellar, J. "Message of the United Nations Secretary General to the World Congress of Women: Toward 2000." Speech presented at the meetings of World Congress of Women, Moscow, 1987.

Reardon, B. "Moving Toward the Future." *Network Newsletter Network* January/February, 1980.

———. *Sexism and the War System.* New York: Teachers College Press, 1985.

United Nations. Convention on the Elimination of all Forms of Discrimination Against Women. 1979.

United Nations. *The Nairobi Forward Looking Strategies for the Advancement of Women.* Vienna: United Nations Division for the Advancement of Women, 1986.

Women for Mutual Security. Press Release. Baghdad, January 10, 1991.

———. Message to the President of the United States. Baghdad, January 14, 1991.

REARDON

CONTRIBUTORS

LORRAINE ELLIOTT is Lecturer in Political Science at the Australian National University, where she teaches courses in international relations and environmental politics. She is author of a book on environmental politics in the Antarctic and a soon-to-be completed textbook on global politics of the environment. Dr. Elliott is Inaugural President of the Australasian International Studies Association.

JULIE FISHER is the author of *The Road from Rio: Sustainable Development and the Nongovernmental Movement in the Third World* (Praeger, 1993). She has been a consultant to many international development organizations and is currently a Visiting Fellow at the Program on Non-Profit Organizations, Yale University.

LINDA RENNIE FORCEY is Professor of Peace and Women's Studies at Binghamton University, and author of *Mothers of Sons* (Praeger, 1987), editor or coeditor of *Peace: Meanings, Politics, Strategies* (Praeger, 1989); *Yearning to Breathe Free: Liberation Theologies in the U.S.* (Orbis, 1991); *Disarmament, Economic Conversion, and the Management of Peace* (Praeger, 1992); and *Mothering: Ideology, Experience, and Agency* (Routledge, 1994). She was a Fulbright Scholar in India lecturing on women and peace in 1992, and she is actively involved in the Consortium on Peace Research, Education, and Development (COPRED) and Chair of the Peace Studies Association (PSA).

LENORE B. GOLDMAN is the founder of Goldman Associates, an organization working with business, government, and nonprofit/nongovernmental organizations. Since 1991 she has worked extensively with women's groups in Hungary, Poland, and the Czech and Slovak Republics.

GEETA RAO GUPTA is Vice President of The International Center for Research on Women and works on the Center's reproductive health projects, including the Women and AIDS Research Program. Dr. Gupta has a Ph.D. in social psychology from Bangalore University in India, and has over ten years of experience in the fields of women's health and women in development. She has authored several articles on gender and reproductive health and has helped develop curriculum on women's health for a graduate program at the Tata Institute of Social Sciences in Bombay, India.

LOIS ANN LORENTZEN is Associate Professor of Social Ethics at the University of San Francisco, where she was the National Endowment for the Humanities Chair for 1995–1996. Her research and articles focus on development ethics and women in grassroots environmental movements, primarily in Central America. She is coeditor of *Liberation Theologies: Postmodernity and The Americas* (Routledge, forthcoming) and *Global Ethics: Theories and Issues* (Wadsworth, forthcoming). She is on the editorial board of *Terra Nova: A Journal of Nature & Culture* (MIT Press).

CLAIRE McADAMS, Ph.D., is a former university teacher of urban and environmental sociology, race/ethnicity, and family/gender courses. Her research and community activism focus on environmental decisionmaking processes and leadership, and the social aspects of housing (expecially CoHousing). Her life experiences as (at various times) neighborhood activist, local appointed official, environmental organization member/participant observation researcher, real estate broker, and fourth-generation family tree farmer, inform her writing.

KATHLEEN M. MERCHANT is currently an Assistant Professor in the College of Human Performance and Development at the University of Nevada at Las Vegas. She conducts research in international nutrition, investigating the effects of nutritional deprivation and reproduction on women. She has authored several research articles addressing issues of maternal nutritional depletion and the effect of maternal stunting on maternal delivery complications.

BETTY REARDON is Director of the Peace Education Program at Teachers College, Columbia University. Long active in a number of international organizations and movements, she has served on the Council of the International Peace Research Association, the Council of the University for Peace, and the International Jury for the UNESCO Prize for Peace Education. Her previous publications are in the areas of women's issues, human rights, alternative security systems, and teaching and learning the skills of peacemaking.

VESNA NIKOLIĆ-RISTANOVIĆ works as a researcher in the Institute for Criminological and Sociological Research, and gives lectures in criminology of women and feminist methodology at the Center for Women's Studies in Belgrade. She is author of the book *Women as Victims of Crimes* (Naučna knjiga, Belgrade, 1989) and coauthor of the books *Social Control and Criminality of Women* (Draganić and IKSI, Beograd, 1992) and *Women, Violence, and War* (IKSI, Beograd, 1995). She is coordinator of the Group for Women's Rights of European Movement in Serbia.

RUTH K. ONIANG'O teaches in the Jomo Kenyatta University College of Agriculture and Technology in Nairobi, Kenya. Her research focuses on women in development and food security in Africa.

MARY J. OSIRIM is Associate Professor of Sociology on The Rosalyn R. Schwartz Lectureship and Director of the African Studies Consortium at Bryn Mawr College. She received her B.A. and Ph.D. degrees from Harvard University in social work and sociology respectively, and received the M.Sc. degree from the London School of Economics and Political Science in sociology. Her teaching, research, and many publications have focused extensively on gender and the family, economic sociology, and the role of entrepreneurship in African development.

HAMIDEH SEDGHI is a Political Scientist and Visiting Scholar at the Institute for Research on Women and Gender at Columbia University, and a Visiting Research Professor at the Kevorkian Center for Near Eastern Studies at New York University. Her research on women in Iran includes the forthcoming *Veiling, Unveiling and Reveiling: Women and Politics in Iran.*

JENNIFER TURPIN is Associate Professor and Chair of Sociology and Women's Studies at the University of San Francisco, where she received the Distinguished Teaching Award in 1993. She is the author of *Reinventing the Soviet Self* (Praeger, 1995), and coeditor of *Rethinking Peace* (Lynne Rienner, 1994), and *The Web of Violence: From Interpersonal to Global* (University of Illinois Press, 1996). She is the Associate Editor of the 4-volume *Encyclopedia of Violence, Peace, and Conflict* (Academic Press, forthcoming), Senior Editor of *Peace Review*, and Chair of the American Sociological Association's Section on Peace and War.

CLAIRE VAN ZEVERN is a recent graduate of the University of San Francisco. She is a 1995–1996 James Irvine Fellow for Sustainable Communities.

ELLEN WEISS, a Public Health Specialist at the International Center for Research on Women, manages the Women and AIDS Research Program funded by USAID, which supports action research projects in seven countries worldwide. She has a M.Sc. in maternal and child health from the University of London and has been working domestically and internationally on AIDS, women's health, and nutrition issues for the last fifteen years. Ms. Weiss has authored several papers on women and HIV/AIDS.

DANIEL WHELAN is a Program Associate at the International Center for Research on Women and works on the Women and AIDS Research Program, in addition to other projects involving women's reproductive health. He holds an M.A. in International Affairs from The American University in Washington, D.C., and has authored various articles on the importance of the HIV/AIDS pandemic to the field of international affairs, and the linkages between HIV/AIDS and human rights in the areas of national HIV/AIDS policies, gender, and violence.

INDEX

243